Places That Matter

Places That Matter

KNOWING YOUR NEIGHBORHOOD
THROUGH DATA

Joan Ferrante

UNIVERSITY OF CALIFORNIA PRESS

University of California Press, one of the most distinguished university presses in the United States, enriches lives around the world by advancing scholarship in the humanities, social sciences, and natural sciences. Its activities are supported by the UC Press Foundation and by philanthropic contributions from individuals and institutions. For more information, visit www.ucpress.edu.

University of California Press
Oakland, California

© 2018 by The Regents of the University of California

Library of Congress Cataloging-in-Publication Data

Names: Ferrante-Wallace, Joan, 1955- author.
Title: Places that matter : knowing your neighborhood through data / Joan Ferrante.
Description: Oakland, California : University of California Press, [2018] | Includes bibliographical references and index. |
Identifiers: LCCN 2017057349 (print) | LCCN 2017058980 (ebook) | ISBN 9780520965928 (ebook) | ISBN 9780520292369 (cloth : alk. paper) | ISBN 9780520292352 (pbk : alk. paper)
Subjects: LCSH: Communities—Research—Methodology.
Classification: LCC HM756 (ebook) | LCC HM756 .F47 2018 (print) | DDC 307.072—dc23
LC record available at https://lccn.loc.gov/2017057349

27 26 25 24 23 22 21 20 19 18
10 9 8 7 6 5 4 3 2 1

To
Diana McGill,
a champion of learner-centered
and action-based education

Contents

	Preface	ix
Chapter 1.	The Project	1
Chapter 2.	Launching the Project	14
Chapter 3.	Things Are Not What They Seem	31
Chapter 4.	The Residents	59
Chapter 5.	Neighborhood Resources	88
Chapter 6.	Basic Research Concepts	115
Chapter 7.	Types of Investigative Research	148
Chapter 8.	Writing the Research Brief	179
	Appendixes	203
	Index	211

Preface

Places That Matter: Knowing Your Neighborhood through Data is for anyone who wants to learn the basic language of qualitative and quantitative research methods and translate that language into action. Engaging with these methods for the first time is especially eye-opening when you try them out in familiar spaces, like a neighborhood. Research methods will turn the familiar into something new so that "even places you know well can take on a touch of the unknown when you arrive there from a different direction" (Milford 2012, 2).

Doing research is always an adventure because it begins with the experience of chaos—of confronting the complexities of the world and the people in it. So the challenge becomes, where do I begin? what do I want to know? how do I ask questions that will guide my efforts? It is the process of working through the chaos that moves us onto the path of discovery.

To do meaningful research requires many decisions, including retractions. When I ask those doing research about what it is like for them, most reply that it is challenging in many ways. When I press them to elaborate, the challenges named include the following:

- the "ton of little details" they must know to do research
- becoming overwhelmed by so many decisions
- the brain shutting down when it comes to this kind of work
- investing so much concentration and other mental energy
- thinking in such a disciplined way
- the time and dedication it takes to become just adequate
- learning the language of research methods,[1] which can seem like a foreign language
- its messiness: the constant need to think and rethink
- not understanding how each part of the research process adds up to reveal the big picture

Places that Matter is written with the goal of easing the many challenges that come with doing research by (1) applying the methods to a place that matters to your everyday life; (2) converting the abstract language of research into action; and (3) coaching you through the process of doing research.[2]

THE PLACE THAT MATTERS

This book uses a place that matters to your life as a vehicle to introduce the methods of research. That place can be the house where you grew up or now live, a café where homework is done, a park, a place of worship, a grandparent's house, or a spot to meet friends. Whatever the choice, the place that matters serves as an emotional anchor that attaches you to the project and to its larger educational and applied purposes. Those purposes are to reveal the power of research methods and the importance of the neighborhood that surrounds your place that matters. Mattering gives purpose to the mental effort and discipline required to internalize the research concepts and move forward. The work of

---

1. Research Methods is a course that is "consistently received by students with as much groaning, moaning, eye-rolling, hyperventilation, and waiver strategizing" (Epstein 1987, 71).
2. Of course, your professors may choose to read sections of the action plan as completed or read only the finalized action plan.

negotiating difficult material is eased when there is an emotional connection to the task at hand.

BUILDING CONFIDENCE

You will engage in experiences that reveal how the methods of research can help you answer questions about the neighborhood that surrounds, or "hugs," the place that matters. This book eases you into the concepts and processes by tying them to questions that need to be answered: What does "place that matters" mean? How do I define the surrounding neighborhood? How will the sociological lens help me see things in this neighborhood that I might never have noticed? How do I collect data and make other kinds of observations to help me learn about the neighborhood needs and draw up a plan of personal action? How do I know if the neighborhood is unusual or typical?

COACHING

Places That Matter coaches you through the process of finding answers to the kinds of questions posed above and using those answers to take an action. That plan addresses the extent to which you currently *support* (or fail to support) the *neighborhood* that surrounds *the place that matters*. That plan also addresses ways to increase or sustain that support. The work you do for each chapter builds toward a finalized plan you may one day decide to implement (see chapter 8).

This book is not a comprehensive overview of research methods. Rather, it seeks to build a solid conceptual and experiential foundation for wanting to learn more. It adopts an action-based learning (ABL), or learner-centered, approach to research. At least four criteria distinguish ABL.

(1) At the center of ABL are overarching questions to guide activities.

ABL projects must be carefully crafted. A carefully crafted project requires you to engage with key questions that ultimately direct your energies in "the service of an important intellectual purpose" (Blumenfeld et al. 1991,

372).³ In fact, the key questions are the most critical ingredients of the project as they also evoke interest and convey the project's essence. For the *Places that Matter* project, there are two key questions:

1. In what ways do you currently *support,* or fail to support, the *neighborhood* that surrounds *the place that matters*?
2. Should that *support* be increased? If so, in what ways?

(2) Learners are invested in the project.

ABL learners have many opportunities to make decisions and take responsibility. There are opportunities to engage with the sociological literature on places, neighborhoods, residents, and households; do investigative research; share experiences and insights; offer and accept feedback; and find ways to share lessons learned with audiences beyond the classroom.

(3) Investigative methods are central.

Potential investigative methods include interviews, surveys, observation, document analysis, conversation, and content analysis. The method that is chosen must deliver the kinds of facts that best support thoughtful and honest answers to the key questions. In other words, the method is chosen with the aim of gathering the best evidence that can be used to build a credible and compelling answer.

(4) ABL changes thinking and behavior.

The project—and its key questions—should be so compelling that it commands attention and cultivates deep interest. Ideally, the lessons learned are so eye-opening that you feel compelled to make subtle or even dra-

---

3. Action-based learning works best when coaches offer clear guidance and meaningful feedback. The job of a coach is to explain the game and offer well-conceived strategies and instructions that increase chances of success and motivate. On the other hand, it is the "players" who play the game, with the coach on the sidelines. Keep in mind that players don't invent the game; they learn how to play it, work as a team, and learn from experience. They also learn from studying and modeling the efforts of those who have been deemed the best at playing the game. But they also bring their own style to the game.

matic changes in your thinking and behavior and share what you have learned. That sharing can entail reaching out to those in a position to change society's fate (Burawoy 2004).

ACKNOWLEDGMENTS

I must thank the hundreds of Northern Kentucky University (NKU) students in my Research Methods, Introduction to Sociology, and other classes who have worked through the exercises in this book. I especially thank NKU students McKenzie Eskridge, India Hackle, Kirsten Hurst, Lauren James, and Joe Keller for testing the instructions that coach readers through the exercises. My colleague, Lynnissa Hillman, has tested the exercises in her sociology classes, and I am grateful for our conversations about how students processed the material. Another colleague, Kristie Vise, read and critiqued this book in its earliest drafts, and I am thankful for her constructive recommendations. The artwork was created by Tabitha Kelly, a graduate of NKU with a BFA in visual communication design and a sociologist at heart. I dedicate this book to Dr. Diana McGill, dean of NKU's College of Arts and Sciences and a champion of learner-centered and action-based education.

At the University of California Press, I thank Maura Roessner (acquisitions editor), Francisco Reinking (production editor), and Sheila Berg (copy editor) for guiding this book through the many stages that lead to publication. I hold the reviewers who read the proposal and drafts of this book in the highest esteem.

REFERENCES

Blumenfeld, P. C., E. Soloway, R. W. Marx, J. S. Krajcik, M. Guzdial, and A. Palincsar. 1991. "Motivating Project-Based Learning: Sustaining the Doing, Supporting the Learning." *Educational Psychologist* 26 (3–4): 369–98.
Burawoy, M. 2004. "Public Sociologies: Contradictions, Dilemmas, and Possibilities." *Social Forces* 82 (4): 1603–18.
Epstein, I. 1987. "Pedagogy of the Perturbed: Teaching Research to the Reluctants." *Journal of Teaching in Social Work* 1: 71–89.
Milford, K. 2013. "Unhomely Places." In Cassandra Clare, ed., *Shadowhunters and Downworlders: A Mortal Instruments Reader.* Dallas, TX: Ben Bella Books.

1 The Project

I do not understand how anyone can live without one small place of enchantment to turn to.

Marjorie Kinnan Rawlings, *Cross Creek*

Do you have a place that matters to you—a specific space to which your sense of self is tied, that evokes strong emotions and meaning? Your first answer might be the name of a town, city, or state. But that is not the answer we are looking for. Rather, identify a specific place or spot in that town, city, or state that matters. What is that place—the home you grew up in, the café you go to every day to do homework, a park in which you relax, the place you worship, your grandmother's house, or the place where you meet friends?

We understand the power of place in our lives when we realize that we are always in some specific place, headed from one specific place to another, planning to go to some specific place, and imagining what a specific place might be like. At any moment, our very being is bound to a place: "I am at a place called work," or "I am at a place called home," "I am on my way to a place called a church," or "I am leaving a place called a bar." Or "I would love to live in a place called Utopia." It is difficult to imagine a person *not* being in some place (Gieryn 2000). In this sense, self and place are intertwined (Flunk, Pease, and Rowe 2011). In fact, people are known in large part by the places they frequent and by their level of attachment to those places (Gieryn 2000). Simply think about how you feel calmed or angered when you learn the place someone you care about is or is about to go.

We often focus on the place that matters most to us and take for granted the surrounding neighborhood. We can think of the neighborhood as the home to the place that matters. It is the neighborhood—the residents, the vacant and occupied buildings, the streets and roads, the green space— that "hugs" the place that matters to you. The neighborhood shapes how you relate to that specific place. In fact, the neighborhood deserves your attention given that it is the backdrop to that place, as the following remarks suggest.

- "Once I get home, I just lock my door because I am afraid to go out."
- "When I am at my local library, I feel connected to the community that supports it."
- "The little park by the river is where I go to just watch people in the neighborhood, just relax."
- "The boys and girls club was a place I went after school to stay out of trouble."
- "I always go to a little nightclub to hear music. I don't tell my parents where it is because they think the neighborhood is a dangerous place."

WHAT YOU WILL DO

Places That Matter guides you through an action-based research experience that is launched by identifying a specific place that *matters* to your life and then asking you to get to know the neighborhood that surrounds it. That place can matter to you now or it could have mattered at a crucial time in your life, but it must be a place with a physical address (as opposed to a virtual address) that you can get to without exerting great effort, time, or expense. That place can be a school, a residence, a café, a hair salon, a bookstore, a park, a place of worship, or a community center. You must have a role that gives you a stake in the place that matters. That role may be as

- ✓ a resident;
- ✓ a member of a church, mosque, or synagogue;

- ✓ an employee (or frequent customer);
- ✓ a friend, relative (grandmother, uncle, parent), or significant other of a resident;
- ✓ a coach of a team whose home field is a park, ball field, stadium, or gym; or
- ✓ a student at a school.

Your place that matters acts as a social, emotional, and physical (as opposed to a virtual) anchor attaching your very being to the neighborhood in which you move about and otherwise live parts of your life. This action-based research project asks you to take a hard look at that neighborhood. After all, not only is the place that matters to you part of a neighborhood, but the health of that neighborhood has a direct impact on quality of life as it relates to that place. For this reason alone, the neighborhood is deserving of your interest and support.

Those who have tested this project have named their grandmother's house, a local library, a school running track, their workplace, a frequented restaurant, and their residence as the place that matters to them. Some reflections about places that matter are given below. Note the personal energy and level of investment that each writer brings to the project.

- I would have to say that the place that matters to me is my grandmother's house. Ever since my father joined the Marines when I was a baby, my family has been on the move. By the time I graduated from high school we had lived in several states and even other countries. I did not get to see my cousins, aunts, and uncles very often. The place we always met up (and still meet up) was a quaint little house at 444 Reunion Road, in Anchor, Iowa.[1] No matter where I was in the world, I knew I could always come "home" to visit with family, and that place remained the same in a life of constant change. Many times, where you live is not where your home is but where your heart is.
- The place that matters to me is Thai Heaven. It is a small, family-owned restaurant in Beanthread, New Jersey. The restaurant, as you can probably guess, serves authentic Thai food. I am absolutely in love with their dishes. They have a very spicy and unique flavor that leaves your

---

1. When the place that matters is a personal residence, I have changed the street address, city, and name to maintain confidentiality.

mouth watering just thinking about it. It is a local favorite, a hole-in-the-wall eatery that one could easily drive right by without noticing. If you were to step inside, though, you would quickly be greeted by the scent of spices, meat, and rice. The owners are two brothers. They came over to America when they were young and decided to start their own business. Their story evokes a strong patriotic feeling in me.

- An important place to me is the Public Library located at 1786 Book Pike in Peaceful, Ohio. The silence of the library brings me peace from my difficult home and school life. In this library, I become anonymous. I am no longer the girl no one talks to at school. I am simply a woman eager to learn. The people sitting next to me on their computers do not care if I sit next to them. I can look at whatever I want, learn whatever I want, and be free from the people who see me in narrow ways. No one asks me why I am there. When I was homeless for a few months, I could go into the library to drink water from the fountain. I want to know something about the neighborhood that supports this library through its tax dollars.

- There are many places in my life that matter, but the one place that matters most to me is the running track at Ikaika[2] High School (1515 Noa i ka[3] Ave.) in Mokupuni Ma, Hawaii,[4] where I went to high school. I still run on the track today. That six-lane track brought me smiles, laughter, tears, and pain. This place birthed my hunger for the sport of track and field. Here, I met many friends who became like family to me. The track was a place where I talked to friends, family, coaches, and spectators. This place really comes alive at night when those big stadium lights shine down, putting runners in the spotlight.

- My place that matters is a local Dairy Queen located on 3 Scoop Street in Spumoni, Indiana, where I have been working since I was sixteen. I chose this place because of how much I have learned by working there. This is the place I grew as a person. I have acquired job skills that I will take with me for the rest of my life. I learned to be responsible. I showed up for every shift and never called in sick, even in the summers when I worked six days a week. I learned how to balance my school, work, and social life. I learned how to save money from my paychecks and keep a budget. I stayed at this job because my coworkers are like a family to me. I also met my boyfriend there. We all have a close bond, and we even hang out in the store when we aren't working. People think we are crazy to spend so much time "at work." We call ourselves the "DQ Crew" and always have each other's backs.

2. *Ikaika* means "strong" in the Hawaiian language.
3. In the Hawaiian language, *Noa i ka* means "free."
4. *Mokupuni Ma* means "ocean."

Figure 1.1. The Power of Supporting Questions to Guide Thinking
SOURCE: Joan Ferrante and Tabitha Kelly

Once the place that matters has been identified your charge is to do research that will answer two core questions:

- In what ways do you currently support, or fail to support, the neighborhood that surrounds the place that matters?
- Should your support be increased? If so, in what ways?

Now that you know the two driving questions, the challenge becomes how to begin. Typically, trying to answer the core questions generates more questions, such as those listed in Figure 1.1: What counts as the surrounding neighborhood? How do I learn about who lives there? What kind of things do I want to know about the residents? These secondary questions generate information that can help you assess the neighborhood's strengths and weaknesses. In turn, you will gain insights about specific areas where support is needed and where your energies might be directed.

THE PROCESS

For now, do not worry if you are unclear about how to frame the secondary questions that will ultimately drive the research you will do to answer the core questions. This book coaches you through the question-asking and question-answering process. Each chapter is broken into a series of modules with related exercises that take between 10 and 90 minutes each to complete. There are step-by-step instructions to guide you through them and to give you experience gathering and interpreting qualitative and quantitative data.

The coaching extends to *subtle skills*—the kinds of skills that can only be taught while doing the project and learning what to do when you run into roadblocks, forks in the road, and dead ends. Subtle skills are taught when someone in the role of mentor or coach shares helpful hints, conveys rules of thumb, and alerts you to challenges that are likely to arise along the way. Each exercise has been tested to ensure that instructions are worded clearly and deliver expected results.

Each chapter concludes with coaching about how to write a 1- to 2-page section of what will eventually become part of an 8- to 10-page research brief. That brief highlights the findings about the neighborhood's needs and what you can do to address those needs. By the start of chapter 8, you will have completed a draft of the research brief. Chapter 8 coaches you through the process of consolidating the six sections created in chapters 2 through 7 into the research brief that evaluates your current level of support and recommends ways you can increase (or sustain) support for the neighborhood surrounding the place that matters. A preview of chapters 2 through 8 follows.

CHAPTER 2—LAUNCHING THE PROJECT—involves asking you to identify a specific *place that matters* to your life. The place can be a school, a residence, a café, a hair salon, a bookstore, a park, a place of worship, or some other place. The next step is to establish the boundaries of the neighborhood that surrounds it. To facilitate the choice of a place that matters and determining neighborhood boundaries, the chapter reviews and clarifies the meanings of four important concepts: *place, matters, neighborhood,* and *support.*

CHAPTER 3—THINGS ARE NOT WHAT THEY SEEM—demonstrates how applying key sociological concepts and sociological perspectives allow you to see in new ways both the place that matters and the surrounding neighborhood. These concepts and perspectives give order to data collecting, observation, and analysis. As such they calm feelings of being overwhelmed and inspire secondary questions to move the project forward. There are also exercises that prompt you to use sociological concepts and perspectives to think in new ways about the neighborhood that surrounds the place that matters.

CHAPTER 4—THE RESIDENTS—places the emphasis on those who live within the boundaries of the neighborhood surrounding the place that matters. It coaches you through the process of creating social and demographic profiles of residents such as the numbers and percentages classified as a specific race, sex, age, disability, income-group, and some other social category. Social categories are treated as human-constructed divisions with real consequences. Such treatment informs the kinds of data gathered and ways of writing about the residents who make up the neighborhood. Knowing about residents' social and demographic characteristics brings to light special issues and needs within the neighborhood.

CHAPTER 5—NEIGHBORHOOD RESOURCES—directs attention to the tangible and intangible resources within the neighborhood. Tangible resources include natural resources (bodies of water, views, parks) as well as the presence or absence of businesses, service-providing institutions, public spaces, and personal resources. Intangible resources include human capital, the neighborhood's reputation, and support systems that allow residents to feel connected to and secure within the neighborhood. Documenting the tangible and intangible resources and their distribution helps gauge the neighborhood's strengths and needs and informs the actions laid out in the research brief.

CHAPTER 6—BASIC RESEARCH CONCEPTS—takes you beyond the largely descriptive methods emphasized in earlier chapters and prepares you to do more complex research. The basic concepts of research covered include units of analysis, target population, sampling, variables, operational definitions, and levels of measurement. Chapter 6 coaches you on how to collect data and make observations. In the process you will establish the number and percentage of 3- to 4-year-olds enrolled in preschool, observe interaction within the neighborhood, determine the neighborhood's reputation, and much more.

CHAPTER 7—TYPES OF INVESTIGATIVE RESEARCH—considers broad types of research (applied versus basic and qualitative versus quantitative). It also considers eight specific and overlapping methods of investigative research each of which can fall under these broad categories. Those methods, distinguished by purpose, are descriptive, interpretive, historical, comparative, correlational, multivariate, experimental, and mixed. Just knowing the many methods opens your eyes to investigative possibilities. No one method should be considered superior or inferior, as each has strengths and shortcomings. The choice of research type depends on the goals of research and the kind of data or observations needed. There are exercises that give you opportunities to practice using some of these methods. So, for example, you will learn to compare the wages of women in your neighborhood to those of men and evaluate that difference. And you will learn to connect something that occurred in the neighborhood's past with the present.

CHAPTER 8—WRITING THE RESEARCH BRIEF—covers how to consolidate the six sections of the research brief drafted in chapters 2 through 7. The research brief is the final product that addresses the core questions: (1) In what ways, if any, do you support the neighborhood surrounding the place that matters to you? (2) Should that support be increased? If so, in what ways? This chapter ends with two sample briefs. One brief centers on a place that matters located in an urban neighborhood undergoing gentrification and the other focuses on a place that matters located in a rural neighborhood.

MEETING THE CHALLENGE

For whatever reason, most people I talk to hate the prospect of doing research because it involves negotiating, creating, accessing, and making sense of data. Doing research demands a high level of proficiency. Yet proficiency is not achieved quickly; it takes dedication, determination, practice (doing), and mindfulness. The work of negotiating difficult material is eased when there is an emotional connection to the task at hand. Identifying a place that matters and taking time to learn about the neighborhood (its residents and resources) serves as an emotional anchor that attaches you to the project and to its larger educational and applied purpose. That purpose is to recognize, appreciate, and take some action to support the surrounding neighborhood as the home to the places that matter in our lives. Even when there is an emotional bridge to ease the work of accomplishing a challenging task, it is important to know that building any kind of proficiency is a steady process that involves at least four stages.

The Four Stages of Proficiency Building

People in Stage 1 are in a state of inertia. Something must happen that motivates them to do something that shakes them from this state and launches them into Stage 2, realization (e.g., "I need to know this!"). Stage 3 is the action stage, as the once inert dedicate themselves to the task at hand. Stage 4 is one of ongoing learning and growth.

1. **Inertia**—People in this stage do not—and cannot yet—understand or anticipate all they will need to know and what they will need to do to become proficient at something. Those in the inertia stage cannot articulate how taking the time and making the effort to learn a skill puts them at an advantage. Consequently, they view learning to do research or other challenges as things they must endure. They dismiss, often with great certainty, that which they are being asked to learn, not seeing (even refusing to see) any value or usefulness.

2. **Realization**—The key to moving into Stage 2 is recognizing that lacking a needed proficiency is a problem. Typically, some critical experience jump starts that recognition. That stimulus may be a job interview in which one fails to demonstrate to a potential employer that one possesses a desired skill. When people are in the realization stage they acknowledge that they do not yet understand or know how to do something, *and* they recognize that this puts them at a disadvantage. They see the value of knowing or being able to do that which they cannot do. Armed with this newfound awareness, they are ready to move to Stage 3.

3. **Action**—At Stage 3, people become learners and take first steps toward achieving proficiency. Here the learner is ready to make a sincere effort, but that effort must be met with clear direction, feedback, and meaningful opportunities to practice. At this stage, there is self-consciousness in the effort as learners must concentrate hard to do the work to address their deficit. There are misunderstandings and misapplications, but overall those in the action stage *get it*.

4. **Growth**—Over time, as people gain more experience, the knowledge and skills that once seemed so difficult to master become second nature. Effort is paying off. The self-consciousness and doubt of Stage 3 eventually dissipate and are replaced with confidence and feelings of accomplishment.

Figure 1.2 illustrates the process of getting to Stage 4. That process can be compared to learning to drive a car. People start out by realizing it is time they learn to drive. The first few times they drive, they must think about every move. There seems to be so much to keep track of: other drivers, knowing the rules of the road, controlling the car, and so on. But after weeks or months of practice, driving becomes automatic. No longer must the new driver think about how far and in what direction to turn the steering wheel, or about how much pressure to apply to the brake. The decision to brake hard or lightly, to turn the steering wheel barely or sharply, happens without conscious effort. With practice, people learn how to drive a car. Likewise, with practice, we can achieve the skill set we are looking to achieve. I hope this book moves you through the first three stages and that at the end of the book, you *get it* and feel ready to take on other projects that will continue to cultivate the desired skills.

Step 1: Inertia
Lacks understanding or dismisses importance of a proficiency

Step 2: Realization
Acknowledges the need for the proficiency

Step 3: Action
Takes first steps toward achieving proficiency

Step 4: Growth
Gains experiences and moves toward full proficiency

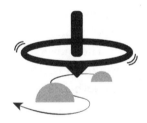

Figure 1.2. The Four Stages of Proficiency Building
SOURCE: Joan Ferrante and Tabitha Kelly

WHY CARE ABOUT THIS PROJECT?

We have already listed skills that this action-based research project will cultivate. But skill-building goals aside, why take the time to learn about the neighborhood that surrounds the place that matters to you? Why take the time to learn whether you support or fail to support that neighborhood?

Clearly people benefit when they can say that there is a place that matters to their lives—a place they spend (and have spent) meaningful time. If they treat the surrounding neighborhood and its residents as the largely unnoticed backdrops to the places they sleep, work, relax, socialize, study, and so on, then they have failed to appreciate the neighborhood as the supportive context. It is in their best interest to care. Here we can point to the "broken window theory," which states, "If the first broken window in a building is not repaired, then people who like breaking windows will assume that no one cares about the building and more windows will be broken. Soon the building will have no windows" (Kelling and Wilson 1982). The point is that some of the very smallest acts can affect the quality of life in a neighborhood and send powerful messages about who cares and what matters. If litter is thrown and left lying in the street or yards, if windows are broken and not repaired. If business owners don't consider that they are trying the patience and goodwill of residents when their customers park in the spaces residents use, And if residents do not support local businesses, these acts send important messages. Just as lapses in caring send messages that affect the quality of neighborhood life, so do *considerate* and other constructive behaviors (Brotherton, French, and Pickering 2013). Those with a stake in a place that matters should feel an obligation to contribute to the quality of neighborhood life and not take it for granted. The University of Kansas Work Group for Community Health and Development (University of Kansas 2014) expresses it best: everyone in a neighborhood can be the source of some asset that benefits the space.

> Everyone has some skills or talents, and everyone can provide knowledge about the [neighborhood], connections to the people they know, and the kind of support that every effort needs—making phone calls, stuffing envelopes, giving people information, moving equipment or supplies—whatever needs doing. This suggests that everyone in the [neighborhood] can be a force for community improvement if only we knew what their assets were, and could put them to use.

REFERENCES

Brotherton, R., C. C. French, and A. D. Pickering. 2013. "Measuring Belief in Conspiracy Theories: The Generic Conspiracist Beliefs Scale." *Frontiers in Psychology* 4 (279). www.frontiersin.org/articles/1-.3389/fpsyg.2013.00279/full.
Fluck, Winfried, Donald E. Pease, and John Carlos Rowe. 2011. *Re-Framing the Transnational Turn in American Studies*. Lebanon, NH: University Press of New England.

Gieryn Thomas F. 2000. "A Space for Place in Sociology." *Annual Review of Sociology*. 26 (1): 463–96.

Kelling, George L., and James Q. Wilson. 1982. "Broken Windows: The Police and Neighborhood Safety." *Atlantic*, March. Retrieved September 13, 2017. www.theatlantic.com/magazine/archive/1982/03/broken-windows/304465/.

Rawlings, Marjorie Kinnan. 1942. *Cross Creek*. New York: Simon and Schuster.

University of Kansas. 2014. "Work Group for Community Health and Development." https://communityhealth.drupal.ku.edu/sites/communityhealth.drupal.ku.edu/files/docs/KU%20Work%20Group%20for%20Community%20Health%20and%20Development%5B2%5D.pdf. Retrieved September 2017.

2 Launching the Project

One of the most crucial tasks in launching a research project is to clarify the organizing concepts. Organizing concepts channel thinking and give focus to the project. For this action-based learning project, there are four organizing concepts: *place, matters, neighborhood,* and *support*. Notice that these four concepts have a prominent place in the two core questions:

1. In what ways do you currently support, or fail to support, the neighborhood that surrounds the place that matters?
2. Should support be increased? If so, in what ways?

In the pages that follow each concept's meaning is clarified. You must know what these concepts mean before you can choose a place that matters, determine the geographic space that constitutes the surrounding neighborhood, and assess your level of support for that neighborhood.

THE CONCEPTS *PLACE* AND *MATTERS*

Place is a very broad and abstract concept. The sociological literature tells us that a *place* is a unique physical location in the universe. That broad definition suggests that a place can be a backyard swimming pool, a bedroom, a neighborhood library, a public park, a police station, a mountaintop, a neighborhood, one of the fifty states, a town, a city, or even the planet Earth (Gieryn 2000). To be more specific, a place is some physical space to which people have assigned a name, a purpose, a reputation, and other meanings. A place can have a reputation for being beautiful or dilapidated, the newest night spot, wheelchair accessible, or solar powered. A place encompasses the people (residents, owners, customers, tourists), the animals (domestic and wild), and the things (coffee, books, food, etc.) you find in and around it.

In *The Great Good Place* (1999), Ray Oldenburg writes about three kinds of places:

- the "first place" is the household in which one lives whether alone or with others;
- the "second place" is the workplace where the employed spend time working in exchange for pay; and
- "third places" are those that function as the anchors of neighborhood life because they draw people in and cultivate interaction. Local libraries, cafés, community centers, public libraries, ice cream shops, and parks qualify as third places.

Places have agentic qualities. Here *agentic* means a kind of force that exerts invisible pressure on people to behave, think, and interact without really questioning why (Gieryn 2000; Werlen 1993). That agentic force is realized whenever people respond in a reflexlike manner. For example, when in a place called a classroom, students just know they should raise their hands and wait to be called on before saying something. When in a place known as a football stadium, rarely if ever does it cross a fan's mind to run out to join the players huddling as they go over plays. To do so violates largely unspoken expectations and draws unwanted attention and scrutiny.

What does it mean for a place to matter? The experience of being in a place depends on whether people believe that they do, or do not, belong there. Here we can make a distinction between feelings of insiderness and outsiderness (Relph 1976). At one extreme is the experience of feeling like an insider. This involves completely blending in, feeling a part of the flow, and moving freely without being noticed, and when noticed, feeling welcome. At the other extreme is feeling like an outsider. This involves feeling threatened, different, or unwelcome. People can experience insiderness and outsiderness with varying intensities. The strongest experience of insiderness involves feeling safe and unscrutinized such that people are not distracted or self-conscious and can immerse themselves in what is going on. The strongest experience of outsiderness involves unsettling sensations of strangeness and separation (Relph 1976). Over time the dynamics of insiderness and outsiderness converge to give a place the reputation for welcoming certain types of people and rejecting others. This reputation can enforce social divisions that exist in larger society (Gieryn 2000).

In sum, a place matters to you when (1) it elicits some emotion, whether it be positive or negative; (2) it exercises agentic power over your thinking, behavior, and interactions; and (3) it sends the message that you are an insider or an outsider.

Exercise 2.1: Choose a place that matters to you

Now that we have clarified the meaning of place and what makes a place matter, you are ready to identify a place that matters to you.

WHAT YOU WILL DO

✓ Choose a place that matters to your life.
✓ Write a personal statement about why that places matters to you.

The chosen place should be one that has had a positive effect on your sense of self and life. Recall the kinds of places named as mattering in chapter 1—a grandmother's house, a library, a running track, a Dairy Queen, a Thai restaurant—and the positive roles these places played in each writer's life. The place you choose should have a physical (as opposed to a virtual) address. It might be a place where you live, work, worship, exercise, sleep, study, relax, socialize, get your hair cut, or otherwise frequent. The place that matters to you should be one that elicits positive emotions. It should be a place where you feel insiderness.

Ideally the place you choose should be within easy driving or walking distance because to truly know the surrounding neighborhood you should walk around and take in what is there. However, there are those among us who are unable to drive or walk to (and around) the neighborhood. If you are in this situation you may be able to learn about a neighborhood through Google Street View.

Exercise 2.2: Write a personal statement about the chosen place

Once you have identified a place, write a statement explaining your choice. In the statement, be sure to name the place and give the address. Explain what about this place matters. In other words, how is this place important to your life? What prompted you to select it? What stake (role) do you have in that place? Are you a home owner, pastor, grandchild, or partner of a resident, director, business owner, school principal, coach, groundskeeper, or frequent visitor, or do you hold some other status? A sample personal statement follows. You will notice that this statement

- ✓ is about 350 to 400 words long;
- ✓ gives the name and full address of the place, including city and state;
- ✓ explains why the place matters;
- ✓ offers some preliminary impressions about the surrounding neighborhood; and
- ✓ presents evidence of insiderness.

Example

I chose my house at 99[1] Home Street, Cincinnati, Ohio, as the place that matters. This house is in a neighborhood known as Northside that attracts local artists and musicians as residents. The neighborhood is located next to a university community. This place matters to me because it is where I spend a great deal of time. I have lived at 99 Home Street for two years. It is a place where I feel safe and secure. I spend many afternoons landscaping the yard with my two dogs who love to be outside with me. Inside my home are many items that once belonged to my grandmother, who died about a year ago.

---

1. The street name and house number are fictitious to protect the identity of the writer.

99 Home Street is in the heart of Northside. My house is within walking distance to many local attractions, restaurants, bars, and a 2-acre park (Jacob Hoffner Park) known for the many neighborhood events that take place there. Those events including a Fourth of July parade, an International Pillow Fight Day (for kids), Art in the Park, a seasonal farmers' market, and music festivals. Sometimes I volunteer to work at events held in the park.

My home has an interesting relationship to the surrounding neighborhood. Before I bought the house, it was in very poor condition. It had gone through many owners over the decades, and unfortunately it had not been well taken care of and fell into disrepair. When it went into foreclosue, the trees and bushes were so overgrown, you wouldn't have known there was a house there. The organization Sustainable Rehab rehabilitated the house, and then I bought it from them. According to the Rehab's mission statement, it exists "to revitalize the community" by taking an interest in abandoned and unlivable homes that they remodel and make energy efficient. Rehab then sells the homes it rehabilitates at an affordable price. I appreciate my home's history. In my role as a home owner I want to learn more about this neighborhood. I am also interested in knowing what I can do to contribute to the surrounding neighborhood's quality of life.

References

Sustainable Rehab. 2018. "About Us." http://cncurc.org/?page_id=21sustainablerehab.org.

THE CONCEPT OF NEIGHBORHOOD

A neighborhood is a kind of community. There are three widely used definitions of community (Macfarlane 1977). One definition presents community as a geographic space or territory that draws people inside to achieve some shared purpose, such as a location to live and call home (the city of Denver), a physical space to work and earn an income (a corporation), or a physical space to share an experience (e.g., Soldier Stadium for a Grateful Dead concert). The people who are residents of Denver, employees of a corporation, or fans of the Grateful Dead are part of their respective communities because they share a purpose or reason for being there. They do not know or feel a sense of attachment to everyone who is inside that space. What makes them a community is that they are drawn into a physical space to achieve some shared purpose (to live, to earn a living, or to listen to music with like-minded fans).

The second definition treats community as consisting of people who share an important social quality, characteristic, interest, or life experience that binds them together (Bryant and Peck 2014). When community is defined in this way, we can speak of the Italian community, the LGBTQ community, a community of alumni, and so on. People considered part of these communities do not have to share a geographic space. It is the shared experience of being perceived, labeled, and treated as a member of a social category that binds members together and sets them apart.

The third definition presents community in an idealized way—a community made up of people who know and interact with one another, who share an identity based on a territory, who feel attached to one another, and who engage in some joint action in the name of their community (MacQueen et al. 2001). When "community" is used in this third sense, it consists of people who are very aware that they share something in common—a something that generates sensations of belongingness and motivates them to act in the name of the community. An example is a place of worship where members agree to eat rice and beans for a week with the goal of donating the money saved to a food bank.

Of the three definitions, the first best captures a neighborhood. For this research project we are interested in the residents, buildings, and other spaces that make up the neighborhood surrounding the place that matters to your life. So we are using the word *neighborhood* in reference to people who live near one another. With this definition in mind, you are ready to determine the geographic space that qualifies as the neighborhood for your place that matters. The decision about where to draw boundaries is based, in part, on existing data. Unless you have the time and resources to survey residents, you must consider the data that already exist before establishing boundaries.

The best source of data is the U.S. Census Bureau, which conducts annual surveys based on of sample of 3.5 million households randomly selected from households across the 50 states, 19,540 cities/towns, 3,144 counties, and 74,135 census tracts that make up the United States. That survey is known as the American Community Survey (ACS),[2] and it collects information on residents' age, race, income, commuting time to work, occupation, disability status, home value, educational attainment, veteran status, and much more. It issues estimates on the residents who live in the nation and in each state, county, city/town (over 2,000 residents), and each census tract.

We could think of the county as the surrounding neighborhood, but counties are very large geographic spaces. They typically encompass many cities and towns that attract very different populations. Since we want to learn about the immediate neighborhood surrounding the place that matters, the census tract is the best option because it is a small, geographic territory that is closest in size to what we might call a neighborhood. Census tracts boundaries are drawn to reflect existing landmarks such as railroad tracks, highways, overpasses, rivers, or industrial complexes that function as physical divides.

Exercise 2.3: Establish the boundaries of your neighborhood
WHAT YOU WILL DO

✓ Make a map of the neighborhood surrounding the place that matters.

✓ Assess how that neighborhood figures into your daily routine.

The first step in establishing a working definition of "surrounding neighborhood" is to establish the census tract number. You can find the census tract number that corresponds to your place that matters by typing the search terms "FFIEC Geocoding System." Then type the address of the place that matters and wait for a map to pop up. The kind of map generated is shown in figure 2.1. Look for the dot (marker) that shows the location of the place that matters. Notice that the marker is inside a set of boundaries and that the tract number is printed inside those boundaries. For this example, the census tract number is 0521.00 and part of Bellevue, Kentucky.

---

2. The U.S. Census Bureau is probably best known for the once-per-decade census of the entire U.S. population. We could use the 2010 census, but it is already more than eight years old.

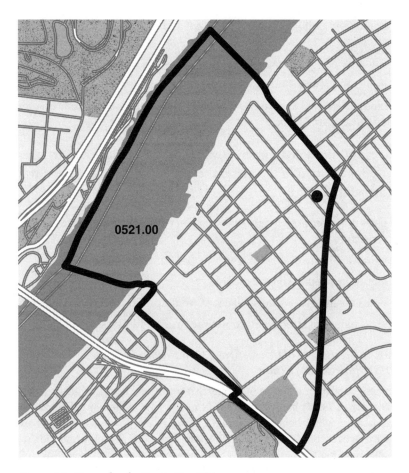

Figure 2.1. Example of a Census Tract Map
SOURCE: Joan Ferrante and Tabitha Kelly

Now that you have a map of the census tract and can see where your place that matters is located within it, you are ready to take a tour of the census tract so you can learn about the streets, structures, public spaces, and landscapes within its boundaries. As you walk around, pay attention to

- who you see outside along your walk or drive;
- businesses, schools, places of worship, public spaces (e.g., parks, community centers);

- homes and buildings that look vacant and in disrepair and those that are not;
- evidence of public transportation, such as bus stops;
- events for which the census tract is known; and
- landmarks (e.g., a monument, a public park, distinctive architecture, a distinctive landscape).

Write a 500-word description of what you see on the tour. An example description (written in the present tense) is given below. As you read it, notice that it

- ✓ gives only some[3] highlights of what lies within the boundaries of the census tract;
- ✓ paints a picture of the housing;
- ✓ mentions people who are outside;
- ✓ notes businesses, schools, places of worship, and landmarks; and
- ✓ gives names of streets and sometimes exact addresses.

Model Description of Census Tract 78 in Northside (Hamilton County), Ohio

I chose to begin my tour at 99 Home Street (my residence), which is part of census tract 78. My home is in a census tract located in the heart of Northside, an urban neighborhood in Cincinnati, Ohio. I drive down Home Street and take a right onto Pitts Avenue. Pitts Avenue has many potholes, and the sidewalks need repair, but the houses are nice two-story structures with well-maintained yards. These houses have no driveways, and residents park their cars on the street. On the corner of Pitts and Chase Avenues is a school and large church building, St. Boniface. As I drive down Chase (a very busy street with a lot of traffic) I notice maintenance crews working on the sidewalks, and I also notice one house for sale. I google that listing and find (according to Zillow.com) that the asking price for homes in this area is in the $229,000 to $289,000 range. I see a gas station and notice that across the street a few women who appear to be white and middle-aged are setting up a yard sale.

I turn left onto Kirby Avenue, where I see a building with a sign that reads Cincinnati Urban Promise. I look this organization up on my phone

---

3. You cannot describe everything.

and discover it exists to meet the spiritual, physical, emotional, and academic needs of individuals, families, and communities. Its mission is to help children in underresourced communities succeed and avoid negative peer pressure. The apartments and homes around Cincinnati Urban Promise are in rough shape and are occupied by people who appear to be lower-income and predominantly Hispanic and black. Some houses have boarded-up windows and are priced as low as $60,000. At the end of Kirby, I move on toward Colerain Avenue and see a sign for Interstate 75. I take a right onto Colerain and then a right onto Florida Avenue, where most of the structures are very nice 2- and 3-story, single-family, wood and brick homes. Some have nicely fenced yards. Most people I see outside appear white. I see a construction crew repairing the porch of the largest house on the street.

This route brings me back to Chase Avenue and onto Cherry Street. The houses appear in good condition. I turn onto Pullan Avenue, which is known to be one of the nicer and wealthier streets in Northside and has the reputation of being owned by those who make up a young professional class that has replaced the blue-collar and low-income people who once lived in these homes. The houses for sale are listed in the $300,000+ range.

I continue exploring and come to Lakeman Street, where I see large multistory wood and brick homes that are at least 90 years old. These homes have character but need routine maintenance. The road is paved and smooth. I turn left onto Blue Rock Street, home to businesses (record stores, cafés, antique stores, and bars) that draw crowds of customers on the weekends. I keep driving until I come to Spring Grove Avenue, where I see old factory buildings, some of which appear abandoned, but others have already been or are being converted into living spaces (loft-style apartments) attractive to those who want to live in urban settings.

Exercise 2.4: How does neighborhood figure into your routine?

Now that you have made a map and taken a tour, it is important to think about how the surrounding neighborhood figures into your daily or weekly routine, including the streets, businesses, and parks you drive, walk, or otherwise travel through regularly. Use the three questions below as a guide.

- What streets within the census tract do you walk or drive through on a routine basis?

- What businesses, public spaces, houses of worship, and so on, do you frequent?
- What markers stand out in the census tract?

If when answering these questions you have doubts about whether a street, building, or other space that you frequent falls within the census tract, simply google "FFIEC Geocoding System" and type the address in to verify that it comes up as being in the same census tract as your place that matters. The model write-up that follows shows how the neighborhood figures into the daily life of the person who resides at 99 Home Street (census tract 78).

Model Description of Census Tract 78 in Northside (Hamilton County), Ohio

- I feel a deep attachment to Jacob Hoffner Park at 4104 Hamilton Ave., Cincinnati, OH 45223, which is only .05 mile from my home address and just outside census tract 78.
- Driving from work, I feel the sensation of being almost home right after I pass the Comet Bar (4579 Hamilton Ave.), which tells me I am entering my home census tract 78.
- Every workday (5 days a week, 2 times a day) I drive from my residence to Lakeman Street, down Blue Rock Street, taking a left at Hamilton Avenue, leaving the census tract to make my way to work. I retrace the route in reverse coming home. There is a sandwich shop (the Melt Eclectic Deli) where I love to eat located right along the boundary of my census tract.
- I often ride my bike starting out at 99 Home Street. On my route, I take Lakeman Street to Blue Rock to Spring Grove and then into Spring Grove Cemetery (a National Landmark), where I ride past "lakes, state champion trees, hundreds of plant species and panoramic views within the park-like setting" (according to the website). While the cemetery is located just outside my census tract, I rely on streets within my census tract to get there.

THE CONCEPT *SUPPORT*

The fourth concept is *support*. We can call people's relationship to the surrounding neighborhood supportive whenever they do something that makes a positive contribution to the quality of life there, whether it is picking up litter or running for the city council or school board. So in assessing the level of support you need to consider

- your track record of getting to know and assist (even in small ways) people in the neighborhood, including shopping local and caring for (not just using) public spaces there; and
- the resources (time and treasure) you contribute to the neighborhood.

It is likely that the level of support falls between two extremes. At one extreme is no support. That is, you (1) know very few, if any residents; (2) have no understanding of the neighborhood's needs; and (3) make no effort to buy local or care for public spaces. At the other extreme is a level of support in which you (1) are highly integrated in the neighborhood (you know many residents; residents know you); (2) understand neighborhood needs; and (3) make every effort to buy local and care for public spaces. Regardless of where you fall on this continuum, your charge in the chapters to come is to educate yourself about the surrounding neighborhood, including its residents and tangible and intangible resources. Your charge is also to reflect on your current level of support. This knowledge will help you understand the strengths, needs, and challenges of the neighborhood and determine in what areas you can extend support and in what ways. For now, begin to write Section 1 of the research brief.

WORKING DRAFT OF THE RESEARCH BRIEF, SECTION 1
Background on Self and Place That Matters

At this point in this chapter you have

- identified a place that matters to your life;
- found the census tract number and made a map;
- taken a walking or driving tour and written up your observations; and
- broadly reflected on your relationship to the surrounding community.

Now you are in position to begin writing a **working draft** of your research brief. A working draft is a work in progress, a preliminary form of an envisioned final document. Referring to the research brief as a working draft indicates you have made a commitment to continually reanalyze, revise, and seek feedback or input until the document is deemed ready for final submission (see chapter 8). Think of the research brief as an executive summary, with each completed exercise as a supporting document.

Section 1 of the research brief will include a concise overview of the project goal. It should include an introduction to the place that matters and a statement about why that place matters. Following that should be a map and a general description of the surrounding neighborhood. Obviously, this working draft is based on what you learned from doing the chapter exercises (which serve as supporting documents). Keep in mind that what you write can only be as good as the effort and thought you gave to completing the exercises. If you rushed to get the exercises done and produced sloppy, uninspired work, your executive summary will reflect that poor effort. Conversely, if you took your time and produced a careful, inspired analysis, your writing will reflect that care. Think of Section 1 as your introduction to the project. The two-page opening of your research brief sets the tone and stage for what will come. Section 1 should include a cover page, a purpose statement, and mention of the chosen place and why it matters to you. It should also include a map of the neighborhood (census tract) and how it figures into your routine.

Cover/Title Page

The cover page of your research brief is the first page and, by extension, the first thing your reader sees. For now, the cover page includes (1) the title of the research project with clarification that this is a working draft and (2) your name and status relative to the place that matters. Deciding on the title is the most difficult part of a cover page. An effective title should capture the purpose of the brief, resonate with readers, and offer hints as to what is to follow. Since the focus of this research project is the census tract or neighborhood and the extent to which you support, or fail to support, that neighborhood, the title should capture this focus.

RESEARCH BRIEF: A PLAN TO SUPPORT CENSUS TRACT 78 IN NORTHSIDE (HAMILTON COUNTY), OHIO[4]

Purpose Statement

The brief should open with a very clear statement of purpose. This opening is arguably the most critical part of the research brief. We do not want anyone who reads this brief to wonder about the guiding purpose. The purpose statement should include the core questions to which you seek answers, basic information about yourself (age, income, race), and a brief overview of your relationship to the place that matters and how that relationship is manifested in your daily and weekly routine. This is your opportunity to describe the place that matters and how you became associated with it. The purpose statement should present your stake or role in the place that matters (e.g., resident, home owner, director). The following model illustrates what an effective purpose statement might look like. Notice that it draws heavily on work already completed.

Model Statement of Purpose

This research was conducted with the goal of addressing two core questions:

(1) In what ways do I, in my role as home owner and resident of 99 Home Street, Cincinnati, Ohio, currently support or fail to support the surrounding neighborhood?
(2) Should support be increased? If so, in what ways?

As a resident, I have an obligation to care about the neighborhood that supports my home and lifestyle. I recognize the neighborhood surroundings are the supportive context of that lifestyle, and I feel an obligation to contribute to the quality of neighborhood life and not take it for granted. I want to be a force for neighborhood improvement.

---

4. If, at this preliminary stage, you have made few if any significant contributions to the quality of life in the surrounding community, you might title the report:
Research Brief
Stepping Up to the Plate to Support Census Tract 78

Model Background Write-Up on the Place That Matters

My house is located in Northside, a neighborhood that is part of Cincinnati, Ohio 45223. I am 32 years old, a college graduate with a major in business management. I currently work for a large retailer as a sales representative earning $38,800 a year. Before buying this house 2 years ago, I rented an apartment in Northside for 7 years. When I decided to buy a home, I felt it was time to put rent payments toward something to own. I believed that buying a home would be a good investment and vote of confidence in the neighborhood. My home on Home Street is in what is considered the heart of Northside and within walking distance of many restaurants, bars, and other local attractions, including the popular Jacob Hoffner Park, a 2-acre public park known for the many neighborhood events it hosts, including a famous Fourth of July parade, an International Pillow Fight Day (for kids), Art in the Park, a seasonal farmers' market, and music festivals.

My home has an interesting relationship to the Northside neighborhood. Before I bought the house, it had gone through many owners over 94 years, many of whom could not afford to maintain it. The county tax records suggest that several owners could not maintain payments, and the house was in foreclosure on a least two occasions in the past 15 years. In 2015 Hamilton County Land Reutilization took possession of the house and turned it over to Sustainable Transformation (ST). The trees and bushes were so overgrown you would not have known there was a house on the lot. ST's mission is "to stabilize and revitalize the community" by taking an interest in abandoned homes slated for demolition, remodeling them and making them energy efficient. ST rehabilitated the house, and then I bought it for $150,000.

Map of Neighborhood and Personal Use of Space

For this action-based research project the neighborhood is defined as the census tract within which the place that matters is located. Recall that you have already written about what spaces within the census tract figure into your daily routine. Include in this section a map and a description of the place that matters. The map should show the census tract boundaries and mark the streets that figure into your daily routine (see figure 2.2). Remember that it is the surrounding neighborhood that is the focus of your investigative research.

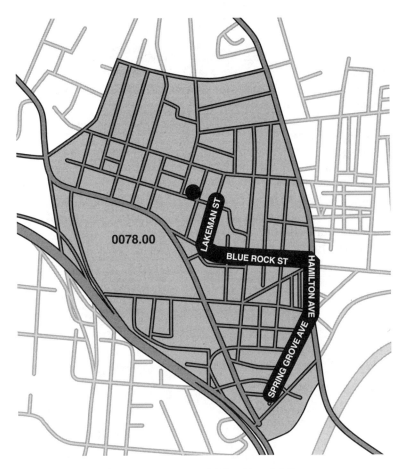

Figure 2.2. Map of Census Tract 78 and Often-Traveled Streets
Source: Joan Ferrante and Tabitha Kelly

Model Write-Up: Census Tract Map and Personal Use of Space

Figure 2.2 shows the spaces within census tract 78 in Northside (Hamilton County), Ohio, that are key to my daily routine, including the streets on which I drive to work, walk, or ride my bike. Those streets are Lakeman, Blue Rock, Hamilton Avenue, and Spring Grove. These streets take me to my favorite eating place, Melt Eclectic Deli, and my favorite place to relax, Jacob Hoffner Park.

REFERENCES

Bryant, Clifton D. and Dennis L. Peck. 2007. "The Sociology of Community," in *21st Century Sociology: A Reference Book*. Sage Publications Inc.

Gieryn, Thomas F. 2000. "A Space for Place in Sociology." *Annual Review of Sociology* 26: 463–96.

Macfarlane, Alan. 1977. "History, Anthropology and the Study of Communities." *Social History* 5 (May): 631–35.

MacQueen, Kathleen M., et al. 2001. "What Is Community? An Evidence-Based Definition for Participatory Public Health." *American Journal of Public Health* 91 (12): 1929–38.

Oldenburg, Ray. 1999. *The Great Good Place: Cafés, Coffee Shops, Bookstores, Bars, Hair Salons, and Other Hangouts the Heart of a Community*. 3rd ed. New York: Marlowe & Co.

Relph, Edward. 1976. *Place and Placelessness*. London: Pion.

Werlen, Benno. 1993. *Society Action and Space: An Alternative Human Geography*. London: Routledge.

3 Things Are Not What They Seem

Imagine a group of sociologists walking the streets of your census tract. They are not content with just looking at what is in their line of vision because they realize that "things are not what they seem" (Berger 1963, 17). They have an uncontrollable urge to go inside the buildings and look in basements and attics, under floorboards, behind walls, and in all the rooms and closets to learn about everything that is hidden from view. The desire to explore things hidden from view captures the language and methods that are the lens of sociology. That lens compels us to leave our comfort zones to talk with people and explore social settings no matter their reputation as desirable, ordinary, or even dangerous. Sociologists understand that gathering data about people and places comes with immense responsibility. They do not gather or use data with the aim of embarrassing, exposing, or disgracing others. Instead sociologists are "interested in understanding for its own sake" (Berger 1963, 17).

This chapter is divided into four modules:

Module 3.1: Five Concepts

Module 3.2: Applying Concepts to Data

Module 3.3: Come to Terms with Margin of Error

Module 3.4: The Four Sociological Perspectives

Each module guides you through the preliminary work of getting to know the neighborhood that surrounds your place that matter. Completing the modules will help you identify areas in your neighborhood in need of support—support that you may be able to provide. The exercises prepare you to answer the core research questions:

1. In what ways do you currently support, or fail to support, the neighborhood that surrounds the place that matters?
2. Should support be increased? If so, in what ways?

You have already done a preliminary tour of the census tract that is home to the place that matters to your life (see chapter 1). Module 3.1 prepares you to do a sociologically guided tour.

MODULE 3.1: FIVE CONCEPTS

Before embarking on this second tour, you will become familiar with five key sociological concepts. The concepts and theorists (in parentheses) are as follows: materialism (Karl Marx), solidarity (Émile Durkheim), social action (Max Weber), color line (W. E. B. Du Bois), and sympathetic knowledge (Jane Addams). The five theorists are counted among the great thinkers in sociology. Those who call themselves sociologists must know these concepts and be able to apply them in the world. While these concepts are considered key to the discipline, there are thousands of other sociological concepts that could drive thinking and channel your vision in new ways.

WHAT YOU WILL DO

- ✓ Read about each of the five sociological concepts.
- ✓ Imagine taking a tour of the census tract with the ghosts of Marx, Durkheim, Weber, Du Bois, and Addams.
- ✓ Imagine a question each theorist would ask or something they might notice.
- ✓ Write up a clear account of each tour referencing census tract and signature terms.
- ✓ Mention how the key concepts help you think about ways you can support your neighborhood.

MATERIALISM

Karl Marx's (1846) concept of materialism places emphasis on things humans produce and on economic activity. Marx saw society as a system of social relations that ultimately mirror economic relations in the workplace and the labor market. From the materialist's point of view, people's social identity and livelihood is ultimately tied to what they do (or to what someone they depend on does), how much they earn, and what part (if any) of the production process they own.

Marx focused on the relationship between capitalists and laborers. This relationship is characterized by the competing and conflicting interests of employers, who are always compelled to find ways to reduce the cost of labor,[1] and employees, whose interests lie with increasing their wages. Marx noted that the wages paid to workers are lower than the true value of their labor since workers deliver a product or service that employers can sell at a higher price than what it costs them to manufacture or deliver. The worker is the one who adds value to the true cost of production (labor, material, facilities, etc.), and the employer reaps that added value in profits—profits that the employer and stockholders pocket or reinvest.

On your imaginary tour with the ghost of Karl Marx, be prepared to answer questions that direct your attention to tensions or conflicts in economic relationships.

- Who are the major employers in the census tract?
- What kind of labor do they require to run their enterprise?
- Speculate on the wages employers pay.
- Is there a conflict (tension) between residents within the census tract rooted in income differences? For example, do some residents see their neighborhood as better or inferior in some way?

---

1. Marx (1973 [1867], 112) wrote, "It is the absolute interest of every capitalist to press a given quantity of labor out of a smaller, rather than a greater number of laborers, if the cost is about the same.... The more extended the scale of production, the stronger this motive. Its force increases with the accumulation of capital."

Exercise 3.1: Tour the census tract with the ghost of Karl Marx

Make at least ONE observation about your neighborhood that addresses economically driven tensions or conflicts. Note that residents of the census tract do not necessarily work at these establishments; they are likely employed outside the census tract. Here we are interested in the kinds of employers inside the census tract that draw in employees, from both inside and outside the tract. See appendix A at the end of the book for a checklist of potential observations. A model write-up follows.

> Focusing on who the major employers in the neighborhood are and what kind of labor they require, Karl Marx notices the Now Hiring signs posted outside different fast-food businesses and grocery stores along 6th Street in census tract 521 located in Bellevue (Campbell County), Kentucky. There is a McDonald's, a Gold Star Chili, an Arby's, a Big Lots, and a Kroger. This method of advertising for *labor* sends an unmistakable message about the kind of positions available: Help Wanted signs do not aim to attract accountants or managers but people "willing" to work for low wages. These are businesses that run like an assembly line. The workers must satisfy impatient customers, which puts them under great stress. This information makes me think that I could support my neighborhood by organizing an "appreciation day" for those who work in minimum wage environments.

SOLIDARITY

The concept of solidarity is associated with the writings of Émile Durkheim. This concept draws our attention to the social ties or social bonds that connect people to others and to society (Durkheim 1897). The most obvious social ties are with people we interact with on a regular basis, including family members, neighbors, coworkers, classmates, and roommates. There are also *instrumental social ties,* or ties with people we do not know well (or at all), such as sanitation workers who pick up and empty household garbage or factory workers in faraway places who make our clothes and electronic equipment.[2] The estimated 200 pairs of human hands that are involved in the process of manufacturing our gym

---

2. For example, if there were no trash collectors it would be impossible to reside in or visit a neighborhood because of the overpowering odor, in addition to other resulting problems that would make the area unlivable.

shoes count as those to whom we have instrumental social ties (Chang 2009). We may not know the sanitation workers, shoemakers, or factory workers, but we have a bond with them nevertheless.

Durkheim also focused on contexts that nurture social ties or solidarity, such as places of worship, neighborhood events (festivals, concerts), and spaces (playgrounds, nature trails). These contexts widen opportunities for people to connect and form new ties. In addition, Durkheim was concerned with economic and other social crises. During times of crisis people's ties are disrupted. During an economic crisis, for example, jobs disappear, and people lose ties to workplaces and communities. Ties with others are also disrupted when long-standing traditions end, when a place of worship closes, when a playground falls into disrepair, or when a business fails.

Because Durkheim looks at the world through the lens of solidarity, when you walk with his ghost around your census tract, be prepared to observe evidence of ties that bind residents to each other and the neighborhood. Durkheim would ask the following questions.

- Are there any activities within the census tract that bring residents together (e.g., some event that cultivates social bonds)?
- Are there organizations within the census tract that cultivate ties among residents (e.g., places of worship, a neighborhood watch group, a home owners' association)?
- To what extent have residents lost or gained a social tie in the past year (e.g., as the result of a business closing, a new business opening, a divorce, or a birth of a child)?
- How are residents tied to others within and outside their census tract who they do not know and will likely never know?

Exercise 3.2: Tour the census tract with the ghost of Émile Durkheim

Your task is to make and write up ONE observation about your neighborhood inspired by the concept of solidarity. See appendix A of this chapter for a checklist of potential observations. A sample write-up follows.

> As Durkheim and I are walking down Fairfield Avenue, one of the main streets in census tract 521, which is part of Bellevue (Campbell County), Kentucky, he points to a now-abandoned movie theater with one screen and seating for

about 80 and asks me to think about how this represents the loss of a social tie for residents in this neighborhood. Durkheim notes that at one time the theater offered residents an activity that facilitated *solidarity* or *social ties* among residents. Residents, especially children, could walk from their homes to the theater, see people they knew, and meet friends from outside the census tract. Now if residents want to see a movie the nearest multiplex is 2 miles away. It is not that far, but to get there they must drive, pay for parking, and pay much higher prices for tickets and snacks. Perhaps I could support my neighborhood by looking into whether there is some organized effort in place to reopen this theater or turn it into something else that benefits the neighborhood rather than sit empty. If such an effort exists, I will join it.

SOCIAL ACTION

The sociologist Max Weber (1922) placed a great deal of emphasis on social action. Actions are social when people behave in some predictable or expected way. That predictability can be enforced by (1) the sacredness of tradition (i.e., something that we have always done and that those before us have always done); (2) deep emotion, which might include faith, love, or attraction to charismatic figures; (3) a code of conduct (i.e., a right and honorable way to do things, such as a professional code of conduct); or (4) the desire to choose the quickest, most efficient means possible (irrespective of negative consequences) to meet a goal (e.g., the quickest way to make a profit).[3]

Because Weber thinks in terms of predictable thought and behavior, he looks for contexts or settings that support a certain way of thinking and behaving. So on your walk with Weber be prepared to field questions about any organization or setting in the census tract that

- ✓ cultivates or honor tradition such as a place of worship;
- ✓ evokes or honor emotion, such as a cemetery or a parade (on the Fourth of July, Veterans Day);
- ✓ requires or rewards a code of conduct (a doctor's office, an extreme fitness training center, a school);

---

3. One might equate this type of action with the behavior of an addict who pursues a drug no matter the cost to self or others (Posner 1997).

✓ demands that a valued goal (winning a game, making a sale) be achieved at any cost.[4]

Exercise 3.3: Tour the census tract with the ghost of Max Weber

Your task is to make at least ONE observation about some behavior or activity that goes on within your census tract that is inspired by a context that promotes one of the four types of social action. See appendix A for a checklist of potential observations. A sample write-up follows.

> In census tract 35.09 located in West Palm Beach (Palm Beach County), Florida, Weber points out that there seems to be many Catholic churches with signs announcing fish fries that draw crowds of people who either eat at the church or pick up food to take home. Driven by the question, Are there any settings in the neighborhood that honor tradition or emotion?, Weber comments that these church-sponsored fish fries maintain *traditions* and spark *emotions*. Weber and I wonder what tradition *motivates* churches to do fish fries and Catholics to abstain from eating meat on Fridays during Lent. The best answer we are able to find comes from Catholicism.com: "The drawing of a symbolic fish in the dirt was a way that the early Christians knew each other when it was dangerous to admit in public that one was Christian. Our Lord cooked fish for His Apostles after His Resurrection, and most of these men were fishermen. After He established His Church, these fishermen became 'fishers of men for the Kingdom of God.'" The fish fries honor this past, and they have become a tradition. Until I walked around with Weber, I never thought about supporting a church fish fry. But now I will try to support this tradition by bringing a friend on a Friday during Lent to eat.

COLOR LINE

In *The Souls of Black Folk* (1903), W. E. B. Du Bois wrote that "the problem of the Twentieth Century is the problem of the color line—the unequal relations of the darker to the lighter races" (13). An honest look at history reveals that the color line has been a "real and efficient cause of misery" (45). Du Bois pointed out that most people decry prejudice and discrimination based on color, but it remains a "heavy fact" that cannot be (and

---

4. Another related question is, are there settings that reject tradition, emotion, or code of conduct to achieve a valued goal in the most efficient way?

has not been) easily dismantled. It is important to point out that Du Bois was concerned with all forms of discrimination and prejudice, not just forms based on skin shade. The color line is most noticeable in racially segregated spaces.

The roots of the color line can be found in prejudice and discrimination once mandated by law. Although these laws have been dismantled, that line is still supported by what became custom or tradition. Du Bois is interested in color lines and other lines of division based on characteristics over which people have little or no control. See appendix A for a checklist of potential observations. As you walk around your census tract with Du Bois be prepared to answer questions such as the following:

- Are certain racial and ethnic groups largely, or even completely, absent from the census tract?
- Do the residents appear to be members of one racial category?
- Are there streets or sports within the census tract known to draw people of a specific racial category?

Exercise 3.4: Tour the census tract with the ghost of W. E. B. Du Bois

Your task is to make at least ONE observation about your neighborhood inspired by the concept of the color line. A model write-up follows.

> As Du Bois and I walk around in census tract 92, Wahiawa (Honolulu County), Hawaii, seeking to answer the question, Is there a color line in this neighborhood?, he notices the seeming absence of a *color line*. He sees a mixture of white-, black-, Hawaiian-, and Samoan-appearing peoples. Du Bois is curious as to what draws such diversity and asks me if I know. I point to the Dole Plantation and its history of bringing low-wage labor from around the world but especially from Asian countries. The U.S. military base is another reason for the diversity of people who live in the neighborhood. But Du Bois is not convinced that there is no color line. He wonders if we would find that a color line exists if we looked at the military and Dole Corporation hierarchies. Maybe one group is at the top and another is at the bottom. This observation makes me wonder whether there are nonprofits within or near my census tract that support soldiers stationed here. This is something I plan to investigate and learn ways I might lend my support.

SYMPATHETIC KNOWLEDGE

The concept of sympathetic knowledge is associated with the writing and work of Jane Addams (1930). She made it her life's work to focus on social problems that result from forces beyond any one person's control. Social problems make themselves known in the disruptions and disadvantages they bring to people's lives and livelihoods. Addams believed social services should be in place, not just for assisting people in times of crisis, but to empower them to stand on their own. She argued that sympathetic knowledge—firsthand knowledge of people, especially the most marginalized—can be acquired from living and working among them. Addams believed sympathetic knowledge is *the* approach to grasping the true gravity of social problems. Sympathetic knowledge rejects easy generalizations and unsubstantiated judgments in favor of a deeper understanding of the situation. This kind of knowledge fuels empathy, which builds understanding and connections among people of different positions in society. Such knowledge increases the chances of responding in effective and empowering ways. See appendix A for a checklist of potential observations. As you walk around your census tract with Jane Addams, she will be asking:

- Do you see evidence of social problems within the census tract that are a response to larger social and economic forces (foreclosures, a food pantry, a social service agency, a Goodwill store, property in disrepair) or marginalized status (low income, lack of documentation, physical impairment)?
- What social services are in place to empower those who are disadvantaged by those forces?

Exercise 3.5: Tour the census tract with the ghost of Jane Addams

Your task is to make at least ONE observation about your neighborhood inspired by the concept of sympathetic knowledge. A model write-up follows.

> As Jane Addams and I aree walking in census tract 703.07, Burlington (Boone County), Kentucky, she notices a nonprofit named the Black Rose Tradition. Addams asks about its purpose, and we learn that it is a local

organization that raises funds to help low-income women who want to deliver full-term, healthy babies. Addams is immediately interested, since her focus is guided by the question, Is someone's life made difficult because of the marginalized status they occupy? She points out that often low-income women do not go full-term; their babies are born premature. This organization seeks to help women have healthy pregnancies and avoid complications. Addams, who is all about *sympathetic knowledge,* is impressed by the symbolism of a black rose and the comfort that symbolism brings to the pregnant women—a rose symbolizing unconditional love and the color black representing the safety of the womb and the power of "dark spaces" to protect the baby from critical gazes. Perhaps I could donate money to or volunteer at the nonprofit the Black Rose Tradition.

MODULE 3.2: APPLY CONCEPTS TO DATA

In completing Module 3.1 above, you experienced the interpretive power of the five signature concepts that allows you to see the surrounding neighborhood in a new light. The point of Module 3.2 is to reinforce the use of those interpretive skills. This time you will again apply the signature concepts of Durkheim, Marx, Weber, Du Bois, and Addams. But now the five concepts will inspire the way you look at census data that apply to the residents of this neighborhood.

WHAT YOU WILL DO

- ✓ Follow instructions about how to access census data on residents;
- ✓ Imagine reviewing the data with Marx, Durkheim, Weber, Du Bois, and Addams looking over your shoulder.
- ✓ Come to terms with the meanings of estimate and margin of error.

Access Census Data on Residents

To access four overview census documents on the census tract (or neighborhood) in which the place that matters is located, follow the instructions below.

1. Google "ACS Data Tables on American FactFinder."
2. Under "Data Profiles (all years, all datasets)," choose the latest five-year data product (DP).

3. You will see the following documents listed (do not check the boxes next to each yet):

> Selected Social Characteristics in the United States
>
> Selected Economic Characteristics in the United States
>
> Selected Housing Characteristics in the United States
>
> ACS Demographic and Housing Estimates

4. Before checking the box next to each, specify the geography of interest (your census tract). Do this by choosing Geographies (at lower left), and then from the dropdown menu (select a geography type) choose "Census Tract-140." Next select the appropriate state, county, and census tract number for your place that matters. Click "Add to Selections." Close the box.
5. Now check the four boxes associated with the four documents listed above and choose View.
6. Move from one document to the next by clicking on the results arrow at the top right of the page.

To prepare for the task ahead, first study table 3.1 below, which contains some estimates taken from the document "Selected Housing Characteristics in the United States" for census tract 4083.01 in Medina City (Medina County), Ohio. Notice that those estimates are the numbers and percentages of householders who moved into their place of residence during each of six time frames. The numbers are called estimates because they are based on answers that a sample of residents gave to a question about what year they moved into their place of residence. Because these numbers and percentages are based on a sample, they never perfectly reflect the actual numbers and percentages.[5] But they are the best *estimates* available.

Now imagine each of the five theorists looking at table 3.1. Which one of these five might find these estimates especially interesting? Durkheim would certainly point to the large percentage of households whose residents moved in before the year 2000 (30.6%) as evidence of households with very strong ties to the surrounding neighborhood. That means that

---

5. See chapter 5 for discussion on sampling.

Table 3.1 Estimates of Year Householder Moved in for Census Tract 4083.01 Medina (Medina County), Ohio

Year Householder Moved into Unit	Estimate (number)	Margin of Error	Estimate (%)	Margin of Error
Occupied housing units	1,305	+/-78	1,305	(X)
Moved in 2015 or later	17	+/-19	1.3%	+/-1.4
Moved in 2010 to 2014	324	+/-86	24.8%	+/-6.2
Moved in 2000 to 2009	564	+/-99	43.2%	+/-7.1
Moved in 1990 to 1999	195	+/-62	14.9%	+/-4.8
Moved in 1980 to 1989	128	+/-49	9.8%	+/-3.7
Moved in 1979 or earlier	77	+/-37	5.9%	+/-2.8

SOURCE: American Community Survey, latest data (2015) accessed Nov. 15, 2017.

almost one in three households has residents who have lived in the census tract for almost 20 years. For now, ignore margin of error columns.

Exercise 3.6: Choose data points that interest each of the five theorists

Look over the four census bureau documents. For each theorist, select ONE estimate that is likely to attract that theorist's attention. Write approximately six to eight sentences for EACH theorist. The write-up for what Durkheim would say about the data in table 3.1 might look as follows:

- As Durkheim and I look over Selected Social Characteristics in the United States, he makes it clear that he is interested in data that tell him something about *solidarity*. He is also interested in any data that provide insights about the strength or weakness of residents' *ties* to others and/or to the neighborhood. Right away, Durkheim notices that there are estimates for the number and percentage of householders who moved in by year. He asks me to add up the numbers and figure the percentage of those who moved in before 2000. I do that, and we see that 400 of the 1,305 householders (30.6%) in census tract 4083.01 located in Medina County, Ohio, moved in before the year 2000. Durkheim thinks this is a evidence that one-third of householders have strong ties to the surrounding neighborhood as they have lived there for almost 20 years. The thought crossed my mind that I could organize a search for the householders who have lived in the census tract the longest and find a way to celebrate the stability they bring to the neighborhood.

Examples of how to apply the signature concepts of Marx, Weber, Du Bois, and Addams to other estimates follow. Notice in each write-up that the estimate and the accompanying interpretation create the need to learn more.[6]

Model Write-Ups for the Other Four Theorists

- As Weber and I look at estimates in Selected Social Characteristics in the United States for census tract 652, located in Ft. Wright (Kenton County), Kentucky, Weber keys in on the number and percentage of residents in my census tract who are veterans. Of the 3,245 people age 18 and over, 241, or 7.4%, are veterans. Weber asks me to speculate about what may have *motivated* veterans to enlist when they did. I thought for a few minutes. Some veterans may have been motivated by *tradition* if they followed in the footsteps of parents or grandparents who also served. For others, the motivation may have been *emotion* (love for country). Still others may have joined because they saw the military as an experience that would instill discipline or a *code of conduct*. Weber reminds me that the data are only estimates of how many residents 18 or over hold veteran status; it cannot tell us the reasons veterans joined and served. Perhaps I could find a business within the census tract—a café, a restaurant, the ice cream shop—whose owner or manager would like to know this population exists and agree to offer resident veterans a discount on any purchase.
- As W. E. B. Du Bois and I look at the ACS Demographic and Housing Estimates, he sees that of the 3,581 residents in census tract 4083.02 in Medina City (Medina County), Ohio, 96.8% (or 3,466 residents) classify themselves as white, 0.9% (34) as black, and 2.5% (93) as Asian. Du Bois wonders where nonwhites live and in what spaces I notice people who appear black and Asian as we are walking. I say to Du Bois, "I am shocked. I never thought of my census tract as having a *color line*." I tell Du Bois that I have never even noticed people who appear other than white. Du Bois tells me that this color line can likely be traced to a time when laws segregated the white- from nonwhite-

---

6. You can check data for yourself by going to the census bureau website to find the listed state, county, and census tract.

classified and our country has yet to recover. This may sound like a cliché, but I would like to have a block party where everyone invites a person who appears to be a different race from themselves to the event.

- In looking over the data in Selected Housing Characteristics for census tract 652 located in Ft. Wright (Kenton County), Kentucky, Jane Addams exercises *sympathetic knowledge* for the 27 (1.6%) of 1,706 households that do not have telephones in the home or access to cell phones. She tells me we must find out how these 27 people communicate with others. Do they borrow a neighbor's phone? Addams says, "Let's go out and walk around the census tract to see how many pay phones there are." This conversation makes me want to learn where pay phones are in the neighborhood and if there are none, identify a place where people without phones could go to make a call.

- When looking over data in Selected Economic Characteristics for census tract 46.01 located in Palm Springs (Palm Beach County), Florida, Karl Marx sees evidence of employers exploiting workers. As we look at the population age 16 and over in the labor force (n = 3,081), Marx quickly notices that 1,978, or 99.4%, of the employed commute and that it takes them an average of 27.7 minutes to get to work. Marx sees this as a cost workers bear—cost in time (55.4 minutes round trip), gasoline, car maintenance, or bus fares. Marx argues that the workers are subsidizing employers by absorbing these costs. This information made me think about how ridiculous it is to drive 55 minutes per day alone. I wonder if my place of worship could have a "find a ride share" night where people "speed dated" to find a person who drives to the same general destination.

Use the above examples as a guide to your write-ups. Notice that the examples are effective because the writer

- ✓ names the document that is the source of the chosen estimate;
- ✓ specifies the census tract number and associated county and state;
- ✓ is clear about the theorist and that theorist's interest;
- ✓ gives the number *and* percentage of residents who share a characteristic (e.g., drive to work alone) in the context of some total population (e.g., those employed);
- ✓ applies an appropriate signature concept; and
- ✓ gets into the spirit of the assignment by imagining a conversation about data with each theorist.

MODULE 3.3: COME TO TERMS WITH THE MARGIN OF ERROR

You have already noticed that the census data (numbers and percentages) are estimates. For example, table 3.1 (above) shows estimates and margin of error (see column headings) for census tract 4083.01 in Medina City (Medina County), Ohio. The table shows estimates of the number of households[7] and the year residents moved in. The number of occupied households in census tract 4083.01 is estimated to be 1,305.

Because estimates are based on a sample of residents' answers to survey questions, we must live with sampling error, or *margin of error*. In this case, the margin of error for the number of occupied households is + or – 78. The margin of error is used to calculate what is called a confidence interval by adding 78 to the estimate of 1,305 and subtracting 78 from that estimate.

1,305 – 78 = 1,227
1,305 + 78 = 1,383

Figure 3.1 depicts the confidence interval for the estimate of 1,305 occupied households, which ranges from a lower limit of 1,227 to an upper limit of 1,383. The confidence interval is typically expressed in terms of a level of certainty: 90%, 95%, or 99%. The census bureau applies a 90% level of certainty.[8] This represents a level of confidence about the probability that the confidence interval contains the actual value or in this case the actual number of occupied households. In the case of census tract 4083.01 we can be 90% confident that the actual number of householders is between 1,227 and 1,383.[9]

---

7. Householders are the people who answered the survey questions about themselves and everyone else who lived in a housing unit, whether that unit is a house or an apartment.
8. We will not go into the details of how confidence intervals are calculated. Our emphasis is on making an interpretation once we know the confidence interval.
9. Think about it this way: If we were to repeatedly resample (each time drawing a new sample, conducting new interviews, establishing new estimates, and calculating new margins of error), the confidence intervals we calculate for *each new sample* would *in theory* contain the value that is the average of all the sample estimates 90% of the time. That is, we can be 90% certain that the average of the estimates is no smaller or no larger than the lower and upper limits of the confidence interval. In the case of census tract 4083.01 we can be 90% confident that the actual size of its occupied households is no smaller than 1,227 and no

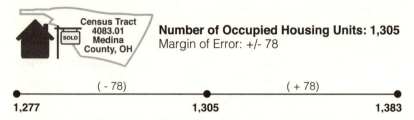

Figure 3.1. Interpreting Margin of Error and Calculating Confidence Intervals for Total Households in Census Tract 4083.01, Medina (Medina County), Ohio
SOURCE: Joan Ferrante and Tabitha Kelly

The point is that the *estimate* is not the actual number of occupied households. The true size is knowable only if we survey every household within the census tract. When using estimates derived from a sample, we must accept uncertainty.

Notice that the logic holds for assessing estimates of the number and percentages of households whose residents moved in during each range of years. The margin of error for the estimated number of households whose members moved in during the year 1979 or earlier is + or − 37. So we can be 90% confident that the *true* number is between 40 and 114 (figure 3.2).

Now turn to the percentage of households (59%) whose members moved in during the year 1979 or before. The margin of error is + or − 2.8%. We can be 90% confident that the true proportion is between 3.1% and 8.7% (figure 3.2).

So how does this uncertainty affect how we interpret the data? Recall that the margin of error and the confidence interval tell us

1. we can be 90% confident that the *true* value falls somewhere on the calculated confidence interval;
2. the narrower the calculated confidence interval, the more confident we can be that the estimate is close to the true value.

---

larger than 1,383. The operating assumption is that if we had the time to take hundreds of samples and make hundreds of sample estimates, the average of those estimates would be the true value of the population size.

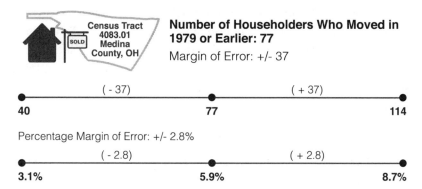

Figure 3.2. Interpreting Margin of Error and Calculating Confidence Intervals for Number and Percentage of Householders Who Moved into Census Tract 4083.01, Medina (Medina County), Ohio

SOURCE: Joan Ferrante and Tabitha Kelly

If you are using estimates to make some decision or recommendation, remember that this estimate is the best measure you have of the number of householders and the year ranges during which residents moved in. We cannot treat this estimate as the actual number, but we can use the confidence interval to think in terms of best- and worst-case scenarios.[10] We can ask, what would be the impact on our thinking and plans if the *true* number of occupied households was as small as 1,227? Or as large as 1,383? Imagine, for example, that you are planning to open an urgent care clinic in the census tract with the goal of serving its households. You can use your estimate to speculate about whether 1,305 households will provide a large enough customer base to support the clinic. But then use the end point of the confidence interval to think in terms of best- and worst-case scenarios. Will the urgent care clinic have enough business if there

---

10. The margin of error (MoE) is not a measure of the quality of the data gathered. It is a reflection of the sample size relative to the total population of interest. Well-designed survey questions with a sample size of 50 or 100 will typically have a larger MoE than a more poorly conceived poll but with a sample size of 5,000. To assess quality of data, you need to know the sample size, how the sample was determined, and the thought put into writing the questions. The census bureau calculates margin of error taking into consideration how "sampling, interviewing, measuring, and modeling contribute to uncertainty" (U.S. Bureau of the Census 2017).

are 1,227 occupied households in the tract? Or will it be overwhelmed with business if there are 1,383 households? Of course, you will need more information than the estimated number of households[11] to decide whether it is worthwhile to put an urgent care clinic in the census tract, but this is a start.[12]

Exercise 3.7: Rethink estimates considering the margin of error

Now that you have a basic understanding of margin of error and confidence intervals, revisit ONE data point from your walk with Durkheim, Marx, Weber, Du Bois, or Addams. But this time pay attention to the margin of error. Use that margin of error to calculate the 90% confidence interval for the chosen estimate. Now incorporate margin of error into that write-up. Two sample write-ups reevaluating estimates in light of margin of error follow. Notice that these sample write-ups

- ✓ are very clear about the estimate being reevaluated;
- ✓ refer to the census tract number, the county, and the state;
- ✓ specify the margin of error;
- ✓ calculate a confidence interval; and
- ✓ state the upper and lower limits of the confidence interval.

Model Write-Ups

- Weber and I looked at the number and percentage of residents who hold veteran status in census tract 652, located in Ft. Wright (Kenton County), Kentucky (from Selected Social Characteristics in the United States). Of the 3,245 people age 18 and over, 241, or 7.4%, hold veteran status. The margin of error for that estimate is +/- 82. We can expect, with 90% confidence, that the true number of veterans could be as low as 159 or as high as 323. The margin of error for the percentage of veterans is +/- 2.4%. We can expect with 90% confidence that

---

11. For example, you will want to know how many people live in these occupied households. But knowing the number of households is a start because a household is an economic unit. Children and those not in the labor force rely on the household and other income-generating members to pay for treatment (or secure health care coverage).

12. Always keep in mind that these census data offer the best estimates we have of a population's social and demographic characteristics.

the true percentage is between 5% and 9.8%. Of course, the end points of the confidence interval represent extreme possibilities.
- When looking over the Selected Economic Characteristics in census tract 46.01 in Palm Springs (Palm Beach County), Florida, Karl Marx and I noticed that an estimated 1,326, or 66.6%, of the population age 16 and over in the labor force (1,991) drive alone to work. We also notice that it takes an average of 27.7 minutes to make that drive (one way), for a total of 55.4 minutes of driving time. When we reevaluate the estimate of the number of commuters driving alone in light of the margin of error, which is +/- 242, we can be 90% confident that the true number of commuters falls between 1,084 and 1,568. The margin of error for the average minutes to get to work is +/- 4.8. We can be 90% confident that the true number of minutes to get to work ranges from a low of 22.9 to a high of 33.5 minutes. These numbers should be considered worst- and best-case scenarios.

It is important to note that while we will be using census data to do other assignments, we will not make direct reference to margin of error every time we create tables. However, depending on what you choose to include in your research brief margin of error is something to be addressed at that time.

MODULE 3.4: THE FOUR SOCIOLOGICAL PERSPECTIVES

To this point you have imagined taking a tour of your census tract with the ghosts of Karl Marx, Émile Durkheim, Max Weber, W. E. B. Du Bois, and Jane Addams. You have reviewed census data with each theorist. This next section introduces you to four major perspectives in sociology: functionalist, conflict, symbolic interaction, and feminist. Each perspective acts as an interpretive tool that focuses our attention on what is going on in the world around us. Each perspective guides thinking by drawing our attention to (1) a key question to focus attention on and (2) a vocabulary to frame the analysis. In this section, we will apply each theory to something within the census tract. This focus ultimately prepares you to answer the two core research questions:

1. In what ways do you currently support, or fail to support, the neighborhood that surrounds the place that matters?
2. Should support be increased? If so, in what ways?

WHAT YOU WILL DO

✓ Read the brief overview of each of the four sociological perspectives.

✓ Imagine that you are collaborating with a functionalist, a conflict theorist, a symbolic interactionist, and a feminist to think about something within the census tract.

✓ Write approximately 6 to 10 sentences applying EACH perspective to the chosen focus.

✓ Make reference to a Google Scholar source (https://scholar.google.com/) that supports your observation. See appendix C at the end of this book for instructions on how to use Google Scholar.

FUNCTIONALIST PERSPECTIVE

Functionalists view "order and stability" as the key force at the center of human activities. The functionalist perspective assumes that society is a system of parts. A part can be *anything* that exists in society—festivals, speed bumps, neighborhood centers, places of worship, police officers, a library, a city council, crime, wealth, and even poverty-level wages. Each part serves a function. That is, it makes some contribution to order and stability. That contribution can be expected (manifest) or unexpected (latent). Functionalists ask, How does a part contribute in expected and unexpected ways to order and stability?[13] The functionalist perspective encourages us to ask the following question:

- Is there something within the census tract that contributes to order and stability?[14]

13. For example, a neighborhood festival can support order and stability because it is where the residents can meet and connect with each other (manifest function). Because people sometimes must park far from the event they have a chance to walk through streets they might not otherwise frequent. As a result, they have an opportunity to observe neighborhood life (latent function).

14. Although not covered here, functionalists also look at expected and unexpected dysfunctions. If we stay with the example of festivals, we expect traffic and litter to be a problem (manifest dysfunctions). A latent dysfunction might be that police use the "chaos" of a

Exercise 3.8: Apply the functionalist perspective

Your task is to imagine collaborating with a functionalist to find something within the census tract that contributes to order and stability and support that observation with at least one Google Scholar reference. One model write-up follows.

> I will be focusing on the Auto Care Shop, which is located within census tract 004 in Oscoda (Iosco County), Michigan. I have asked a functionalist how an auto repair shop can promote order and stability within a neighborhood. We have noticed that the shop is filled with many customers. I told the functionalist that locals seem to admire and want to support the shop because it is family-owned and has been around for 50 years. We found Google Scholar sources (https://scholar.google.com/) that describes how locally owned businesses give residents confidence and a sense of pride. The functionalist tells me that local businesses that have been around for a while contribute to the health of the neighborhood in ways that chains and transnationals cannot.
>
> **Reference**
> Anselin, Luc. 1988. *Spatial Econometrics: Methods and Models*. Dordrecht: Kluwer Academic.
> ———. 1995. "Local Indicators of Spatial Association—LISA." *Geographical Analysis* 27: 93–115.

CONFLICT PERSPECTIVE

As we might expect, conflict theorists view conflict as the central force shaping the structure of human activities. The conflict perspective assumes that human activities are structured to advantage some and disadvantage others as people compete to take or maintain control of some scarce and valued resources. Those in advantaged positions work to protect their own interests against the competing interests of their disadvantaged counterparts. Typically, the advantaged rationalize their relative good fortune as resulting from their hard work and minimize any external factors that might have contributed to their success. Conflict theorists ask,

---

festival as an opportunity to call a strike to secure higher wages. Such an action would be a latent dysfunction to the neighborhood but a latent function to the police.

Who benefits from the way human activities are structured? Who is disadvantaged by that structure? With regard to the place that matters, the conflict perspective encourages us to ask

- Are there ways that the place that matters advantages some and disadvantages others?
- Does the place that matters hold a valued resource that some people in the neighborhood can access and others cannot?

Exercise 3.9: Apply the conflict perspective

Your task is to imagine collaborating with a conflict theorist to make at least one observation about the neighborhood related to valued resources or advantaged/disadvantaged groups. Include support from at least one Google Scholar source. A sample write-up follows.

> The conflict theorist I am with is fascinated by the library that lies within census tract 501.01 in Oneonta (Blount County), Alabama, and encourages me to ask, Does the library hold some valued resource that some groups could not access if it were not for the library? Whenever I walk into the library, I notice that the chairs in front of the computers are always occupied, and there are often waiting lists. This library offers patrons free access to that highly valued resource. It is my impression that those who cannot afford personal computers and internet service obtain access to them in the library. Searching Google Scholar, we found an article pointing out that "public libraries have evolved into a primary source of Internet access in many communities, generating wide-ranging impacts in the communities that public libraries serve."
>
> **Reference**
> Bertot, John Carlo, Charles R. McClure, and Paul T. Jaeger. 2008. "The Impacts of Free Public Internet Access on Public Library Patrons and Communities." *Library* 78 (3).

SYMBOLIC INTERACTION PERSPECTIVE

Symbolic interactionists see social interaction as the central force guiding society and society as ultimately a web of interactions. Symbolic interactionists assume that people are social beings, meaning that a sense of self emerges and evolves from interacting with others. Moreover, we can think of the human biography as a chronicle of the millions of interactions people have had with others. Over the course of interaction, the involved parties interpret each other's behaviors and actions considering the context or setting.

Symbols and *context* are important to any interaction. Symbols are the mechanisms by which people communicate with each other. A symbol is anything to which people assign meaning; for instance, a wave of the hand can mean many things, including hello, come here, go away, or good-bye. Depending on the situation or context, along with subtle changes in the way the hand is waved, that wave can have a deeper meaning, such as "Good-bye until we meet again" or "Good-bye, I never want to see you again." The wave could also mean, "Hey, I see you." The central questions guiding the symbolic interactionist perspective are, What meanings do people assign to their own and others' words and behavior? How does context shape action and interpretations?

A symbolic interaction perspective puts the focus on the spaces and interactions within the census tract. Symbolic interactionists ask

- What kinds of interactions occur within and around those spaces?
- What meanings do residents assign to something inside the census tract?
- How does a setting within the census tract shape interaction and interpretation?

Exercise 3.10: Apply the symbolic interactionist perspective

Your task is to imagine collaborating with a symbolic interactionist to make at least one observation about your neighborhood related to symbolic meaning, interaction or interpretation. Include support from at least one Google Scholar source. The write-up should incorporate Google Scholar research to enhance the analysis. A sample write-up follows.

> Within census tract 132.02 in Orlando (Orange County), Florida, is a funeral home. I am with a symbolic interactionist. We did a little research and found that this funeral home is part of a large corporation called the Dignity Memorial®, a network of more than 2,000 licensed providers in North America. I was totally surprised because I thought it was a unique place, not part of a national chain. My symbolic interactionist collaborator suggested we ask, What meanings do people assign to this funeral home and its services?

According to the Google Scholar article, "Selling in a Dying Business," funeral homes use advertising and marketing strategies that nudge patrons toward "customized burial options." Although price is not mentioned, it is clear that marketing language influences how burial options are considered. The *legacy package* sounds much more impressive than the *tribute package* and, to no surprise, is more expensive. The symbolic interactionist asks, "Can you see that the funeral home manages to convey the higher value of the legacy package versus the tribute package by the words it pairs with each? The legacy burial option offers something that lasts forever, and the tribute burial option offers a moment of respect."

Reference

Beard, Virginia R., and William C. Burger. 2017. "Selling in a Dying Business: An Analysis of Trends During a Period of Major Market Transition in the Funeral Industry." *OMEGA—Journal of Death and Dying* (December 13).

Dignity Memorial®. Customized Funeral Planning. www.dignitymemorial.com /en-us/search/location-finder.page.

FEMINIST PERSPECTIVE

The feminist perspective puts gender at the forefront of any analysis. It focuses on forces that underly inequalities rooted in the binary (two-category) classification of gender. That classification system assumes people naturally identify with, and should be perceived as belonging to, one of two categories: male or female. For the most part, this two-category system marginalizes and undervalues labor, bodies, and statuses considered feminine and celebrates and values labor, bodies, and statuses considered masculine. This binary system also marginalizes family forms and relationships that depart from ideals rooted in heterosexual norms and in beliefs about how males and females should think, feel, and behave. The feminist perspective focuses on gender-based inequalities, including the penalties and privileges that empower one gender and disadvantage another. It also considers intersectionality, the complex intersection between a person's gender and other statuses such as race, age, disability, and class. In focusing on the census tract, the feminist perspective compels us to ask questions such as

- In what ways, if any, does something inside the census tract that privileges or disadvantages one gender over another?

- Is there something inside the census tract that liberates people from the binary system of gender expectations?

Exercise 3.11: Apply the feminist perspective

Your task is to imagine collaborating with a feminist to make at least one observation about gender-based inequality or constraints of the binary system of gender expections. Provide support for this observation from a Google Scholar source. A sample write-up follows.

> I am with a feminist who is walking through Sawyer Point Park in census tract 265 in Cincinnati (Hamilton County), Ohio. She asks, "Does the park do anything to liberate the grip of the binary system of gender expectations?" The feminist is impressed when I tell her about the Cincinnati Gay Pride Celebration held in June. We google Cincinnati Pride and learn that its mission is to affirm the LGBTQ community's "importance to the Greater Cincinnati area by giving expression to our community's rich history and diversity and renewing our dedication to promoting acceptance of all individuals regardless of sexual orientation, gender identity or expression." According to Johnston and Waitt (2015), parks and other parade settings act as spaces where binary norms are transgressed in a supportive, celebratory context.
>
> **Reference**
> Cincinnati Pride. 2018. Mission Statement. www.cincinnatipride.org/mission.html.
> Johnston, Lynda, and Gordon Waitt. 2015. *The Spatial Politics of Gay Pride Parades and Festivals: Emotional Activism*. Aldershot: Ashgate.

Each of the four perspectives pushes us to ask different questions about something within the census tract and its relationship to the neighborhood. Like the four examples above, your write-up should

- ✓ be clear which perspective is being applied;
- ✓ make reference to a guiding question;
- ✓ refer to a signature concept;
- ✓ reflect the spirit of the assignment, which is to image a collaboration with a theorist;
- ✓ state the census tract number, city/place, county and state; and
- ✓ include some Google Scholar research to enhance your analysis and a citation.

WORKING DRAFT OF THE RESEARCH BRIEF, SECTION 2

Key Observations

Recall that you have already written a draft of Section 1 of your research brief that included an introduction to the project, a statement of purpose, and background on your place that matters. In Section 2 of your research brief draft, choose at least three observations that stand out from your tour with the ghosts of each of the five theorists, from the census estimates you chose in "collaboration" with each theorist, and from the imaginary consultation with the sociologists from each of four major perspectives. These observations and estimates should be such that they offer some preliminary clues about what in your census tract needs support (core question #2). Therefore, in writing the Section 2 draft of your research brief, the first step is to review the work you have done in conjunction with the exercises in this chapter and draw from that work. As you review, always keep in mind that you are writing a section that helps you to answer the two core questions:

1. In what ways do you currently support, or fail to support, the neighborhood that surrounds the place that matters?
2. Should support be increased? If so, in what ways?

Also remember that the research brief is a proposed plan of action, and it is up to you whether you will follow through on that plan. Your charge is to learn enough about your neighborhood to know its needs so that you can find ways to support it. In writing Section 2, keep in mind that you are making preliminary observations. As you learn more about your neighborhood, you will revise your thinking and the working draft.

When writing up three highlights, be sure to acknowledge the concept or theorist that inspired each observation or choice of data point. Refer to the theorist in parentheses. After completing the draft, conclude with a summary paragraph that connects the three highlighted observations to some trends that seem to be affecting your neighborhood. The data and observations referenced in this model write-up may or may not have appeared in this chapter. This is one illustration of what a write-up should look like.

Model Write-Up, Section 2

The three most significant preliminary observations about census tract 78 in Northside (Hamilton County), Ohio, are the following:

1. According to ACS Demographic and Housing Estimates, there are 1,531 housing units in census tract 78 (the home census tract). This includes rental and home owner units. Of that number, 28.7% (n = 439) are counted as vacant. (Durkheim would see vacancy rates as one measure of social ties lost. People once rented or owned the units that are now vacant. For whatever reason—a new opportunity or a loss— they have "abandoned" the place in which they once lived. While some level of vacancy is healthy, too much vacancy is a sign of distress.) I plan to investigate why more than one quarter of the properties are vacant and take what I learn to a neighborhood organization in a position to address chronic vacancy.

2. On my tour of home census tract 78, I noticed an obvious divide between the have and have-nots. As one example, there is the nonprofit Cincinnati Urban Promise, "with a mission of helping children in under-resourced communities succeed and avoid negative peer pressure." The apartments and homes around Cincinnati Urban Promise are in rough shape and are occupied by people who appear to be lower income and predominantly minority—Hispanic and black. Some houses have boarded-up windows and, for the most part, need major repair. This section is in stark contrast to Pullen Avenue, which is known to be one of the wealthier streets in Northside, with homes occupied by a young professional class (late 20s to 30s); most appear to be white, but there are hints of diversity. (This observation is inspired by Du Bois, noted for the color line concept.) This makes me wonder, is it possible to learn what skills residents in the two parts of the census tract possess and then set up a venue for trading services (e.g., tax preparation for painting a room)? That might just weaken the divide.

3. My home was one of many that have been renovated by a nonprofit organization, Sustainable Transformation (ST). The organization's goal is to fix up and sell homes that have been labeled eyesores at an affordable price. I am someone who earns about $35,000 a year, so I and others like me benefit from this nonprofit's mission. My house is occupied because of ST and contributes to the stability of the neighborhood by increasing property values, feelings of safety, and curb appeal. (This observation is inspired by Jane Addams's theory of sympathetic

knowledge, which supports solutions that empower.) I want to find a way to support the organization that helped me obtain affordable housing.

Summary: The three preliminary observations suggest that census tract 78 is part of a neighborhood in transition. Specifically, the census tract is part of the larger national trend that values urban or high-density living over suburban or rural living. This trend is associated with a process known as gentrification, where socially and economically disadvantaged populations are pushed out by more advantaged populations. This trend includes what has been called a generational bifurcation, as urban environments are attractive to both older and younger adults.

Reference

Moos, Markus. 2015. "From Gentrification to Youthification? The Increasing Importance of Young Age in Delineating High-Density Living." *Urban Studies* 53 (14): 2903–20.

REFERENCES

Addams, Jane. 1930. *The Second Twenty Years at Hull-House*. Google E-book Free.
Berger, Peter. 1963. *An Invitation to Sociology*. New York: Anchor.
Du Bois, W. E. B. 1903. *The Souls of Black Folk: Essays and Sketches*. Google E-book Free.
Chang, Leslie T. 2009. *Factory Girls: From Village to City in a Changing China*. New York: Random House.
Durkheim, Émile. 1897. *Suicide*. New York: Free Press.
Marx, Karl. 1973 [1867]. *Karl Marx on Society and Social Change: With Selections by Friedrich Engels*. Chicago: University of Chicago Press.
Marx, Karl, and Friedrich Engels. 1970 [1846]. *The German Ideology*. New York: International.
Posner, Richard A. 1997. "Rational Choice, Behavioral Economics, and the Law." *Stanford Law Review* (May 1): 1551–75.
U.S. Bureau of the Census. 2017. "A Basic Explanation of Confidence Intervals."
Weber, Max. 1978 [1922]. *Economy and Society*. Vols. I and II. Berkeley: University of California Press.

4 The Residents

In this chapter, we turn the lens of sociology on the residents and households inside the census tract or surrounding neighborhood. Recall that the goal is to answer the two core questions:

1. In what ways, if any, do you support the neighborhood surrounding the place that matters to you?
2. In what ways might you increase your support for this neighborhood?

You cannot answer these questions without knowing something about the census tract. In this chapter, there are three learning modules that focus on the residents and households in your census tract and compare them with other geographic spaces such as a nearby census tract, the county, the state, or the nation. Comparison allows you to know if the census tract is unusual or typical relative to other geographic spaces.

MODULE 4.1: LEARN ABOUT THE RESIDENTS

One way to learn about residents in your census tract is to establish the numbers and percentages classified by race, sex, age, disability, income, or

60 CHAPTER FOUR

other social category. In the pages that follow we consider the social importance of categories and consider how sociologists think about them.[1] Sociologists define social categories as human constructions with real consequences. That is, categories are things people have invented and made to matter. Categories matter when people learn to explicitly or implicitly rank each as more or less valuable on some continuum of social worth. Social worth may be conveyed in terms of beliefs about which category is filled with people who possess athletic talent, make the best students, or are deserving of a second chance. The sociological point of view influences the way you will think, write, and speak about categories.

WHAT YOU WILL DO

✓ Complete 4 exercises about residents in your neighborhood.

✓ Before beginning each exercise read background information.

✓ Find appropriate census data from the American Community Survey (Factfinder) to create tables and figures.

✓ Interpret the data.

Background on Disability or Impairment

The U.S. Bureau of the Census, the agency that conducts the American Community Survey from which you extract data for this research project, defines a disability as a long-lasting physical, mental, or emotional condition that makes it difficult for a person to do activities such as walking, climbing stairs, dressing, bathing, learning, or remembering. These conditions can also impede people from being able to go outside their homes alone or to work. It is important to know that sociologists make a distinction between disability and impairment. As you will see, this distinction challenges the census bureau's definition of disability.

Sociologists define **disability** as something society has imposed on people because of the way technology has been applied to solving

[1]. The exercises in this chapter walk you through the steps to obtain the racial composition, age-sex composition, and household-type composition of a neighborhood. Other social categories such as educational attainment and occupation are explored in subsequent chapters.

human problems. To elaborate: inventors and engineers have created any number of technologies with the goals of assisting humans to do some activity faster and with less effort. Inventors and engineers, however, do not think about everybody when they conceive a technology. A bicycle, for example, helps remove barriers of time (to travel somewhere) and of fatigue humans experience from getting there by foot, but it is a technology that was originally designed for people with two functioning legs. What if the bicycle had originally been designed to pedal using arms and hands. If that had been the case, people with *and* without functioning lower limbs could have benefited. Instead bicycle inventors helped only some people overcome barriers of time and fatigue.

In contrast to a disability, which is societally imposed, sociologists define **impairment** as a physical or mental condition that stands in the way of doing something, absent technical assistance. To illustrate: a person confined to a wheelchair has an impairment when it comes to walking, as the person with fully functioning legs walks without assistance. Even though wheelchair-bound people need assistance moving from one place to another, they are often not impaired, for example, with regard to cooking. Yet because stoves are designed for people who stand to cook rather than sit, wheelchair-bound persons have a disability imposed on them.

The sociological distinction between impairment and disability is important when interpreting data on the number and percentages of people with disabilities. We do not want to portray the category "disabled" as filled with residents helpless in every area of life. We do want to think of ways a neighborhood might inadvertently impose disability in the way its public spaces are designed such that people who have trouble standing or walking cannot access and enjoy those spaces. This distinction between "disability" and "impairment" pushes us to keep the following questions about the neighborhood in mind:

- How many residents are counted as disabled?
- Does the neighborhood impose disability by the ways it designs access to public spaces?

Exercise 4.1: Determine the number and percentage of residents in your census tract who are counted as disabled

Go to the census bureau website (see appendix D for directions) and request "Table DP02, Selected Social Characteristics in the United States" (latest 5-year estimates) for your census tract. Scan the document until you find the estimated total number of civilian noninstitutionalized residents, and then scan down until you see the number classified as disabled. (Later you may want to look at types of disability and the characteristics of those counted as disabled by age, sex, and racial classification.) Write a statement that describes the estimated number and percentage of all residents counted as disabled in your census tract. An example using census tract 401, Akron (Hale County), Alabama, follows.

> There are 1,512 residents in census tract 401 in Akron (Hale County), Alabama. Of these 1,512 residents, 385 are estimated to be disabled. That is 25.5% of all residents—the equivalent of about one in every four. This percentage tells me that more than 25% of the residents have difficulty doing one or more of the following activities: walking, bathing, learning, or remembering.

You may wish to visualize the disability data using a pie chart. There are many pie chart apps (see, e.g., Google "create a pie chart free"), or you can use the pie chart function in Microsoft Word. A pie chart brings to mind a pie divided into slices. The number of slices and the size of each slice relative to the others allow viewers to see the contribution of each slice to the overall total. A pie chart for census tract 401 in Hale (Hale County), Alabama, would have two slices. One slice would be 25.5% (disabled classified) of the pie, and the other slice would be 74.5% of the pie. Pie charts work best as a visual tool when there are six or fewer categories (slices). Too many slices can make the chart look cluttered and confusing.

While by any standard 25.5% of residents with a disability is high, is it unusually high? One way to find out is to compare it with to geographic area such as another census tract, the county, the state, or even the nation (See appendix B for directions about how to do this). The disability rate in an adjacent census tract (census tract 400) is 20.4%; it is 16.3% for Hale County, Alabama, and 12.4% for the United States. It is safe to say that 25.5% is high, especially when compared to state and national estimates.

It is important to ask why the disability rate for census tract 401 is especially high. One answer might be that census tract 401 has a higher proportion of disabled because a high portion of its residents are age 75 and older. That age group is more vulnerable to disabilities. The importance of finding out why is covered in subsequent chapters.

Background on Racial Categories

The census bureau and the U.S. government recognize only five official racial categories (plus an "other" category) and two official ethnic categories. These racial categories and their official definitions are as follows:

> **American Indian or Alaskan Native**—any person having origins in any of the original peoples of North America, which by some estimates includes more than 2,000 distinct groups
>
> **Asian**—any person having origins in any of the original peoples of the Far East, Southeast Asia, or the Indian subcontinent
>
> **Black**—any person having origins in any of the black racial groups of Africa
>
> **Native Hawaiian or other Pacific Islander**—any person having origins in any of the original peoples of Hawaii or the Pacific Islands
>
> **White**—any person having origins in any of the original peoples of Europe, North America, or the Middle East
>
> **Other**—a race other than the five listed above

The government officially recognizes two ethnic categories.[2] The two officially recognized ethnic categories are Hispanic/Latino and non-Hispanic/non-Latino. The category Hispanic includes persons with a heritage, nationality, lineage, or country of birth that aligns with 19 Central

---

2. The U.S. Census Bureau does ask an ancestry question. The intent is to determine "a person's ethnic origin or descent, 'roots,' or heritage, or the place of birth of the person or the person's parents or ancestors before their arrival in the United States." So it is not clear when respondents say they are German or Jamaican what that means. The U.S. Census Bureau (2016) states that the intent "is not to measure the degree of attachment the respondent has to a particular ethnicity. For example, a response of 'Irish' might reflect total involvement in an 'Irish' community or only a memory of ancestors several generations removed from the individual. A person's ancestry is not necessarily the same as his or her place of birth; i.e., not all people of German ancestry were born in Germany (in fact, most were not)."

and South American countries once under Spain's control (U.S. Bureau of the Census 2015).³

From a sociological point of view, race, including Hispanic ethnicity, is not a physical quality we are born with. Rather **race** is a concept, or a belief, about what certain physical differences mean. That is, those with the power to do so decided to call differences in hair texture and eye shape "race" and to invent unequal categories to divide people. The unequal treatment accorded to categories is what gave them great social importance.

When you walk around your neighborhood you might think you know someone's race just by noting skin shade, hair texture, eye shape, and color. But race is not what it seems, and people are more complex "racially" than the checklist of categories presented as options. Consider the cases of Caitlin, Porter, and JJ.

- Caitlin knows she appears to be *just black* and said she does answer "black" when asked her race. But Caitlin knows that in addition to being black, she is French, German, and Native American. Catlin's mother could pass as white, and her father is biracial, black and white. Therefore, Caitlin considers herself black, Native American, and white (in that order). She feels that she is forced to choose *just black* as her race because of her appearance.
- When people ask JJ his race, he says he is biracial. When people tell JJ he is white, he replies, "No, I'm half black."
- Porter wrestled with being black because he has a very light complexion. But his father told him, "A little dab will do you," which means that just a drop of African blood makes you black. That saying always stuck with Porter, which is why he proudly embraces his black culture, even as people challenge his "blackness."

The racial category to which you and others are assigned is actually the product of three factors: chance, context, and choice (Haney Lopez 1994). **Chance** includes things not subject to human will, choice, or effort. We do not choose our biological parents or our ancestors, nor can we control the physical characteristics we inherit from them (e.g., by chance the 44th president of the United States, Barack Obama, is the son of a mother considered white and a Nigerian father considered black, appears "black," and

---

3. Brazil is excluded because it is a former Portuguese colony.

is not "white enough" to be thought of as a biracial president.) **Context** is the social setting in which racial categories are recognized, created and contested. (In the United States, Obama is widely recognized as the country's first black president; in Hawaii, the state of his birth, Obama (2007) writes in his autobiography about blending in as a native Hawaiian until he moved to Indonesia, where he was perceived as just American; later, when he moved to Kansas, Obama realized he was black. In Brazil, Obama would likely be recognized as being multiracial, brown, or perhaps even white.) **Choice** is the act of choosing from a wide range of possible behaviors or ways of presenting oneself. When Obama first ran for office in 2008, he presented himself as a black candidate but "chose" (out of necessity) to also present himself as someone raised by white grandparents from Kansas. He never referred to himself as white or biracial for complex reasons that we cannot cover in this book.[4]

Since 2000, Americans have had the option of identifying with more than one of the six official racial categories. Still, almost 20 years later, 97% of Americans identify with one racial category alone. On the surface, it seems normal to many Americans to think of themselves and others as belonging to only one race. However, if we probe long enough, we will find that every person in the United States has a story of how they became the race they check from a list. And those seemingly personal stories are intertwined with a history that began with Jamestown (1607). The United States has systematically divided its population into racial categories for over 400 years. This means that everyone who now lives or who has ever lived in the United States (since Jamestown) has been categorized by race. In fact, we can count the experience of being categorized as something that binds all Americans together (even as it divides them).

For more than four centuries racial categories were treated as real and meaningful ways of dividing humanity. Americans have been taught to see themselves and others as members of one racial group alone (even though we now have the opportunity to legally identify ourselves as more than one of the official categories). For instance, President Obama is not *just*

---

4. All racial categories, when closely examined, are arbitrary at best. The statements above are not a criticism of President Obama but of the American system of racial classification. People do not fit neatly into categories. We have learned to enforce and sustain artificial boundaries by reminding people what race they appear to be.

black, but the long-held American belief that everyone belongs to one race makes us forget the distinctiveness of Obama's background and celebrate him as our first black president.

From a sociological point of view, everyone has been *racialized*. The term "racialized" is key to understanding the concept of race because it suggests that over time the United States has succeeded in convincing people that they are members of a certain racial category. Our personal identities, relationships, interactions, experiences, social settings, and organizations are racialized, and in a racialized society people "are never unaware of the race of a person with whom [they] interact" (Emerson and Smith 2000, 7).

You might be tempted to argue that race is an illusion and that racial categories have no meaning. There is no doubt that in a biological sense race is an illusion, but it is an illusion with real and profound effects on lives, identities, and perceptions. In light of its more than 400-year history, it would be naive to think that race and racial categories could not matter.

These thoughts about race encourage us to ask and answer the following questions:

- Into what racial categories do residents classify themselves?
- Is there evidence that residents have rejected the categorical vision of race by identifying themselves as more than one race?
- Is the neighborhood racialized so that almost all the residents who live there classify themselves as one race?
- Do the data suggest that there is a color line?

Exercise 4.2: Determine the number and percentage of residents by racial category

Go to the census bureau website and request B03002 Hispanic or Latino Origin by Race (see appendix D for instructions). Create a table for your neighborhood modeled after table 4.1 below. This table features residents of census tract 1082.21 located in Edmond (Oklahoma County), Oklahoma. Note that table 4.1 gives the number and percentages of residents who are Hispanic and non-Hispanic and the number and percentage who identify as each race. The rule of thumb is to rank the racial categories in the

Table 4.1 Residents by Ethnic and Racial Category, Census Tract 1082.21
Oklahoma County, Oklahoma

Racial Category by Ethnic Classification	Number in Tract 1082.21	% Tract 1082.21	% State of Oklahoma	% United States
Non-Hispanic	7,610	95.4%	90.4%	82.9%
White	6,410	82.5%	67.3%	62.3%
Black or African American	435	5.4%	7.1%	12.3%
Two or more races	409	5.2%	6.9%	2.2%
American Indian/ Alaskan Native	302	3.8%	1.9%	.7%
Asian, alone	54	0.7%	1.8%	5.1%
Some other race	0	0.0%	.1	.2%
Native Hawaiian/OPI,	0	0.0%	.1	.2%
Hispanic	363	4.6%	9.6%	17.1%
White	165	2.1%	5.7%	11.3%
Two or more races	90	1.1%	0.9%	0.8%
Black	62	0.7%	0.1%	0.4%
Some other race	46	.6%	0.3%	4.5%
Total, all residents	7,973	100.0%	100.0%	100.0%

SOURCE: American Community Survey, latest data (2015) accessed Nov. 15, 2017.

census tract from largest to smallest in number and percentage. In this table, you will be weighing your census tract percentages against associated percentages for the state and the nation to learn how your census tract's racial-ethnic composition compares.

Model Interpretation

In census tract 1082.2 in Edmond (Oklahoma County), Oklahoma, there are an estimated 7,973 residents, 95.4% of whom identify as non-Hispanic and 4.6% of whom identify as Hispanic. Of the total population, 82.5% (n = 6,410) classify themselves as non-Hispanic white, making it the majority racial category. The next largest category in the census tract consists of the 5.2% (n = 409) who self-classify as non-Hispanic black (5.4%), followed by the two-or-more-races category. When we compare the percentages to the state of Oklahoma and the nation, we see that the percentage of those classified as non-Hispanic white is 15.2% higher than the state and 20.2%

higher than the nation. We also see that the percentage of Hispanic classified is 5% less than the state and 12.5% less than the nation. Note that 165 of the 363 (45.4%) Hispanic-classified persons identify as white.

Background on Age-Sex Composition

Age-sex composition relates to the number and percentage of residents who self-classify as male and female in each age category. Here it is useful to know how sociologists think about age and sex.

AGE COMPOSITION

We typically think of age as the time that has passed in years, months, and days since a person was born. However, age is more complex than that, as people of the same age vary by physical well-being (e.g., some people 65 and older have the heart of healthy and much younger persons, and some 25-year-olds have the heart of a much older person). Age also has a social dimension, measured by the kinds of things people do and can do (e.g., a person is 90 years old but goes to work every day or competes in marathons). When we examine a neighborhood's age composition we typically consider the size of age cohorts relative to each other. Age cohorts are commonly broken into intervals that can be five years in length (0–4, 5–9, 10–14) or ten years or longer. When the focus is on age composition we ask questions like the following:

- How many people are in each age group?
- Does one or more age cohort seem to dominate the neighborhood?
- Does the age composition suggest the residents are disproportionately young, middle age, or aging?

SEX COMPOSITION

A neighborhood's sex composition is the number and percentages of residents who check the box Male or Female. But what does it mean to check male or female when asked, "What is your sex?" While we cannot know everything that goes on in the minds of respondents, we can speculate that it depends on the meaning they assign to the word *sex*. Respondents may be thinking about their reproductive organs or their gender or some combination of the two. From a sociological point of view, sex and gender have very different meanings. **Sex** refers to the genitalia, chromosomes, and other biological markers that we use to distinguish people as male or female. These physical characteristics can be ambiguous such that people can possess biological markers we associate with both the male and the female sex. **Gender,** on the other hand, refers to the socially created expectations that specify the physical, emotional, and behavioral traits that make someone masculine, feminine, lesbian, bisexual, gay, transgender, or questioning. Gender is a fluid identity because people conform, challenge, undo, and redo gender expectations.[5] Also, it is important to keep in mind that two categories cannot capture the gender diversity subsumed under the answers "Male" and "Female," the only options to the question, "What is your sex?" Thus this census data can tell us the following:

- How many and what percentage of residents are counted as male and female.

AGE AND SEX COMPOSITION

While looking at just the sex or just the age composition of a neighborhood can be useful, it is better to consider age *and* sex composition together. That way we can learn the answer to the following question:

- Is there a noticeable sex imbalance for any of the age groups?

---

5. Whether we realize it or not, almost everything we do is evaluated according to whether it meets or departs from expectations about what is masculine or feminine (e.g., "He waves like a woman"; "She sits like a man"). When someone departs from gender expectations, it is not the expectations that are considered unreasonable. Rather, it is the so-called violator who is criticized for being different or unreasonable. However, when enough people (a critical mass) violate gender expectations, we undo the old expectations and redo gender in light of the new reality.

For example, we cannot assume that females are always the primary caregivers as more men are assuming this role. When men take on the role of caregiving and enter into a domain thought to belong to women, gender is being "undone." But that does not mean that caregiving is now a genderless activity; it still has a gendered component such that tasks that involve physical strength (such as lifting an elderly person from his bed) are likely relegated to men and tasks that involve bathing and intimate exchanges remain the domain of women (Björk 2015).

70 CHAPTER FOUR

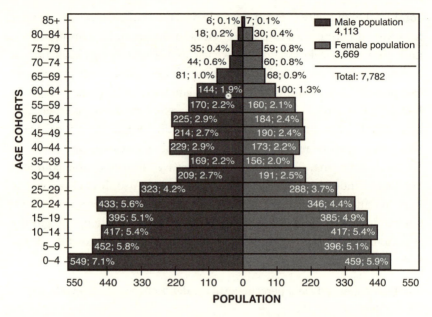

Figure 4.1. Population Pyramid for Census Tract 1, Wade Hampton, Alaska
SOURCE: American Community Survey, latest data (2015) accessed Nov. 15, 2017.

It is common to use a population pyramid to depict a neighborhood's age-sex composition. A **population pyramid** divides the population into a series of 5-year age cohorts. One side of the pyramid shows the number and percentage of females in each 5-year age category, and the other side shows the corresponding number and percentage of males. This visualization allows us to recognize, at a glance, the most prominent and least prominent 5-year age cohorts in a neighborhood as well as cohorts with gender imbalances.

Figure 4.1 depicts a very young population since the six largest age cohorts consist of residents who are under the age of 30. Adding up all the percentages of males and females under 30 reveals that 29.4% of the female population and 33.2% of the male population are younger than 30. Notice that for both males and females, the proportion of the population age 65 and over is very small relative to other age categories but especially when compared to the five youngest age categories. Notice too that men

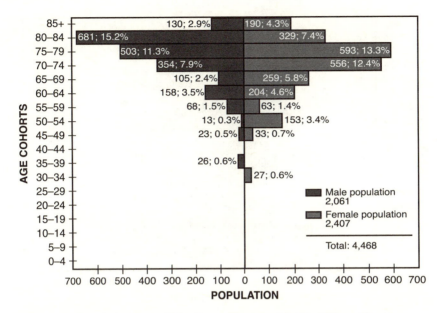

Figure 4.2. Population Pyramid for Census Tract 9108 in The Villages (Sumter County), Florida

SOURCE: American Community Survey, latest data (2015) accessed Nov. 15, 2017.

outnumber women by 444 and that in each age cohort the men outnumber women until age 70.

Figure 4.2 shows a pyramid that reflects a disproportionately older population. The census tract is in the state of Florida, and this is likely a retirement neighborhood. Females outnumber males by 346. In fact, females outnumber males in every age cohort except ages 80–84. Notice also that the proportion of the population 60 years of age and under is very small relative to the older cohorts and that there is no resident who is age 30 or under.

Figure 4.3 shows a population pyramid in which the age-sex composition is almost rectangular in shape, showing relatively equal percentages for each age cohort. Most notably, the youngest age cohorts are about the same size except for the oldest age cohorts.

Keep in mind that age-sex composition is dynamic since residents are always aging. Some communities have young professionals or retirees as residents, but that population will not stay forever young or old. Once we

72   CHAPTER FOUR

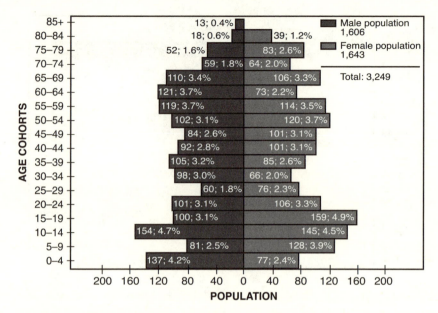

Figure 4.3. Population Pyramid for Census Tract 3731 in Bluejacket (Craig County), Oklahoma

SOURCE: American Community Survey, latest data (2015) accessed Nov. 15, 2017

know the age-sex composition of a neighborhood we can think about the needs of various age-sex cohorts.

Exercise: 4.3: Determine the age-sex composition of your neighborhood

For this assignment, you will establish the age-sex composition of your census tract. To do this, go to the census bureau website and request Table B01001, Sex by Age, for each census tract that makes up your neighborhood. The directions to access these data are slightly different from the steps you have taken to access data to this point.

1. Google American FactFinder Census.
2. Scroll down to the link to American Community Survey, then select "Get data."

3. Click arrow head button at geographies.
4. Choose "Census Tract-140" from the drop-down menu for "Select a geographic type," then select the state, select the county, and select the census tract *number*. Click "Add to Selections." Close the box.
5. In the search box type in "B01001 Sex by Age"
6. Check the box for the most recent 5-year data set
7. Select "View."

Here you can decide how you want to group the ages. You may choose to group the residents of your census tract in 5-year or larger age segments. One option is to think in terms of life stages. One life stage model divides the human life span into six broad categories, as shown in table 4.2, which features census tract 2116 in St. Louis (St. Louis County), Missouri. You may decide that there is a better way to divide the residents of your census tract.

Model Interpretation

Table 4.2 shows that the female residents of census tract 2116 in St. Louis (St. Louis County), Missouri, outnumber males by 338. The residents are 47.2% male and 52.8% female.[6] These percentages are in line with the nation: 49% male, and 51% female. We can see the largest imbalance between the numbers of women and men in tract 2116 in the age 40–64 cohort where women outnumber men by 147. Almost 27% of the residents are in the young adulthood stage. Another 29.5% are in the middle adulthood stage. These percentages are similar to percentages for the nation.

MODULE 4.2: LEARN ABOUT THE HOUSEHOLDS

You have now established the disability, race, and the age-sex composition of residents for your census tract. While it is important to know something about residents as individuals, it is also important to learn something about the households in which they live. The U.S. Census Bureau defines a household as comprising people (one or more) who occupy a housing unit. A housing unit can be a house, an apartment, a single room, or a group of

---

6. The percentage of females is calculated by dividing the total number of females by the total population; the same calculation is used to find the percentage of men(e.g., 5,904 ÷10,718 = 55.1%; 4,811 ÷10,718 = 44.9%).

Table 4.2 Sex Composition of Age Cohorts for Census Tract 2116 in St. Louis (St. Louis County), Missouri, and Nation

Life Stage	Socialization Needs	Males (no. and % of residents)	Females (no. and % of residents)	Total (no. and % of residents)	Difference (males-females)
Infant–age 4 Infancy Early Childhood Preschool	Need for reliable caregivers (infancy); gaining personal control over physical skills (learning to walk, talk, run) and successful exploration of the environment around them are key needs and achievements.	134 (2.2%) (U.S. = 3.2%)	164 (2.7%) (U.S. = 3.1%)	298 (4.9%) (U.S. = 6.3%)	-30
Ages 5–14 Youth	Need to negotiate/cope with a new social world (beyond the family) and with academic demands (rigors of school)	496 (8.1%) (U.S. = 6.6%)	515 (8.4%) (U.S. = 6.3%)	1,011 (16.6%) (U.S. = 12.9%)	-19
Ages 15–19 Adolescence	Need to develop a sense of self (e.g., to learn I am good at sports; I am known as someone who is always smiling)	252 (4.1%) (U.S. = 3.4%)	302 (4.9%) (U.S. = 3.3%)	554 (9.1%) (U.S. = 6.4%)	-50
Ages 20–39 Young Adulthood	Important to form intimate, loving relationships with others (partners, close friends, children, pets)	842 (13.8%) (U.S. = 12.7%)	794 (13.0%) (U.S. = 13.3%)	1,636 (26.8%) (U.S. = 25.8%)	48
Ages 40–64 Middle Adulthood	Need to create and nurture things that will outlast them	826 (13.5%) (U.S. = 16.1%)	973 (15.9%) (U.S. = 16.8%)	1,799 (29.5%) (U.S. = 32.9%)	-147
Ages 65+ Maturity	Need to look back at life and feel a sense of fulfillment and perspective (a person is shaped by time, place, and circumstances)	334 (5.5%) (U.S. = 6.1%)	474 (7.8%) (U.S. = 7.7%)	808 (13.2%) (U.S. = 13.8%)	-140
Totals		2,884 (47.2%) (U.S. = 49.0%)	3,222 (52.8%) (U.S. = 51.0%)	6,106 (100%)	-338

SOURCE: American Community Survey, latest data (2015) accessed Nov. 15, 2017.

rooms designated as distinct living quarters. This means that the occupants consider their living space private and not to be shared with others who live in the same structure. The occupants of a household have direct access to that dwelling from an outside door or through a common hall.

WHAT YOU WILL DO

- ✓ Complete 3 exercises about the households in which residents live.
- ✓ Before doing each exercise, read background material on household types and other characteristics such as income.
- ✓ Look up appropriate census data to create tables and figures.
- ✓ Interpret the data.

Background on Household Type

The U.S. Census Bureau divides households into two major categories: "family" and "nonfamily." A household is considered a family household when its members are related to each other by law, blood, or adoption. A household is considered a nonfamily household when people living together are not related by law, blood, or adoption (e.g., lodgers, roommates). A person living alone also counts as a household. The census bureau considers the following household types:

Male-headed households WITH children under 18
Female-headed households WITH children under 18
Married couple WITH children under 18
Female-headed households, NO children under 18
Male-headed households, NO children under 18
Married couple, NO children under 18
Single-person household
Unmarried partner household, including same-sex

Sociologists recognize that there is no one household type that is recognized universally as *the* way to live. If we apply a historical and a global lens to households, we will quickly see that a variety of household forms have always existed. The most celebrated but historically short-lived household type in the United States comprises a married heterosexual couple with children. Currently that household type represents only about

76 CHAPTER FOUR

20% of all households in the United States, meaning that 80% depart from that "ideal." The census tract you study may mirror this national trend or depart dramatically in favor of one form or another. Living arrangements are best evaluated not by whether they conform or deviate from some ideal arrangement but by the well-being of the people who make up a household. Researchers looking at data on household composition ask the following kinds of questions:

- Is one household type dominant within the neighborhood?
- What are the numbers and percentages of children under age 18 in each household type?

Exercise 4.4: Find the number and percentage of household types in your neighborhood

Create a table using table 4.3 below as a model. Go to the census bureau ACS website (see appendix D for directions) and retrieve Table S1101 Households and Families (latest 5-year estimates). Before you begin, study the column headings on the retrieved table. Notice that sometimes just the number of households under each type is listed and sometimes just the percentage. If a percentage is listed, be sure to multiply the percentage by the total number of households to calculate the number for a certain type.

Model Interpretation

In census tract 2116 in St. Louis (St. Louis County),,Missouri, the one-person household is the most common household type (n = 560) and the highest percentage (23.7%), followed by female-headed households (476, or 20.1%). The least common household type is same-sex partner households. There are an estimated 26 (or 1.1%). Note that the estimates in this table were made after June 26, 2015, when the U.S. Supreme Court declared same-sex marriage legal.[7] When the tract percentages are compared to the nation's percentages, the percentage of female-headed households in census tract 2116

---

7. In the case *Obergefell v. Hodges* the Supreme Court ruled that bans on same-sex marriage are unconstitutional. The ruling made same-sex marriages legal in all 50 states, Washington, DC, and U.S. territories (except American Samoa) but not on all Native American tribal lands.

Table 4.3 Number and Percentage of Household Types, Census Tract 2116 in St. Louis (St. Louis County), Missouri, Compared to U.S. Percentage

Household Type	No.	% Tract	% U.S.
Single resident living alone	560	23.7	27.6
Male-headed households WITH children under 18	37	1.6	2.3
Female-headed households WITH children under 18	476	20.1	7.1
Married couple WITH children under 18	252	10.7	19.4
Female-headed households, NO children under 18	271	11.5	5.8
Male-headed households, NO children under 18	139	5.9	2.5
Married couple, NO children under 18	408	17.3	28.8
Unmarried other-sex partner households	135	5.7	5.6
Unmarried same-sex partner households	26	1.1	.4
Total households	2,363	100.0	100.0

SOURCE: American Community Survey, latest data (2015) accessed Nov. 15, 2017.

stands out as significantly higher (20.1% vs. 7.1%). The percentage of married couple households with children under 18 is considerably lower than the percentage for the nation (10.7% vs. 19.4%), as is the percentage of married couple households with NO children under 18 (17.3% vs. 28.8%).

Note: there may be specific household types in table 4.3 to which want to draw special attention. For example, you might choose to focus on households with children under 18. You could create a pie chart focusing only on three household types where children under 18 live. To do this, begin by calculating the total number of households with children under 18. For census tract 2116 the total number of households with children under 18 is 765. Of those 765, an estimated 476 (62.2%) live in female-headed households; 252 (32.9%) live in married couple households. About 5% (n = 37) live in male-headed households.

BACKGROUND ON HOUSEHOLD INCOME

Dividing households into income categories and examining how income is distributed offers insights about the degree of inequality. Social inequality exists when valued resources are distributed unevenly across a population. Inequality is a problem when there is a pattern that suggests some are accorded an unfair or excessive advantage. Since the 1970s income inequality between the wealthiest 20%, 10%, 5%, 1%, and .01% and the rest of the population has grown significantly in the United States. Many analysts predict continued widening of income gaps between the most advantaged income categories and other income categories. This widening is fueled by the "rise of mechanized intelligence (an ever-faster internet, artificial intelligence and computer programs that can quickly perform vast data calculations), which means that the economy will be passing along most of the higher rewards to a relatively small cognitive elite who have mastered these machines. High-income earners of tomorrow will be those who complement the speed and power of machines" (Network 2015).

One way to examine the income differences in a neighborhood is to divide households into five categories called quintiles. Each quintile represents 20% of households in the neighborhood. The first quintile contains the 20% of households with the lowest incomes, while the fifth quintile contains the 20% of households able to secure the highest incomes. In between are the second, third, and fourth quintiles. The census bureau also estimates the household income of the top 5%.

The census bureau defines **income** as total money secured by all members of a household combined in the past 12 months from the following sources: wages, salary, tips, bonuses, self-employment; interest, dividends; net rental income; royalties; social security; supplemental security income; public assistance received by check or electronic transfer; retirement, survivor or disability pensions; and any other sources (Guzman 2017).[8] We can ask the following questions about income distribution.

- How is income distributed across households?
- How much do the top 5% and 20% of households earn relative to the households in the lowest-earning 20%?

One way to look at the distribution of household income in your census tract is to look at (1) the mean household income for each quintile, (2) the range of income within each quintile, and (3) the share of all household income each quintile controls. The mean quintile income is the average

---

8. For the complete list, see "Guide for the American Community Survey": www.surveys/acs/methodology/questionnaires/2015/guide15.pdf.

income of all households in a quintile. Typically, sociologists compare the average household income of the lowest quintile with the average income of the highest quintile to determine the degree of income inequality. For example, if average household income is $200,000 for the highest quintile and $10,000 for the lowest quintile households, then we can say that for every dollar secured by those living in the lowest quintile, those in the highest secure $20.

The census bureau also calculates the share of all household income that each quintile pulls in. Typically, the share of the lowest quintile is compared to the share of the highest quintile to estimate the level of inequality. A criticism of these measures of inequality is that neither takes into account differences in household size and number of earners. That is, while 20% of households are in each quintile, the number of people and the number of earners in those households vary. Obviously, the number of earners affects the total amount of income a household secures, and knowing the number of people in the household (including nonearners) speaks to how many that income supports.

Exercise 4.5: Determine how income is distributed across households

You can access latest 5-year estimates on the mean income and share of all household income by quintile by requesting

- ✓ Table B19081, Mean Household Income of Quintiles
- ✓ Table B19082, Shares of Aggregate Household Income by Quintile
- ✓ Table B19080, Household Income Quintile Upper Limits

Using table 4.4 below for census tract 12 in Cookeville (Putman County), Tennessee, as a model, create a table for your census tract and give an interpretation as shown below.

Model Interpretation

The mean income of the lowest quintile in census tract 12 in Cookeville (Putman County), Tennessee, is $11,219, and the mean income of the highest quintile is $265,938. The average household in the highest quintile

Table 4.4 Estimates of Household Income Distributed across Quintiles and Top 5% for Census Tract 12, Putnam County, Tennessee (Compared to % of U.S.)

Quintile	Mean Income	Range within Quintile	Share of Aggregate Income Tract 12	Share of Aggregate Income U.S.
1st quintile	$11,219	Less than $18,705	2.63%	3.17%
2nd quintile	$29,282	$18,706–$40,176	6.86%	8.42%
3rd quintile	$49,168	$40,177–$61,360	11.52%	14.37%
4th quintile	$71,914	$61,361–$88,107	16.85%	22.83%
5th quintile	$265,938	$88,108–$157,380 (this range excludes top 5%)	62.13%	51.21%
Top 5%	$728,938	$157,381+	42.71%	22.81%

SOURCE: American Community Survey, latest data (2015) accessed Nov. 15, 2017.

secures 23.7 times more income than the average household in the lowest quintile. The most dramatic differences are between the top 5% and the lowest quintile in census tract 12, where the top 5% of households, on average, secure 64.97 times more income than the average household in the lowest quintile. This means that for every dollar secured by the average household in the lowest quintile, the average household in the top 5% secures $64.97.

The range of incomes within quintiles gives you some idea of the diversity of household incomes within a quintile segment. Note that the second quintile can earn as little as $18,706 or as much as $40,177, a difference of $21,471. The greatest difference within a quintile can be found with the highest. The range is from $88,108 to $157,380 (minus top 5%), for a difference of $69,272. If the top 5% were included, the upper limit of that range exceeds $728,938 (its mean income).

The share of income secured by the households in the lowest quintile of census tract 12 is 2.63%, compared to 62.3% in the fifth quintile. To put it another way, households in the highest quintile secure 23.7 times more income than households in the lowest quintile. When we compare the percentage share of income for each quintile in census tract 12 against the percentage share for each quintile in the U.S., we can see that income inequality for census tract 12 is higher. Most notably, the top 5% of households in census tract 12 secure 42.71% of all income, compared to the 22.9% secured by the top 5% within the United States.

What Do Ratios Comparing Highest- and Lowest-Income Households Mean?

What does it mean for the top income quintile to secure 23.7 times more income than the lowest quintile? The answer is, it depends on context. Some argue that extreme differences are very harmful to social stability and that there must be some mechanism (taxation; special programs) in place to redistribute income. Others maintain that income inequality drives economic growth and innovation. The better those at the top do, the greater the resulting innovation and creativity that ultimately benefits everyone in the larger society (Weinberg 2011).

This research project examines income inequality at the neighborhood level. So you have to think about what income inequality means in the space of a few square miles. If the degree of income inequality is low, it is likely that the census tract draws residents of similar income levels such as those who can afford high-priced houses or who are attracted to low-cost or subsidized housing. In high-poverty neighborhoods, for example, where virtually everyone is poor, there is high income equality. That kind of income inequality is very problematic because

> the school you are likely to have access to is more likely to be of subpar quality. Your exposure to crime and its negative consequences for health and wellbeing is greater. The potential for victimization—the stress associated with everyday life, the stress associated with raising your kids—is greater. Many of those secondary effects have been found to be associated with inequality. (Small 2014, 1)

When there is income inequality, it could be the outcome of deliberate planning to create mixed-income neighborhoods that are "inherently integrationist" and imbued with the spirit of positively affecting the lives and well-being of all residents (Thurber, Bohmann, and Heflinger 2017). On the other hand, that inequality could reflect an income-segregated neighborhood where certain streets within it are home to the high-, middle-, or low-income residents.

There is some evidence that mixed-income neighborhoods are settings that benefit those in lower-income households. Unlike mixed-income neighborhoods, homogeneous-income neighborhoods are filled with residents with similar incomes. When the high- and middle-income residents separate themselves from those with low income, it may "leave the poor with relatively few jobs . . . or reduce the extent to which the rich confer positive spillovers on the poor" (Wheeler 2008, 1; see also Wilson 1987; Benabou 1996). Such income segregation narrows the variety of role models, opportunity networks, and voices that advocate for the schools and neighborhood amenities. While mixed-income neighborhoods offer more opportunities than low-income communities, they offer fewer advantages than what can be found in high-income communities (Vesselinov et al. 2017).

MODULE 4.3: ESTABLISH YOUR SOCIAL LOCATION

As a researcher, you hold narrative and interpretive power over residents and households in the census tract you are studying and writing about. Therefore, it is important for you to recognize your positionality, or **social location** (the social categories you occupy), relative to the residents in the census tract. It is also important to recognize that positionality shapes perceptions and limits experiences with and understanding of those whose positionality is different. For example, imagine a 20-year-old male named Sam who identifies as black and lives at home with two working parents. When Sam encounters Callie, an unmarried female with children who identifies as Asian, he must take steps to see a unique person instead of a faceless category. This recognition of uniqueness should not mean that Sam should ignore Callie's experiences that come with being perceived and treated as a category. But Sam must avoid overgeneralizing about her social category such that he sees a stereotyped version of that category.

WHAT YOU WILL DO

✓ Begin by reading the background on social location.
✓ Follow instructions for doing an analysis of your social location relative to the residents in your census tract.

Social Location

Remember that you hold narrative and interpretive power over residents and households in the census tract you are studying and writing about. As a researcher it is your job to avoid "us versus them" interpretations. Instead, make a point of recognizing shared characteristics across groups. To assume, for example, that men on average earn more than women fails to acknowledge that some women earn more than some men, that there are workplace settings where men and women are paid equally, and that some men in the labor force are losing ground to some women. Recognizing complexity and similarities across categories does not mean that there is no pattern of inequality (Fitzsimmons and Callan 2016). Similarly, to assume that those classified as disabled are helpless in every area of their lives denies this category of people their humanity and uniqueness. Always assume that "things are not what they seem" (Berger 1963, 23).

Also keep in mind that people move into and out of categories. People age. People who are married may be thinking about or may be in the process of divorcing. Residents with a high school degree may go on to college. Renters become home owners; home owners become renters; people lose their homes. People change jobs, putting them into a new occupational category, and they become parents. It is equally important to recognize that people occupy multiple and intersecting categories. Our social location is defined as the intersection of race, sex, age, class, and other categories.

We have learned that it is important to think about our social location relative to the people we are studying and writing about. As researchers, we should take time to reflect on how much experience we have with the various categories of people we are studying.

Exercise 4.6: Establish your social location

The data you need in order to analyze your social location in the larger context of the neighborhood you are studying can be found in the tables you have already created. Reflect also on the social categories with which you have had limited to no experience.

Model Social Location Write-Up, Example #1

In census tract 12 in Cookeville (Putnam County), Tennessee, I am one of 9,177 residents. Of those 9,177 residents, I am one of

- 1,233 (13.5%) counted as disabled;
- 642 (7%) counted as age 22–24;

- 4,752 (51.8%) counted as male;
- 8,867 (96.6%) who classify themselves as white.
- Of the 2,600 households in census tract 12, I am part of a household that is
- in the 3rd quintile ($40,177–$61,360).
- one-person, which makes up 769 (21.4%) of all households.

Reflection: I have no experience with those who identify as black males. There are 58 black males who live in my census tract. I have had no direct experience with those 75 years of age or older as my maternal grandparents died in a car accident when I was a baby and my paternal grandparents are in their late 60s. That age group makes up 17.5% of residents (n=1605). As far as I know, I don't know anyone who lives in a household that is in the lowest income quintile (less than $18,705), 20% of my census tract. As a conscientious researcher, I must take steps to learn about, interact with, and consult people who occupy these categories. I cannot assume I know the needs of people in categories with which I am unfamiliar. I realize that failing to do to my homework (acquire sympathetic knowledge) limits my ability to think and write in a sociologically conscious way about the data gathered on these populations.

Model Social Location Write-Up, Example #2

In census tract 225.00 in Woodlawn (Hamilton County), Ohio, I am one of 3,956 residents. Of those 3,956 residents, I am one of the

- 2,407 (60.8%) who classify themselves as black or African American
- 2,160 (54.6%) counted as female
- 32 (0.8%) classified as a 20-year-old female
- Of the 1,661 households in census tract 225, I live in a household that is one of
- the 305 (18.3%) considered female householder, no husband present, family
- the 785 (47.3%) who live in renter-occupied housing units
- those in the second income quintile ($35,765–$55,449)

Reflection: I have little to no experience with the disabled, including the 385 residents (10.3%) in my census tract counted as such. I have had only the most minimal interaction with residents classified as Asian. There are 161 residents (4%) in my census tract who are counted as Asian. I do know someone who appears to be from India who manages the gas station I frequent. The extent of my interaction is "$15 on pump 3" and "Thank you." There are 89 homes valued over $300,000. I don't know anyone with an income high enough to live in and keep up such a house. The reflection has taught me that based on my own experiences, I am not qualified to write and speculate about the disabled, the Asian classified, or wealthy home owners. If I had not completed the assignment, I would have unthinkingly written about these groups as if I knew what their lives were like.

WORKING DRAFT OF RESEARCH BRIEF, SECTION 3

Residents and Households

Now we are ready to highlight key findings about the residents and the households in the surrounding neighborhood. These highlights will be included in this section of the research brief. Because every neighborhood is different, it is difficult to offer precise instructions on how to know what constitutes a highlight. However, keep the following points in mind.

- You cannot include everything you learn about the census tract in your research brief, so you must make choices about what to include.
- Typically, the age-sex composition data offer clues about the life cycle needs of those who live there. Each age cohort has needs associated with their place in the life cycle. Are there organizations and opportunities within or near the census tract that support those needs?
- Think about whether the census bureau estimates support the observations you made while touring the census tract with the five classic sociologists.
- Avoid making claims that the data cannot support. For example, the census data that you have gathered cannot tell us about the diversity of people who occupy each of the age, race, household, educational, or other categories. At this point, we cannot conclude that those with college degrees live in the wealthiest households or that people who live alone are mostly females age 65 and older. In later chapters, we will learn how to determine more about who makes up each category, but for now we have a very broad understanding of the demographic and household makeup of this neighborhood.
- Always keep in mind that this section of the research brief is preliminary and is open to refinement and revision.

Model Write-Up, Section 3

- Census tract 78 in Northside (Hamilton County), Ohio, is home to 2,411 residents who live in 1,166 occupied households.
- The age distribution of the 2,411 residents shows that the 30- to 34-year-old age cohort is the largest. It appears that those 19 and under are overshadowed by those in the 20- to 39-year-old age groups.
- 41.8% of households are single resident, meaning that the residents of these households live alone; 7.9% of households (n = 93) consist of a married couple with children 18 and younger; 9.0% (n = 217) are unmarried partner households.
- 65.5% of residents identify as white and 24.8% as black; 3.4% identify with more than one race. There are very few who self-classify as Hispanic.
- The average income of the bottom 20% of households is $11,219 in census tract 78. In contrast, the average income of the top 20% of households is estimated to be $265,132. The average income for the top 20% is 23.6 times that of the bottom 20%.
- The bottom 20% of households in census tract 78 secure 2.63% of all income. Compare this with the households in the top 20%, which secure 63.13% of all income.

The estimates I have chosen to highlight correspond to observations I have made while walking around census tract 78. One can readily observe that there are streets where residents appear economically disadvantaged and other areas populated by those with enough income to move into new apartment buildings and rehabilitated homes. School-age residents are noticeable around schools but less evident around the business districts, which draw white-appearing residents and outsiders who can afford luxury coffees, healthy foods, and beverages. The streets known for low-income housing are disproportionately occupied by people who appear to be black and Hispanic.

REFERENCES

Benabou, Roland. 1996. "Heterogeneity, Stratification, and Growth: Macroeconomic Implications of Community Structure and School Finance." *American Economic Review* 86: 584–609.

Berger, Peter. 1963. *An Invitation to Sociology.* New York: Anchor.

Björk, Sofia. 2015. "Doing, Re-doing or Undoing Masculinity? Swedish Men in the Filial Care of Aging Parents." *NORA—Nordic Journal of Feminist and Gender Research* 23 (1): 20–35.

Fitzsimmons, Terrance W., and Victor J. Callan. 2016. "Applying a Capital Perspective to Explain Continued Gender Inequality in the C-Suite." *Leadership Quarterly* 27 (3): 354–70.

Guzman, Gloria G. 2017. "Household Income." *American Community Survey Briefs*. U.S. Bureau of the Census.

Lopez, Ian F. Haney. 1994. "The Social Construction of Race: Some Observations on Illusion, Fabrication, and Choice." *Harvard Civil Rights–Civil Liberties Law Review* 29 (1).

Obama, Barack. 2004 [1995]. *Dreams from My Father: A Story of Race and Inheritance*. New York: Three Rivers Press.

Small, Mario. 2014. "Q-and-A with Mario Small." *Colloquy* 7 (Spring). https://gsas.harvard.edu/colloquy-magazine/spring-2014.

Smith, Christian, and Michael O. Emerson. 2000. *Divided by Faith: Evangelical Religion and the Problem of Race in America*. New York: Oxford University Press.

Thurber, A., C. R. Bohmann, and C. A. Heflinger. 2017. "Spatially Integrated and Socially Segregated: The Effects of Mixed-Income Neighborhoods on Social Well-Being. *Urban Studies* (March): 0042098017702840.

U.S. Bureau of the Census. 2016. "Codes, Lists, Definitions, and Accuracy." American Community Survey.

Vesselinov, E., M. C. Lennon, and R. Le Goix. 2017. "Is It All in the Eye of the Beholder? Benefits of Living in Mixed-Income Neighborhoods in New York and Los Angeles." *Journal of Urban Affairs* 18 (August): 1–23.

Weinberg, Daniel H. 2011. "U.S. Neighborhood Income Inequality in the 2005–2009 Period." U.S. Bureau of the Census, Report No. ACS-16. www.census.gov/content/dam/Census/library/publications/2011/acs/acs-16pdf.

Wheeler, Christopher H. 2008. "Urban Decentralization and Income Inequality: Is Sprawl Associated with Rising Income Segregation Across Neighborhoods?" *Federal Reserve Bank of St. Louis Regional Economic Development* 4 (1): 41–57.

Wilson, William J. 1987. *The Truly Disadvantaged: The Inner City, the Underclass, and Public Policy*. Chicago: University of Chicago Press.

5 Neighborhood Resources

A **neighborhood resource** is anything within the boundaries of a neighborhood (in this case a census tract) that represents a source or a *potential* source of benefits to residents and to the neighborhood as a whole. The word *potential* is important because the mere existence of a resource does not guarantee that residents know its value or will benefit from it. A resource's quality and functionality are important to realizing its benefit. For example, a neighborhood may have a park with a playground but if parents are afraid to let their children go there because its equipment is in disrepair or because it is located in a high crime area, that resource is not benefiting the neighborhood or its residents. For this research project, becoming familiar with neighborhood resources is an important step in assessing neighborhood needs and areas in need of support. Recall that the two core questions guiding this research project are

1. In what ways do I support, or fail to support, the surrounding neighborhood?
2. Should that support be increased? If so, in what ways?

One way you can assess your current level of support to the neighborhood is to think about the resources you currently draw on and how you support that inventory of resources.

Background on Neighborhood Resources

Neighborhood resources can be classified in two broad categories, tangible and intangible. **Tangible resources** are resources that take a physical form: economic (income, revenue), natural (a lake, a view, coal, mines), businesses (fuel, fresh food), buildings (school, health care), landmarks, and public spaces (parks, neighborhood centers). **Intangible resources** include human capital, the neighborhood's reputation, and forces of support or cohesion. These two broad categories of resources are interdependent: tangible resources can yield intangible resources, such as feelings of security or pride; and intangible resources such as human capital can attract businesses.[1] In this chapter you will complete five modules that will help you identify some tangible and intangible neighborhood resources. In the process, you will learn about your neighborhood and gauge its strengths and weaknesses.

MODULE 5.1: TANGIBLE ASSETS

In assessing economic resources at the neighborhood or census tract level, we can determine the sources of income that sustain residents and their lifestyles. Sources of income include wages, salary, tips, self-employment income, interest, dividends, net rental income, royalties, social security, supplemental security, public assistance, retirement, survivor or disability pensions, and the catchall category, "any other sources" (U.S. Bureau of the Census 2016). If residents are disproportionately dependent on one or two income sources, it could signal vulnerability, especially during an economic downturn. We also consider how much of this income households expend

---

1. Of course, some residents, groups, and communities are better at providing, noticing, and accessing resources than others.

on rent, mortgages, and other expenses such as electricity, insurance, and water. If households devote a high share of income to such expenses, they have less income to spend on other necessities and on luxuries.

WHAT YOU WILL DO

- ✓ Complete two exercises about residents' tangible assets.
- ✓ Read background information about sources of income and housing costs.
- ✓ Find appropriate census and other data sources to create tables and inventories.
- ✓ Make interpretations that are consistent with the examples provided.

Background on Sources of Income

The census bureau asks questions on individual and household income secured on a regular basis (not counting capital gains). The amount of income the census bureau records is that secured before income taxes, union dues, or social security are paid or deducted. This figure does not include food stamps, health benefits, subsidized housing, or any other noncash benefit that reduces outlay (a company daycare, tuition, or medical benefits). The census bureau cannot control for respondents underreporting income that is off the record (gifts, family members subsidizing living costs, underground economy).

Exercise 5.1: Determine sources of income

In this assignment, you will establish the combined income of all residents by source and then rank order these sources from highest to lowest. You will also establish what percentage of households secure income from each source. To access the data, go the census bureau website (see appendix D for specific instructions) and request the following tables for your census tract:

- ✓ wages and salary (Tables B19062 and B19052)
- ✓ self-employment income (Tables B19063 and B19053)
- ✓ interest, dividends, and net rental income (Tables B19064 and B19054)
- ✓ social security (Tables B19065 and B19055)

- ✓ supplemental social security (Tables B19066 and B19056)
- ✓ public assistance (Tables B19067 and B1957)
- ✓ retirement (pension) income (Tables B19069 and B19059)
- ✓ other income (Tables B19070 and B19060)

Viewing the various sources of household income allows us to establish which sources of income the neighborhood most and least depends on (e.g., is the neighborhood heavily dependent on public assistance income? social security? or wages and salaries?). The total aggregate income by itself tells us very little because it must also be understood in the context of the number of residents and households. Knowing these numbers will allow you to know the average income per resident (no matter the age) and also per household. So be sure to get those numbers for your census tract.

When writing your assessment of sources of income, avoid opinions that are unfounded, untested, or accusatory (e.g., "Too many people are on public assistance in this neighborhood"; "There will be no social security for me"). Instead, use statements like, "The primary source of income in this neighborhood is wages and salary (86.9%), with a relatively small percentage coming from supplemental social security and public assistance." Your job is to report the facts.

Model Interpretation

We can see from the data in table 5.1 that the 1,829 households in census tract 7001.04 in Prathertown (Montgomery County), Maryland, secure $243.1 million in annual income. That averages to $132,917.50 per household and $41,514 per resident. Just under 87% of that total comes from the category "wages and salary." Each of the other sources account for less than 3% of the grand total. We can see that 93.4% of households depend on wage and salary income. About one quarter of all the households secure money from interest, dividends, and rentals. Very little of the total income is from public assistance and supplemental social security.

Background on Other Tangible Assets

When thinking about the strengths and needs of a neighborhood as a whole, it is useful to take an inventory of specific kinds of tangible assets residents possess that when aggregated offer insights about the neighborhood's

Table 5.1 Sources of Income for Census Tract 7001.04 in Prathertown (Montgomery County), Maryland

Source of Income	Aggregate Amount Tract # 7001.04 Households = 1,829 Residents = 5,856	% of all income	Number (and %) of Households Claiming This Source of Income
Wages & Salary	$211,196,300	86.9	1,708 (93.4%)
Retirement (pension)	$5,936,800	2.45	167 (9.1%)
Self-Employment Income	$6,674,800	2.75	249 (13.6%)
Interest, Dividends and Rental Income	$5,343,000	2.2	477 (26.1%)
Social Security	$4,034,400	1.66	221 (12.1%)
Supplemental Social Security	$329,500	0.14	60 (3.3%)
Public Assistance	$17,400	0.0	40 (2.2%)
Other	$2,960,200	1.22	200 (10.3%)
Total of all sources	**$243,106,100**	**(100.0)**	

SOURCE: American Community Survey, latest data (2015) accessed Nov. 15, 2017.

strengths and challenges. If, for example, you are interested in knowing the extent to which residents are ready for an emergency or a disaster, then you can do an inventory of tangible assets such as those shown in figure 5.1. Currently these results on household readiness are available only at the national level. However, this list will offer ideas about what kinds of items to include in an inventory if such an assessment were to be completed on the local level.

Exercise 5.2: Inventory tangible resources

The U.S. Census Bureau collects data on some tangible assets listed in table 5.2. The estimates you need to complete this table can be found in the following documents: Selected Economic Characteristics, Selected Housing Characteristics, and ACS Demographic and Housing Estimates (see appendix B for instructions). The number and percentage of residents or households without these tangible assets cannot tell us how those

Figure 5.1. U.S. Bureau of the Census Assessment of Households' Readiness for Emergencies
SOURCE: U.S. Bureau of the Census

Table 5.2 Number and Percentage of Residents / Households with No Access to Selected Tangible Resources, Census Tract 106 in San Francisco (San Francisco County), California

Limited Resource	%
No landline or cell phone service	3.1
Does not own home	87.4
No vehicle	64.4
No health insurance (residents)	13.6

NOTE: Households: 1,872. Residents: 3,591.

SOURCE: American Community Survey, latest data (2015) accessed Nov. 15, 2017.

Table 5.3 Number and Percentage of Households Considered Cost Burdened in Census Tract 106, San Francisco (San Francisco County), California

Household Type	n	No. and % Expending 30% or More of Income
With mortgage payments	110	58.2% (n = 64)
Owned free and clear	126	61.9% (n = 78)
Pay rent	1,549	41.6% (n = 644)
All households	1,872	41.2% (n = 786)

SOURCE: American Community Survey, latest data (2015) accessed Nov. 15, 2017.

without them manage. These numbers only tell us how many and what percentage of households with these assets struggle to secure them. One exception is the percentage of households that struggle to pay for housing. The census bureau collects data on households that dedicate 30% of income to meet housing-related expenses. Households are considered cost burdened when their housing-related costs total more than 30% of their household income. Such households may have difficulty affording other necessities such as food, clothing, transportation, and medical care. These data can be found in "Selected Housing Characteristics."

Model Interpretation of Tables 5.2 and 5.3

On the surface it seems that the most alarming estimate presented in table 5.2 is that 87.4% of households in census tract 106 in San Francisco (San Francisco County), California, are renter occupied, meaning that only 13.6% are owner occupied. Another potentially alarming finding is that 64.4% of households are without a vehicle. However, since census tract 106 is part of the city of San Francisco, neither figure should be surprising. In that city, there are many opportunities to take public transportation. And San Francisco is known for housing that is unaffordable. Table 5.2 also shows that 13.6% of residents are without health insurance, and 3.1% have no access to a cell or landline. Table 5.3 reveals that 41.2% of households are considered cost burdened. That is, these households dedicate 30% or more of their income to housing-related expenses. The median housing costs for households with a mortgage is $2,000 per month; without a mortgage, those costs are $600. For those who rent, the median rent payment is $935 per month (see the document Selected Housing Characteristics). The 41.2% of households that expend one-third or more of their household income on housing-related expenses may have difficulty affording other necessities such as food, clothing, transportation, and medical care.

MODULE 5.2: INTANGIBLE ASSETS

WHAT YOU WILL DO

✓ Complete two exercises about residents' intangible assets.

✓ Read background information.

✓ Access relevant census data or data from other sources.

✓ Make interpretations modeled after examples.

Background on Human Resources

Human resources are often referred to as human capital that people within a neighborhood possess, including skills, talents, knowledge, and willpower (energy, willingness to act). Human capital is something to be drawn on and managed to meet the needs of a neighborhood and to help communities adapt during times of change and crisis. A complete inventory of human capital is impossible to create, but we can easily inventory some kinds of human capital, most notably educational attainment, enrollment in schools, and knowledge specializations. Human capital also encompasses occupational diversity. A neighborhood is occupationally diverse when its residents hold a wide variety of jobs that are representative of occupational categories. In a labor market characterized by change and insecurity, a neighborhood is vulnerable if its residents are heavily concentrated in one sector such as health care and absent from others such as construction. A neighborhood benefits when its residents possess a diversity of skills and perspectives. In assessing the human capital within a neighborhood, we may ask the following questions.

- What educational credentials do residents possess?
- How many residents are currently enrolled in school and at what levels?
- For those with four-year degrees, what is their area of study?

Exercise 5.3: Inventory residents' educational attainment

The census bureau provides estimates of the educational credentials residents age 24 and over possess and the numbers of residents enrolled in school at all levels. Here we focus on educational attainment. The census bureau also provides estimates of the number and percentage of residents employed in broad occupational categories and the broad areas of academic study (college major) for those residents with at least a four-year degree. Go to the census bureau website to access DP 01, Selected Social Characteristics in the United States, *and* Table B15012, Total Fields of Bachelor's Degrees Reported (see appendix D for instructions).

Create an inventory of education credentials for your neighborhood modeled after table 5.4 and an inventory of knowledge specializations. The data in this table are for census tract 10, located in Gaston (Whitfield County), Georgia.

Model Interpretation of Table 5.4

The data show that very few (2.74%) residents age 24 and over have earned a four-year degree. Almost half (48.8%) of the residents have *not* earned a high school diploma. Table 5.5 shows the fields of study for the 76 residents in this neighborhood with bachelor's degrees. That number includes those who have also attained graduate and professional degrees.

Table 5.4 Educational Credentials for Residents Age 24 and Over, Census Tract 10 in Gaston (Whitfield County), Georgia

Educational Attainment	n	%
Less than high school	1,351	48.8
High school graduate	751	27.1
Some college or associate's degree	591	21.3
Bachelor's degree	50	1.8
Graduate or professional degree	26	0.94
Total population 25 and over	2,769	100.0

SOURCE: American Community Survey, latest data (2015) accessed Nov. 15, 2017.

Table 5.5 Broad Bachelor's Degree Fields for Population Age 25 and Older, Census Tract 10 in Gaston (Whitfield County), Georgia

Degree Field	n	%
Computers, Mathematics, and Statistics	25	32.9
Biological, Agricultural, and Environmental Sciences	0	0.0
Physical and Related Sciences	0	0.0
Psychology	0	0.0
Social Science	4	5.3
Engineering	0	0.0
Multidisciplinary Studies	0	0.0
Business	18	10.5
Education	0	0.0
Literature and Languages	0	0.0
Liberal Arts and History	0	0.0
Visual and Performing Arts	29	38.2
Communications	0	0.0
Total number with bachelor's degree	76	100.0

SOURCE: American Community Survey, latest data (2015) accessed Nov. 15, 2017.

Model Interpretation of Table 5.5

Almost one-third (32.9%) of the 76 residents with four-year and advanced degrees are concentrated in the fields of computers/mathematics/statistics. Almost 40% (38.2%) studied visual and performing arts. If we assume that diversity in fields of academic study is something to be valued because it brings diverse viewpoints and skills, then this neighborhood has a very narrow perspective as 9 of the 13 fields have no representation.

We could use census data to inventory other kinds of human capital that capture (1) efforts to protect the environment (environmental consciousness), (2) readiness for a knowledge economy, and (3) personal investment in a neighborhood. Suggested items to inventory are listed below. We have already inventoried some items on this list, and you can find data on all the items on the census bureau website (google "American Community Survey subjects included in survey," choose the appropriate link, and then enter appropriate geographic information to access estimates).

Environmental consciousness

- work at home
- carpool to work
- walk or ride bike to work
- take public transportation

Readiness for a knowledge economy or economic changes

- enrolled in school (at various levels)
- access to the internet
- access to cell and landline service
- college degree
- occupational diversity

Behaviors that suggest personal investment in the neighborhood

- added a baby to the household in the past year
- moved to the neighborhood in the past year
- own a home
- have children under 18

Challenges to neighborhood well-being

- unemployed but looking for work
- drive to work alone (drain on resources)
- spend more than one hour going to and from work (drain on time, contributes to traffic congestion)
- no health insurance
- more than 30% of household income used to meet household-related expenses
- need help getting dressed
- no access to the internet
- no access to phone service, including cell or smart phones

MODULE 5.3: NEIGHBORHOOD REPUTATION

WHAT YOU WILL DO

✓ Complete one exercise about your neighborhood's reputation.

✓ Read background information on landmarks.

✓ Follow instructions for doing a cultural analysis of a landmark

Background on Neighborhood Reputation

The reputation—founded or unfounded—of a neighborhood, including the reputation of certain streets, affects both the neighborhood and its residents' lives (Wutich et al. 2014). Reputation can be negative, positive, or unremarkable. Negative reputations can have stigmatizing consequences, which means that the reputation has a discrediting effect on the neighborhood and the residents. "Discrediting" means that the reputation is such that people have difficulty seeing the neighborhood as anything but what the reputation says it is. Because the stigma extends to the residents, it can carry over to any setting where a person's place of residence becomes relevant (e.g., job applications). A neighborhood with a very positive reputation benefits its residents because they are perceived as a reflection of that reputation. Communities with positive reputations can escape scrutiny such that existing tensions and problems within them remain hidden. In thinking about neighborhood reputation, ask the following questions:

- What is the reputation of the neighborhood?
- In what ways might this reputation be harmful or helpful to the neighborhood and/or the lives of its residents?

In chapter 6 we will look at a specific method of data collection, content analysis, to help establish neighborhood reputation in a systematic way. For now, we will consider landmarks that figure into a neighborhood's reputation.

Background on Landmarks

By **landmark**, we mean some monument, distinctive building, public space, unique architecture, or natural scenery that is considered special in some way to the neighborhood. A landmark holds symbolic power in that it conveys something important about the neighborhood. A landmark is considered a valuable resource when it bestows positive recognition—recognition that residents feel as pride, high status, honor, or prestige. A landmark is considered a detriment when it bestows negative recognition or evokes sensations of shame, embarrassment, low status, or dishonor. In this case, it is viewed as something to hide or to be explained. To really understand a landmark, it is important to do research on its origin and what qualities it conveys that has kept it "alive" and influential.

A landmark can function as a marker (e.g., "If you pass the abandoned building that was once the Marianne Theater you have gone too far"). Or it can be a space where something happened that catapulted the area into national or international attention—a police officer was shot, the police shot an unarmed person, or a movie was filmed at this location. Landmarks are often easily seen and recognized as unique to that neighborhood. Landmarks can draw outsiders in (e.g., "If you are in the vicinity you *must* stop and see the Ark Encounter[2] or the 9/11 Memorial").

2. A theme park in Grant County, Kentucky, which houses a full-scale model of the Ark described in Genesis.

Landmarks figure into what it means to be a resident. The landmark may be something that only locals know about, or it may attract visitors to the area. In this regard, the symbolic value of the landmark can be as important to those beyond the locality, or it may tie the locality to something larger (e.g., for some very small towns a landmark may be a McDonald's franchise that ties the neighborhood to a global corporation).

When thinking about the power of a landmark it is important to consider its cultural significance. A landmark qualifies as material culture, which sociologists define as the natural and human-created objects to which people have attached meaning. Its symbolic value lies with what the landmark conveys beyond the object itself. The landmark may convey one or more of the following:

- **values**—some shared and general conceptions of what is good, right, appropriate, worthwhile, and important with regard to conduct, appearance, or some state of being (e.g., "We value service and sacrifice to country"; "We value slow-cooked food from a family recipe"; "We value a time when . . . "; "This event sends the message [right or wrong] that we value one kind of people over another").
- **beliefs**—conceptions that people accept as true, concerning how the world operates and where the individual fits in relation to others (e.g., "We believe children need a safe place to play"; "We believe our schools should provide the best education"; "We believe that a successful football team is important to the neighborhood").
- **norms**—written and unwritten rules that specify behaviors appropriate and inappropriate to a social situation (e.g., "On this day we gather around the monument to pay respect to . . . "; "This is a park for people to bring their dogs to play").

The landmark can serve as a cultural anchor, something that elicits consensus among residents regarding its importance but at the same time elicits debate and disagreement over its meaning (e.g., a liquor store may be a place everyone sees as a landmark, but some people may applaud it because shoppers from another state can avoid paying higher sales taxes there while others may condemn it for promoting tax evasion). To think about the cultural significance of landmarks within a neighborhood, we ask questions such as the following:

- Are there landmarks in the census tract? Do these landmarks matter to people who live outside the tract?
- What larger message do the landmarks convey?
- Do any of the landmarks qualify as cultural anchors?

Exercise 5.4: Do a cultural analysis of a landmark

For this assignment, we apply the sociological perspective on landmarks and culture to write a 1.5-page analysis of a landmark in your neighborhood. Be sure to indicate if the landmark has importance beyond the locality—that is, if it has importance to a city/town, county, state, or region or the country. There may be many landmarks to consider. Analyze the landmark(s) drawing on the vocabulary in the previous section (norms, values, and beliefs). Your write-up should include a photograph with a caption. An example analysis of a landmark follows. Notice that this analysis has a number of important qualities; in particular, the author

- is clear about the landmark and its location (address and specific census tract in the neighborhood);
- describes the landmark and its importance to the census tract and beyond;
- uses the language of culture to drive the discussion; and
- includes references.

Model Example 1: Presidents' Park: A Landmark in Census Tract 655.01, Edgewood (Kenton County), Kentucky

Presidents' Park is located at 283 Dudley Road, Edgewood, KY 41017. This landmark is located in census tract 655.01. Presidents' Park is a place for family, friends, and neighborhood residents to gather for recreation, relaxation, and celebration. The park was designed to accommodate residents of any age. If we think in terms of *material culture,* the 20-acre site has four shelters that residents can rent for events (the Adams, Jefferson, Madison, and Washington Shelters). In addition, there are a variety of sports facilities, including baseball diamonds and basketball, tennis, and volleyball courts. The park also has a hiking trail and two playgrounds for young children. The main attractions are the clock tower and what is known as the Presidential Walkway. The clock tower can be seen from the road and acts as a landmark for the park, the census tract, and the city of Edgewood.

Presidents' Park features a walking tour around the Presidential Walkway, which chronicles the history of our past and current presidents. There is a cement slab for each president with a brief description of his accomplishments during his time in office.

Of course, the park is more than the material objects. Aspects of *nonmaterial culture* are evident as well. According to the brochure, this park was founded on the *belief* that people of all ages deserve a safe place for recreation and entertainment. It also places *value* on neighborhood as it brings residents together for concerts, fireworks, outdoor plays, and other festivities. A park designed for all ages and a walkway that honors *all* presidents regardless of party affiliation convey the message that high value is placed on unity, patriotism, and inclusiveness. These values of patriotism and respect for the past are evoked as people walk through the Presidential Walkway. It is a *norm* that people make no disrespectful comments about any of the presidents as they walk and that they start with the first president and make their way to the last.

References

City of Edgewood. 2017. http://edgewoodky.gov/parksrecreation/presidents-park/.

———. 2017. Presidents' Park Brochure. http://edgewoodky.gov/wp-content/uploads/2013/05/Presidents_Park_Brochure.pdf.

Model Example 2: The Carlisle Building: A Landmark in Census Tract 9568, Chillicothe (Ross County), Ohio

The historic Carlisle Building is located at 9 South Paint Street in Chillicothe, Ohio. This building sits on the corner of Paint and Main Streets. The Carlisle Building did not start out looking the way it does today. It began as a small wood-framed building in 1809. In 1817 a prominent Chillicothe merchant, John Carlisle, purchased the property. And in 1830 John's son Andrew built a two-story building to replace the original and added on over the years. In 1885 the building was torn down, and the four-story "crown jewel" was built in its place. This beautiful landmark has housed many area merchants and restaurants. Tragically, in 2003 a fire nearly destroyed the building. It sat in ruins for nearly 10 years. Many investors considered repairing it, but the damage was very extensive. Finally, in 2013, the local hospital, determined to make improvements to this material culture, worked with a developer to repair the building.

The Carlisle Building symbolizes the change and growth our city has experienced. Like the small wood-framed building that became the immaculate four-story Romanesque "castle," our neighborhood has also evolved.

Chillicothe has grown from an Indian village to Ohio's first capital, and now we are picking ourselves up from the opioid epidemic and repairing ourselves to become once again a city of pride and success.

The neighborhood values resilience, and the building became a symbol of that. The current developer put it this way: "The Carlisle Block Building, that blight in the center of town, represented a failure every time anyone looked at it. Now that building represents success." Today the building is being used as office space for the Adena Health System and 32 apartments that house visiting doctors. By restoring the Carlisle Building, the neighborhood hopes to attract young medical professionals to the area, thus improving our health services, which will affect not only the local neighborhood but also the whole region.

References

Zager, Masha. 2016. "Broadband Communities." March. www.bbcmag.com/2016mags/Mar_Apr/BBC_Mar16_POTM_Carlisle.pdf.

MODULE 5.4: SUPPORT AND COHESION RESOURCES

WHAT YOU WILL DO

- ✓ Complete an exercise about support and cohesion resources.
- ✓ Read background information.
- ✓ Write about the support and cohesion resources in your neighborhood modeled after the example.

Background on Support and Cohesion Resources

Social and cohesion resources provide a sense of belonging or attachment to a neighborhood. They are in place to address local needs. If residents spend a significant amount of time socializing, relaxing, working, consuming, and otherwise participating in neighborhood life, then it is safe to assume that people feel an attachment and a connection to that neighborhood.

Third places within a neighborhood qualify as cohesion resources. Recall from chapter 2 that third places function as anchors supporting and facilitating interaction. Ideally, a third place is free or very inexpensive and does not require people to make purchases to hang out there. Third places provide food, have patrons who are counted as regulars, are accessible such that it takes little time or effort to get there, and have a culture that both supports long-standing patrons and welcomes newcomers (Oldenburg 2001). Examples are community centers, coffee shops, restaurants, malls, hair salons, recreation centers, places of worship, schools, libraries, and parks (Jeffres et al. 2009). All offer residents the incentive to spend their time in the neighborhood rather than go elsewhere.

Then there are neighborhood- or community-serving organizations dedicated to providing medical, educational, cultural, spiritual, and social services. People are connected to their neighborhood when goods and services are accessible (e.g., desirable places to work; health care facilities, museums, theaters, restaurants, shops and gyms). However, these resources must not only be available; they must be affordable and located in safe and welcoming settings. To examine the resources in a neighborhood that offer residents opportunities to feel connected, we can ask the following kinds of questions.

- What are third places within the boundaries of the census tract?
- What nonprofit agencies are in the neighborhood?
- Are their public spaces within the boundaries of the neighborhood? Who uses those spaces?
- What businesses are in the neighborhood?
- Are there other sources of cohesion in the neighborhood (e.g., a sports team, an annual parade, a neighborhood watch group)?

Exercise 5.5: Identify support and cohesion resources

For this exercise, you will focus on the nonprofit agencies that exist within the boundaries of the census tract or neighborhood. You can secure a list of nonprofits using GuideStar.com, the world's largest source of information on nonprofit organizations. To find nonprofits in your neighborhood, visit the website www.guidestar.org and enter the city and state of the place that matters (e.g., Northside, Cincinnati, Ohio). As you look over the list, focus on identifying nonprofits located within the boundaries of your neighborhood. If there is doubt about whether a nonprofit is located in your census tract, enter the address in the FFIEC Geocoding System that you used to establish your census tract (see appendix E). Keep in mind that while GuideStar is the best resource on nonprofits, it is up to nonprofit agencies to register and submit their mission statements, tax forms, and programs offered. As you make your list, eliminate nonprofits with Post Office addresses and without an assigned category label such as mental health, youth, addiction. Also eliminate any private grant-making foundations. If the GuideStar search yields more than 50 listings, you may choose to select a sample for analysis, such as every fourth listing. A sample write-up of nonprofits by categories for census tract 532 in Newport (Campbell County), Kentucky, follows. The category tells us the kind of support and cohesion resources each offers.

Model Write-Up

In Guidestar, I used the search term "Newport, Kentucky" to secure a list of nonprofits. I found eight with addresses in census tract 532 that attracted my interest.

- Wave Foundation, Inc., Museum & Museum Activities
- Newport Southbank Bridge Co., Historical Societies and Related Activities
- New Beginnings Christian Counseling Services, Counseling Support Groups
- East Row Pool & Social Club, Inc., Swimming, Water Recreation
- Brighton Center Properties, Inc., Human Service Organizations
- Motherless Child Foundation, Inc., International Relief
- Corinthian Education and Community Development Corporation, Community Service Club
- South Bank Partners, Inc., Economic Development

From this list, two attracted by attention, and I chose to learn more about them: Brighton Center and Newport Southbank Bridge Co.

Newport Southbank Bridge Co., listed in the National Register of Historic Places, opened in 1872 as a railroad bridge named Newport and Cincinnati Bridge and then opened in 1896 to streetcars and automobile traffic with a pedestrian walkway. Because the bridge suffered from neglect and deterioration, it was closed in 1987 to railroad traffic and then in 2001 to automobile traffic. It became a pedestrian and bicycle traffic only bridge in 2003. The city of Newport, Kentucky, in partnership with an economic development group (Southbank Partners) invested in making the site a gathering place known as Purple People Bridge.

Brighton Center Properties, Inc., is located at 741 Central Avenue, Newport, Kentucky, in census tract 532. Brighton Center strives "to create opportunities for individuals and families to reach self-sufficiency through family support services, education, employment, and leadership." Established in 1966 to aid the growing poor population then moving to Newport from Appalachia, the Brighton Center has continued to grow and adapt to changes in the neighborhood. Today the nonprofit offers adult and early childhood education, workforce development, substance and domestic abuse recovery for women, affordable housing, financial education, and counseling. In 1997 Brighton Properties was opened as a subsidiary of Brighton Center, Inc., to provide and maintain affordable and quality housing for low-income residents in northern Kentucky. Brighton Properties supports subsidized apartment communities in Newport, including Two Rivers Apartments (Elm St.) and Saratoga Place Apartments (Saratoga St.). Half of the apartments in each complex are reserved for residents over 55 years of age. One of the Brighton Center's biggest fund-raising events is the Holiday Drive. The foods, used toys, clothing, and other items collected are distributed to families in need. This Holiday Drive also offers opportunities to "adopt a family" and to make a child's holiday wishes come true. Volunteers are vital at each of these events for sorting, stocking, setup, cleanup, and so on. In this way, the Brighton Center not only gives back to the neighborhood through charity, counseling, and education but also offers opportunities for residents to give back to their neighborhood in a tangible way.

References

Brighton Center, Inc. 2015. "Brighton Center: A Community of Support." www.brightoncenter.com/.

GuideStar USA. 2014. "Brighton Center." www.guidestar.org/organizations/61-0673886/brighton-center.aspx.

Sonnenberg, Elissa. 2006. "Purple People Greeter." *Cincinnati USA*, 14.

Background on Global and Local Businesses

Businesses located in a neighborhood count as an economic resource because they present employment opportunities and pay local taxes. For this research we think of businesses as brick and mortar operations that vary in size and range from small and local to large transnational corporations.

Transnational corporations are multicountry, even global, in reach. They can be counted among the world's largest employers or employ only a small number. The quality that makes a company transnational is a presence in more than one country. The largest transnational corporations make global-scale decisions about "what people eat and drink, what they read and hear, what sort of air they breathe and the water they drink, and ultimately what societies will flourish and which city blocks will decay" (Barnet 1990, 59). In thinking about transnational corporations in your neighborhood, consider not only global corporations like Proctor and Gamble, McDonald's, BP, or Starbucks but also newer ventures such as Airbnb and Uber.

Transnational businesses draw our attention to the intersection between the global and the local. This intersection is often described using the concepts of globalization and glocalization. **Globalization** is the ever-increasing flow and exchange of goods, services, people, money, information, ideas, and culture across national and international borders. **Glocalization** is the process by which those exchanges are launched from one country and then make their way to some local setting in another country. Globalization and glocalization are tied together because globalization encompasses a countless number of instances of glocalization. McDonald's is a transnational or global corporation because since 1955 its fast-food outlets have made their way to 32,000 local settings in 121 countries. Upon arrival in local settings, the residents embrace, modify, or resist the transplanted product. Thinking about the influence of transnational corporations, globalization, and glocalization in the neighborhood can prompt us to ask questions such as

- Are there transnational corporations or businesses located within the boundaries of the neighborhood?
- Are their locally owned businesses within the boundaries of the neighborhood that have a transnational presence?

Exercise 5.6: Inventory businesses

You can find a list of businesses with operations in your neighborhood by going to Yelp and using as a search term the name of the city of which your census tract is a part (e.g., Northside, Cincinnati, Ohio). Look over the list to identify businesses located inside the boundaries of your census tract. Note that the list includes churches and nonprofit organizations. To check whether a listing is actually in your census tract, enter the address in the FFIEC Geocoding System that you used to establish your census tract (see appendix E). Which businesses on the list do you support?

Model Write-Up Inventory of Businesses in Census Tract 78, Northside (Hamilton County), Ohio

Yelp lists 450 businesses in Northside; many are restaurants, cafés, bars or taverns, boutiques, and other local shopping opportunities such as Shake-It Records. Many Northside businesses appear to be independently owned. There appear to be only a handful of businesses that are franchises or branches of some regional, national, or transnational corporation. They include Ace Hardware, Taco Bell, White Castle, KFC, PNC, and BP. There are also several hair salons, a family-owned pharmacy (Shaeper), and shoe repair and consignment shops.

I have frequented Sidewinder Coffee (4181 Hamilton Ave.), Melt Eclectic Deli (4165 Hamilton Ave.), Northside Tavern (4163 Hamilton Ave.), and Shake-It Records (4156 Hamilton Ave.). After scanning Yelp.com Northside businesses, I plan to add at least two businesses to the list of those I support: Shaeper Pharmacy and Awesome Time Shoe and Leather.

MODULE 5.5: SOCIAL CHANGE

WHAT YOU WILL DO

✓ Complete an exercise about changes to your neighborhood.

✓ Read background on social change.

✓ Follow model example to write about a key social change.

Background on Social Change

Communities are not static; they are constantly shifting and changing. Any analysis of a neighborhood must consider change. We observe change when we notice a shift in population—a specific demographic moves out or dies, another moves in. We observe it when a new business closes and falls into disrepair, when a new subdivision breaks ground, when a new highway exit opens, when bike lanes are added, when roads fall into disrepair, or when an election brings in new leadership. No matter the change, we notice it in a physical sense but also in the ways people relate to each other.

When sociologists study neighborhood change, they seek to identify triggers of the change and the consequences. Virtually every neighborhood has been affected by globalization or glocalization, urbanization, the changing economy (from manufacturing based to knowledge based), increasing uncertainty in the labor market, stagnant wages, gentrification, changing demographics (e.g., an aging population, a baby boom, a baby bust), grassroots social movements, economic pressures on communities to become tourist destinations, and technological innovations. Each of these changes brings new opportunities to some and painful dislocations and disruption to others. Think about your neighborhood in terms of social change and ask

- What major triggers of change are affecting your neighborhood?
- Is there evidence of noticeable change in your neighborhood?

To assess the consequences of change, it is always helpful to turn to the five key sociological concepts for direction (see chapter 2). The five key concepts prompt us to look for changes in solidarity (social ties disrupted—strengthened or weakened), labor (jobs lost or gained, wages and benefits lost or gained), social action (traditions revived or lost; emotions heightened or depressed; codes of conduct weakened or strengthened; speed, efficiencies, and cost reductions to make profits at any cost), and color lines dissolving or solidifying. But know that there are thousands of concepts you could draw on and apply to any analysis of change.

Exercise 5.7: Identify a significant and visible change in your neighborhood

As you walk or drive through your neighborhood, what is the most visible change you notice? You might see a ground breaking, the opening of a new apartment complex, a once-vacant space recently turned into retail space, or buildings being repurposed (e.g., an elementary school is now a senior citizen residential complex). You might notice that once-smooth roads are now poorly maintained.

Model Write-Up: Monmouth Row Apartments: A Symbol of Social Change for Census Tract 532, Newport (Campbell County), Kentucky

Monmouth Row Apartments, located at 415 Monmouth Street, Newport (Campbell County), Kentucky, is part of census tract 532. This apartment complex with 101 units was constructed by Towne Properties, a corporation with a 50-year record of building condominiums, apartments, and commercial and recreational properties. Towne Properties sells an urban lifestyle with high-end amenities and services. It targets residents who want to live in a city but with a small-town feel.

Monmouth Row Apartments is one of Towne Properties' newest developments. These one- and two-bedroom luxury apartments cost between $1,085 and $1,640 per month to rent. Monmouth Row Apartments is located near restaurants, a bookstore, and a movie theater and is within walking distance of downtown Cincinnati. The apartment complex melds modern amenities with historic architecture. The apartments have fueled urbanization and drawn a new *demographic* of residents into the area. Monmouth Row Apartments is part of a series of complexes, including another that will transform the abandoned middle school into a space supporting 200 units. Both complexes are part of a larger social change known as gentrification, a "process by which higher income households displace lower income households in a neighborhood, changing the essential character . . . of that neighborhood" (Barton 2014, 1).

References

Barton, Michael. 2014. "An Exploration of the Importance of the Strategy Used to Identify Gentrification." *Urban Studies Journal* 53 (1): 1–20.

"Photos: Inside Newport's Monmouth Row Apartment Development." 2014. *RCN: River City News,* July 18.

Schools, E. 2015. "Who Cares about the Neighborhood?" PhD dissertation, University of California, Berkeley.

Towne Properties Asset Management Co. 2011. "Towne Properties." www.towne-properties.com/TowneHome/Index.aspx.

———. 2014. "Monmouth Row." www.monmouthrow.com/.

WORKING DRAFT OF RESEARCH BRIEF, SECTION 4

Neighborhood Resources

Now you are ready to highlight key findings from your inventory of neighborhood resources. You are also ready to reflect on your personal use of these resources and your level of support. As you worked your way through the chapter's exercises you learned about the tangible and intangible resources within your census tract. Now review your findings, keeping the core research questions in mind. Those core questions are

(1) In what ways do you support, or fail to support, the neighborhood surrounding the place that matters?
(2) Should that support be increased? If so, in what ways?

This inventory will help you assess what you contribute and take away from the neighborhood. Keep the following points in mind as you write up Part 4 of the research brief:

- You cannot write about everything. Be purposeful and selective.
- The inventory of businesses will help you establish what businesses you use and support.
- The inventory of residents' tangible and intangible assets offers insights about neighborhood strengths and vulnerabilities—insights that can inform your plan to increase your support. The inventory of nonprofits located in the neighborhood may include organizations you already support or that offer opportunities for engagement.
- Avoid making claims the data cannot support. For example, the household income estimates you secured cannot be used to make claims that your census tract consists of especially wealthy or economically disadvantaged households. To make those claims you will have to compare it to household incomes in surrounding census tracts or other geographic areas such as the county, state, or nation. We will do those kinds of comparisons in upcoming chapters.
- Consider how the significant social change you identified figures into the neighborhood's strengths and vulnerabilities.
- Always keep in mind that this is a preliminary inventory of resources and therefore open to refinement and revision.

Model Write-Up, Section 4

Census tract 78 is the heart of Northside. This tract is home to 2,411 residents. There are 1,519 housing units, but 353, or 23.2%, are vacant. That makes a total of 1,166 occupied units. This is a neighborhood where residents' combined income from all sources is $99.3 million per year. That translates to $41,174 per person and $65,353.80 per household. Sixty-eight percent of this aggregate income is from wages and salary. The next largest source is pension and social security combined ($13.9 million), which accounts for 28%.

In the neighborhood 157, or 13.4%, of households do not have a vehicle, and 10.6% have no health insurance. Just about 400 (n = 398), or 34.1%, of occupied households are considered cost burdened; that is, residents pay 30% or more of their household income to meet expenses. Almost 30% (29.6%) of the 561 residents who are age 24 and older have a bachelor's degree or higher, with the three highest fields of study being Visual and Performing Arts (84, or 14.9%), Engineering (63, or 11.2%), and Liberal Arts and History (50, or 8.9%). The least represented fields of study are Biological Sciences (22, or 3.9%), Physical and Related Sciences (16, or 2.9%), and Multidisciplinary Studies (9, or 1.6%).

Of the list of businesses in Northside, I frequent Sidewinder Coffee (4181 Hamilton Ave.), Melt Eclectic Deli (4165 Hamilton Ave.), Northside Tavern (4163 Hamilton Ave.), and Shake-It Records (4156 Hamilton Ave.). After scanning Yelp.com Northside businesses, I plan to add at least two businesses to the list that I will support: Shaeper Pharmacy and Awesome Time Shoe and Leather.

GuideStar lists about 8 nonprofits located inside the boundaries of the neighborhood. All have missions related to housing or community outreach. Five are especially notable and are worthy of my support. Cincinnati Northside Community Urban Redevelopment Corporation (CNCURC) focuses on increasing home ownership. CAIN (Churches Active in Northside) attempts to build a more "vibrant community" by providing various resources such as food and crisis assistance. Wordplay Cincinnati, located in the business district of Northside, is a creative writing and learning center for K–12 students. Finally, Happen Inc. and Happen Toy Lab Program offer free art programs and the chance to invent toys. Children can draw on the massive supply of recycled toy parts and seek advice from "toy professors."

The most noticeable symbol of change in the neighborhood is the multi-million-dollar Gantry Complex. The Gantry is a mixed-use complex, with 131 apartments and 8,000 square feet of street-level retail space. It consists of three buildings on Hamilton Avenue and Blue Rock Street that once housed a lumberyard and railroad depot. The apartments capitalize on a swelling millennial population attracted to urban living and convenience. According to the Gantry's website, studio apartments range from $683 to $970 a month. The most expensive units are two-bedrooms ranging from $1,230 to $1,545 a month. A retail space fills the remaining gap in Northside's business district, and the influx of money has boosted the neighborhood economy. But in a neighborhood where 40% of residents pay 30% or more of their income for housing costs and that is actively promoting housing for millennial professionals, there is concern about how the Gantry apartment influences the cost of rent and other housing in Northside.

REFERENCES

Barnet, Richard. 1990. "Defining the Moment." *New Yorker*, July 16, 45–60.
Jeffres, Leo W., Cheryl C. Bracken, Guowei Jian, and Mary F. Casey. 2009. "The Impact of Third Places on Community Quality of Life." *Applied Research in Quality of Life* 4 (4): 333.
Oldenburg, Ray, ed. 2001. *Celebrating the Third Place: Inspiring Stories about the Great Good Places at the Heart of our Communities*. New York: Da Capo Press.
U.S. Bureau of the Census. 2016. "Code Lists, Definitions, and Accuracy." American Community Survey.
Wutich, Amber, et al. 2014. "Stigmatized Neighborhoods, Social Bonding, and Health." *Medical Anthropology Quarterly* 28 (4): 556–77.

6 Basic Research Concepts

To this point we have identified the place that matters, established the census tract that is the surrounding neighborhood, learned about the residents and the households in which they live, and inventoried some of the tangible and intangible neighborhood resources. We have mostly relied on census data—data already collected and available. We have also gathered some observational data guided by the five signature concepts from classic theorists and by the four sociological perspectives. This chapter presents data gathering in a more systematic way, giving emphasis to decisions that must be made when doing more complex investigative research. Those decisions relate to establishing a unit of analysis and a target population to study. There are decisions to be made regarding sampling and data gathering. Finally, variables and a hypothesis must be established.

What follows is NOT a step-by-step guide for how to make these decisions. Rather consider it an overview of the kinds of decisions researchers must make when they collect data. These decisions are not made in any particular order or even one at a time. Sometimes decisions are made simultaneously. As an analogy, think about the skills and knowledge people must possess to drive a car to some destination. There is no agreed upon order about what to do and when. Every action is contingent on the situations that arise along the way, and the driver must continually assess options, draw on skills, and make a series of decisions before eventually getting to the destination.

The exercises you have completed in chapters 1 through 5 involve descriptive research. Just as its name suggests, the aim of descriptive research is to describe. Since these exercises involved becoming familiar with the surrounding neighborhood or census tract, descriptive research was ideal. In this and the chapters to come we will think in more complex ways about gathering data and making interpretations.

MODULE 6.1: UNIT OF ANALYSIS AND TARGET POPULATION

What You Will Do

✓ Read about unit of analysis and target populations.

✓ Complete two exercises.

✓ Present data and observations consistent with the model examples.

✓ Make interpretations modeled after examples.

Unit of Analysis

The **unit of analysis** relates to the "who" or "what" that is the object of research. A unit of analysis can be individuals, groups, households, territories, artifacts, documents, or social interactions. Knowing you have these choices about who or what kinds of things to study offers options and inspires creativity. It is important to know that the choice you make directs the kind of data collected and what you can say about it.

Individuals are perhaps the most well known unit of analysis. When studying individuals, researchers focus on the characteristics, attitudes, behaviors, and opinions of some predetermined number of people. The unit of analysis is individuals if we choose to ask residents, "Do you have a physical condition that substantially limits one or more basic physical activities such as walking, climbing stairs, reaching, lifting, or carrying?"

Likewise, if we ask women ages 15 to 49 whether they have given birth in the past year, the unit of analysis is also individuals.

Groups consist of people who share common traits and/or interact with one another in meaningful ways. When the unit of analysis is the group, we are interested in the group, not the individuals per se who make up the group. Although you may ask questions or collect data from the individuals who make up the group being studied, you will present that data in a way that tells us something about the group. For example, you might want to determine whether men in your census tract are more likely than women to have a physical condition that substantially limits one or more basic physical activities such as walking, climbing stairs, reaching, lifting, or carrying. If you study a neighborhood crime watch group, you can report on the average length of time members have been residents, the ratio of male to female members, the average age of members, and the percentage of members who reported suspicious activity within the past day, week, month, or year. You can also make observations about how members relate to one another.

Households, like groups, are studied apart from the individuals who comprise them. Households include all those who share the same place of residence. When the unit of analysis is households your interest lies in understanding something about the household as a unit. So you gather data with an eye to using it to know about a household, such as total household income (i.e., the combined income of all people living in the household). We could also gather data that yield insights about household structures or types (e.g., female-headed households with children under age 18 or multigenerational households). Or you could establish the percentage of households that pay more than 30% of income to meet housing-related expenses (e.g., mortgage payments, insurance).

Territories are spaces marked by known boundaries. Examples of territories are countries, states, counties, cities, census tracts, neighborhoods, streets, buildings, public spaces, and classrooms. When the unit of analysis is territories, you are interested in the characteristics of that territory. The unit of analysis is a territory if you are interested in learning the rate of bedbug infestation on a street, the poverty rate of a census tract, the income distribution of a county, or the racial composition of a state.

Artifacts or traces include any physical evidence that is the result of some action or activity. In other words, artifacts are any objects humans have made, such as artworks, items of clothing, and tools. Artifacts can also be flowers planted in the front yards of homes, fences marking property lines, litter along a stretch of riverbank, broken windows in abandoned buildings, or a landmark erected to honor a person or a historical event. The unit of analysis is an artifact if your research involves establishing the number of fenced-in yards per every 100 residential properties or if it involves weighing trash picked up. When studying artifacts researchers ask questions like, What messages does an artifact—such as a Humvee or a moped—send about what the owner values? Is there evidence that an artifact—such as a Confederate flag or the American flag—has a uniting or dividing effect on the larger society?

Documents are written or printed materials, such as signs; news headlines; articles; blogs; bumper stickers; birth, death, and marriage certificates; license plates; property valuations; and laws or ordinances. The documents can be records of past activity (marriage licenses issued before sending soldiers off to war) or records that document someone's position (e.g., legal driver, political affiliation). Local ordinances are also examples of documents. Ordinances act as windows into the kinds of issues or behaviors a neighborhood has deemed important enough to impose formal sanctions for violating such as fines, jail time, and other penalties. An ordinance may mandate that teens not be outdoors after 10:00 P.M. or that all owners or keepers of dogs act to keep them off another's property. Another kind of document is news headlines. When the headlines are about your neighborhood they can serve as a window onto its reputation.

Social interactions include encounters or relationships between two or more people in which the involved parties take the social context and each other into account before acting. Interaction is considered social when the parties can expect certain behavior and responses from others. If you study doctor-patient relationships or police-resident encounters, that unit of analysis is a social interaction. Again, remember that the focus is on characteristics or outcomes of an interaction, not on the individuals involved. If you are studying the doctor-patient relationship, you might collect data on the percentage of visits in which a doctor issues a prescription or the percentage of visits in which patients requests a special treatment or medication. If studying police-resident encounters, you might collect data on the percentage of all encounters over the course of a week that are conversational and do not involve any form of disciplinary action.

Target Population

Once you determine the unit of analysis, then you must state the **target population**—the population targeted for research. The population targeted may be be specific individuals, groups, households, territories, artifacts, or interactions. If the unit of analysis is individuals you must specify the types of individuals you are studying and in what context. The individuals could be high school age students at a specific school or schools (St. Mary or Jefferson County in Wakefield, Missouri). Here the aim might be to learn the percentage of students planning to attend college. Likewise, if the unit of analysis is artifacts, then be clear about the kind of artifact and in what context (see figure 6.1). The artifact might be trash discarded along the banks of a 10-mile segment of the Mississippi River or trash discarded along the entire 2,350 miles of the Mississippi River. You may want to know the weight of trash collected per each mile of the riverbank targeted for study. If you decide to compare trash discarded along riverbanks of major cities, then both artifacts and territories are the unit of analysis.

Exercise 6.1: Identify a unit of analysis and a target population

In this exercise territories are the unit of analysis. You will identify two territories or census tracts to study: (1) the census tract that is home to your place that matters and (2) a bordering census tract. For illustrative purposes, tract 9501 in Okolona, Mississippi, is the home census tract and census tract 9502 in New Houlka, Mississippi, is an adjacent census tract. Both tracts are in Chickasaw County. You can identify an adjacent tract number by doing a Google search for FFIEC Geocoding System. In the address box, enter the address of the place that matters. When the map comes up you will see the home census tract number and also the numbers of adjacent tracts. Select one of the adjacent tracts.

The target population is 3- and 4-year-olds who live in the two census tracts, 9501 and 9502. Specifically, you want to know the percentage of

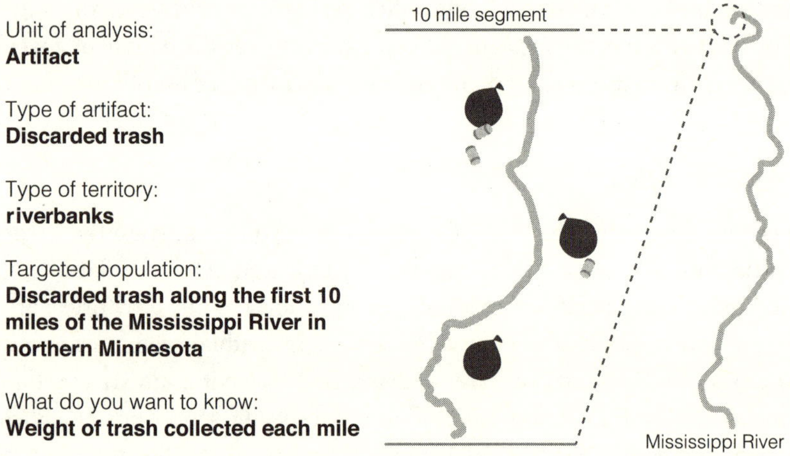

Unit of analysis:
Artifact

Type of artifact:
Discarded trash

Type of territory:
riverbanks

Targeted population:
Discarded trash along the first 10 miles of the Mississippi River in northern Minnesota

What do you want to know:
Weight of trash collected each mile

10 mile segment

Mississippi River

Figure 6.1. Unit of Analysis and Target Population
SOURCE: Joan Ferrante and Tabitha Kelly

3- and 4-year-olds enrolled in preschool and if the two tracts differ in significant ways. Knowing the percentage for the home and adjacent census tracts is useful because it tells you where the home census tract stands in comparison to another. In addition, the comparison will offer insights into whether the home census tract is at an advantage or a disadvantage relative to another tract.

Why is it important to know about preschool enrollment? Research has shown that a tie to a nursery school or preschool is critical (Arteaga et al. 2014). Specifically, the research shows that in comparison to children who do not go to nursery school or preschool, children who do go are

- less likely to fail a grade or to be placed in special education;
- more likely when they reach adulthood to secure higher-paying jobs;
- less likely to be abused and neglected; and
- less likely to engage in delinquent acts as teens.

Use the census data from Table S1401 School Enrollment (latest 5-year estimates) to create a table that shows for both census tracts the number and percentage of 3- and 4-year-olds enrolled in preschool for both tracts. Use table 6.1 as a guide for your write-up. Note that Table S1401 gives you

Table 6.1 Number and Percentage of 3- and 4-Year-Olds Enrolled in Preschool, Census Tracts 9501 and 9502 in Chickasaw County, Mississippi

	Number of Children Ages 3 and 4	Number of Children Enrolled in Preschool	Number of Children NOT Enrolled	Percentage Enrolled
Census tract 9501	91	49	42	53.8
Census tract 9502	47	0	47	0.0

SOURCE: American Community Survey, latest data (2015) accessed Nov. 15, 2017.

the data you need to fill in column 2 (number of children enrolled in preschool) and column 4 (percentage enrolled). You can use these data to calculate the number of children ages 3 and 4 enrolled (column 1) and the number not enrolled (column 3).[1]

Model Interpretation

Just over 53.8% of 3- and 4-year-olds in census tract 9501 are enrolled in nursery school or preschool versus 0.0 percent in census tract 9502. That is a 53.8% difference. For census tract 9501 to equal census tract 9502's enrollment rate of 53.8%, it would have to enroll 25.2[2] more students.

Knowing this difference in enrollment rates may prompt us to consider what is it about census tract 9501—its residents or households—that explains its relative success over census tract 9502. Perhaps residents in census tract 9502 have a higher or lower median household income than those in census tract 9501. To check if there are household income differences between two tracts, go the census bureau website and access Table B19013, Median Household Income in the Past 12 Months, for each census

---

1. The census bureau table (S1401 School Enrollment) presents the number of 3- and 4-year-olds enrolled in preschool as well as the percentage of the 3- and 4-year-old population enrolled. You can use these data to calculate the % of children ages 3 and 4 is (number of 3- and 4-year-olds enrolled / number ages 3 and 4) * 100). To calculate the percentage of children ages 3 and 4 enrolled for census tract 9501, do the following: (49/91) *100 = 53.8%. To calculate the number of children not enrolled, subtract 49 from 91, which is 42.

2. To get this number, simply multiply the number of 3- and 4-year-olds in census tract 9502 by .538 (47 *.538 =27).

tract. The median household income for census tract 9501 is $26,116 and for census tract 9502 it is $35,022, an $8,906 difference. The census tract with the highest median income is the one where parents of 3- and 4-year-olds are not enrolling them in preschool. It is also the census tract where there is a greater percentage of married couple households (49.1% vs. 31.0%) and where there are fewer female-headed households (18.8% vs. 27.0%). See the document "Selected Social Characteristics in the U.S." for household type data.

MODULE 6.2: SAMPLING

WHAT YOU WILL DO

✓ Read background information on sampling.

✓ Complete one exercise about how to select a sample.

✓ Select a sample and specify criteria.

Once you have identified a unit of analysis and a target population, the next step is selecting the **sample,** or subset of individuals, groups, households, artifacts, territories, documents, or interactions, from the population targeted for study. While it might be nice to gather data on everyone or everything that is part of the targeted population, doing so is usually too time consuming or too expensive.[3] For example, if your target population consists of residents ages 3 and 4, you probably do not have the time or resources to knock on every household door to learn how many 3- and 4-year-olds live in your census tract. Your only realistic option is to select a sample.

Sometimes there is no need to take a sample and gather data because the data you need already exist. For instance, we used American Community Survey data (on the census bureau website) to find estimates of the number of 3- and 4-year-olds enrolled in preschool. Even when

---

3. The 10-year national census is an example of research that attempts to "sample" every household and person in the United States. One advantage of taking a census instead of a sample is that in theory you can be certain a census represents the population, because it is the population. Still, even though every householder in the United States is required to answer census questions, an unknown number refuse or cannot be found.

data are available you must know the sampling method the census bureau used to secure that data. That is because it will help you assess **generalizability,** the degree to which the estimates obtained from a sample are representative of the targeted population. Generalizability is an important concept to understand because the degree to which your findings are generalizable depends on how you sample. For example, imagine that you observe that a library in your census tract is an invaluable resource to residents in the neighborhood. You want to verify your hunch, so you decide to find out how many residents use the library. You cannot talk to everyone who comes to the library, so you decide to interview a sample. Greeting patrons on a Saturday as they enter the library and asking them to fill out a short survey about the library's resources is one way to sample patrons. But if the day you choose to distribute the survey happens to be a Saturday when an all-day event for children is scheduled, the results of your study would not represent or be generalizable to all library patrons. When making decisions about how to sample patrons, you must select days and times that capture the diversity of patrons and that enhance your ability to generalize about census tract residents (your target population). Consider that there are two broad methods of sampling: random and nonrandom.

Random Samples

Random samples are those in which everyone or everything that makes up a target population has an equal chance of being selected. Ideally, you should strive to obtain a random sample, since theoretically this sample would be representative of the target population; that is, the sample should reflect the distribution of characteristics (age, income, sex, etc.), behaviors (e.g., commute to work alone or carpool) or attitudes (e.g., toward taxes) of those who are part of the target population. Random samples, however, are not easy to secure. A truly random sample depends on knowing the size of the target population and having a complete list of every person (students, residents, 3-year-olds), household, or thing (tax documents, birth certificates) that makes up the target population. Only after you obtain a complete and accurate list are you able to assign numbers to each case and draw a random sample.[4] If done correctly, a random sample should yield results close to what you would find if you studied everyone or everything making up the target population.

To illustrate how random samples are secured, let's assume that you want to study parents of preschool-age children who live in your census tract to learn why some of them send their children to preschool and others do not. You might be able to secure a list of preschoolers and their parents' names from the local school system. From that list, you can select a random sample of parents to interview. However, the list has shortcomings: you cannot be sure that residents who send children to preschool send them to the school that gave you the list. Moreover, a list of parents who have not enrolled their 3- and 4-year-olds in school does not likely exist. It is not feasible to knock on the door of every household in the census in search of these parents. However, if you have a complete list of all households, you could randomly select a portion of the households, knock on each door, and ask an adult if there are 3- or 4-year-olds who live in the household and whether they are enrolled in preschool. As you might imagine, some residents will not be home, will not answer the door, or will refuse to answer your questions. So, while in theory random samples might seem to be the ideal way to learn about a target population, they are not easy to secure in practice.

To this point you have relied on census estimates for information on residents and households.[5] While the U.S. Census Bureau uses random sampling and has a reputation for delivering high-quality estimates, all data have shortcomings. For one thing, the smaller the territory within the United States, the less reliable the estimates. The best estimates, then, are for the nation as a whole, followed by state and county. The least reliable estimates are for census tracts. We know also that census data can be one

---

4. There are formulas for determining the ideal size of the sample that take into account an acceptable margin of error and level of confidence (90%, 95%, or 99%). The formula cannot account for resources (time and money) required to administer a random sample. If resources are limited researchers may sacrifice sample size to save money, but the trade-off is accepting a higher margin of error and a lower level of confidence.

5. The U.S. Census Bureau uses random sampling to secure data on households and residents living in census tracts, counties, states, and other geographic areas. As we know, samples yield estimates, not the true value. Census data are arguably the best source of information on the residents and households in the United States.

to two years old by the time it is released. Still, the census bureau offers the best data available on residents and households.

Nonrandom Samples

Given the challenges of securing a random sample, researchers often settle for a nonrandom sample. **Nonrandom samples** are those in which the members of the target population do not have an equal chance of being selected for study. Nonrandom sampling is used when a researcher does not have the time or resources to take a random sample or when there is no list of those in the target population from which to draw a random sample. Nonrandom sampling can be purposive, convenience, snowball, and case studies.

Purposive sampling involves selecting a nonrandom sample of individuals, groups, households, territories, traces, documents, or interactions that are part of the target population. The sample is established with an eye toward learning more about the target population. Perhaps the researcher knows some parents who have 3- or 4-year-olds who are not enrolled in preschool. The researcher may ask those parents to do an interview or to fill out a questionnaire.

Another type of nonrandom sampling is **convenience sampling.** This technique requires researchers to select subjects from a target population based on convenience or their availability. If researchers are interested in studying patrons who support local businesses, they may choose to survey patrons who come out to shop onSmall Business Saturday®—a national day set aside in November to celebrate and support local small businesses. Those patrons constitute a convenience sample. While the patrons at this event are not likely to be representative of all patrons, a sample offers some insights about those who support local businesses.

Snowball sampling, sometimes called referral, networked, or word-of-mouth sampling, is used when the target population consists of a very small number of people. If researchers are interested in the population of 3- and 4-year-olds who are not enrolled in preschool, they may try to identify a parent with a child of that age not enrolled in preschool. Once that parent is secured, the researcher can ask that parent to refer another parent with a child not enrolled in preschool. With each contact, the researcher gathers more recommendations and the sample snowballs in size.

A **case study** is nonrandom sample of one. Case studies give an in-depth analysis of one person, experience, or process. They focus on a specific individual, family, household, street, business, or landmark, or some other thing. Case studies tell a detailed story. Sometimes researchers compare two case studies (e.g., a household with a preschooler enrolled in school vs. a household with a preschool-age child not enrolled).

Exercise 6.2: Select a sample of times to observe a third place

For this exercise, you will choose and observe a third place within your census tract. Recall from chapter 2 that **third places** function as the anchors of neighborhood life because they draw people in and cultivate interaction. Local libraries, cafés, community centers, public libraries, ice cream shops, and parks qualify as third places. You will determine the times and days to observe a chosen space. The goal is to learn more about those who frequent this space and how people interact within or use that space. Because it is impossible to observe a chosen space 24/7 or for an unlimited number of days, it is important to select a sample of times to observe and interview patrons. In your write-up you will describe how you would sample times and days and offer a rationale for the type of sample. Remember that this is a plan for how to draw a sample and not something you will carry out for this project. If you want to secure a random sample that is generalizable and minimize margin of error, consult a sample-size calculator that tells you the size. One calculator can be found using the search terms "Survey Monkey sample size calculator."

> *Model Write-Up on Selecting a Sample*
>
> The Culver City Skate Park on Jefferson Boulevard in Culver City, California, is an important neighborhood resource. It is open Monday through Friday from 12:00 noon to 7:00 P.M. or sunset and Saturday and Sunday from 9:30 A.M. to 4:30 P.M. or sunset. One goal is to learn the proportion of patrons using the skate park during the summer months (May 15–September 15) who live in census tract 7025.02. My plan is to ask patrons as they arrive at the park to type their addresses in the FFIEC Geocoding System, which will tell me the resulting census tract number. I plan to select a random sample

of times to be at the park. The park is open 82 days during the summer months, for a total of 574 hours. I will assign each of the 574 hours a number (e.g., May 15, 12:00–12:59) and randomly select a predetermined number of one-hour segments based on a desired confidence interval of 90% and a margin of error of 4%. According to a sample size calculator (see www.surveymonkey.com/mp/sample-size-calculator/), I need a sample size of 246 one-hour times. The +/- 4% means that the estimate of the percentage of patrons who are residents of the census tracts will be +/- 4%.[6]

MODULE 6.3: DATA-GATHERING STRATEGIES

WHAT YOU WILL DO

✓ Complete three exercises about data-gathering strategies.

✓ Read background information on strategies of gathering data.

✓ Engage in appropriate data-gathering tasks.

Data Gathering

Data gathering is guided by a plan for accessing or collecting information on a target population. Researchers take care to gather or acquire data that is reliable and accurate. The most common methods of data-gathering are (1) using existing or archived sources, (2) observation, (3) asking questions (interviews and questionnaires/surveys), and (4) content analysis.

EXISTING OR ARCHIVED SOURCES

These sources give researchers access to data. The source can be an organization, group, or individual that gathered the data for some specific purpose, obviously without considering purposes for which others might one day use it. Examples of archived sources are census data, historical documents (diaries, photos), websites, news and magazine articles, property tax data, comments posted on a website, and business listings. We have already accessed data that the U.S. Bureau of the Census archived for public use. The census bureau collects data on residents and households for

---

6. Researchers may not have the time or resources to be at the park for 246 hours, so they may settle for a convenience sample. That is, they select a typical week (e.g., the second week of June) and collect data on patrons' presence for that week.

reasons that are outlined in "Questions on the ACS Form and Why We Ask," which can be found by searching the web. Know that the various uses for which businesses, nonprofit agencies, and ordinary people have used this archived census data are incalculable.

ASKING QUESTIONS: QUESTIONNAIRES OR SURVEYS

Questionnaires or surveys are data-gathering tools used to secure information from individuals who agree and take the time to complete them. Questionnaires are **self-administered** when respondents complete them on their own initiative. They may fill out a questionnaire they see inside a magazine or come across online without the researcher being present and prompting them to do so. Self-administered questionnaires are economical because the researcher does not use time to ask the questions directly. However, as with any data-gathering strategy, there are limitations. Many people ignore the chance to take the survey, fail to answer all the questions, misinterpret wording, or rush to complete it.

Surveys or questionnaires are considered **researcher administered** when researchers are present to distribute, monitor, and collect them. If a respondent needs clarification, the researcher is there to assist. Sometimes researchers read the questions and record the answers. The presence of a researcher can influence respondents' answers or put pressure on respondents to complete the survey when they do not wish to.

No matter how it is administered, a questionnaire can include fixed-choice and/or open-ended questions. **Fixed-choice** questions include a list of answers from which respondents choose (e.g., check one; check all that apply). In contrast, **open-ended questions** ask respondents to answer in their own words. Fixed-choice questions are useful when the researcher's aim is to gather very specific information, such as respondents' demographic and social characteristics (race, sex, age, income), behaviors (e.g., number of times they have visited the local library), or opinions (e.g., "On a scale of 1 to 5 where 1 means 'not very important' and 5 means 'extremely important,' how important is a local grocery store to your day-to-day life?"). Fixed-choice questions yield standardized answers, which limit a researcher's ability to know why a respondent answers a question in a certain way. Open-ended questions, by contrast, allow respondents the opportunity to generate and clarify their answers. The downside to open-ended questions is that very few respondents take the time to write polished statements. Often respondents just write a few words and leave the researcher guessing about what they meant to say.

ASKING QUESTIONS: INTERVIEWS

Interviews involve a researcher asking respondents questions and recording answers. Interviews can take two forms, structured and unstructured. The questions asked in a **structured interview** are determined before the interview takes place. The interviewer does not vary from the "script" in order to ensure that all respondents have the same experience. Questions may also be open-ended ("Tell me about a time that you recall feeling particularly connected to your neighborhood") or fixed-choice ("How often do you frequent the skate park? Never, less than once per year, once every 6–12 months, once every 2–6 months, once a month, more often than once a month"). In **unstructured interviews,** key questions are still predetermined, but the interview takes on conversational qualities, with the key questions serving as guides, and the researcher asking follow-up questions.

To learn about how residents relate to a third place in your neighborhood such as a business, a public space, or a house of worship, you can conduct short interviews with residents or patrons.[7] To illustrate, you might stop people and ask open-ended questions about special restaurant we will call Thai Smile.

- What words comes to mind when you think of Thai Smile?
- What about Thai Smile stands out as something you are sure to tell others about?
- When you mention you are going to Thai Smile to eat, what is a typical comment or reaction?
- What, if anything, would you change about Thai Smile?

OBSERVATION

Observation is a form of data gathering that involves all the senses: looking, listening, tasting, touching, and smelling. Observation allows the

---

7. If that neighborhood resource is in the news, you may be able to do a content analysis of the news articles to learn about its reputation.

researcher to experience a setting, an environment, or some other situation. As with all data-gathering strategies, there are downsides to observation research, since the mere presence of the researcher taking notes, looking, or just sitting alone and off to the side watching can affect how those being observed behave if they become aware that they are being watched or if they become distracted by the researcher's presence.

Observational research takes two forms. **Participant observation** requires the researcher be an active participant. This approach allows the researcher to understand and experience directly what it means to be part of the group, setting, or process. For example, if researchers want to understand the importance of a youth center to a neighborhood, they might volunteer as a mentor so they can interact with the young people and get to know them. **Nonparticipant observation** involves a researcher looking on but not participating as interactions and activities take place. For instance, a researcher might decide to observe people as they come and go from a third place with the goal of understanding how that place serves the surrounding neighborhood. There are at least four observational strategies: (1) time oriented, (2) event oriented, (3) situation oriented, and (4) stream-of-consciousness oriented.[8]

In **time-oriented observation**, the researcher may choose to observe during a specific time frame such as over the course of a year, a month, a day, or a shorter time span. If you are interested in the number of times you leave your house to do something inside the census tract versus outside of it over the course of a typical week, you are engaged in time-frame observation. You might choose to observe for one week the times of day you come and go and for what purposes. How many times do you leave your house to do something within the boundaries of the census tract? These observations will give you some sense of the role the surrounding neighborhood plays in your life during a typical week. Of course, you must choose a week considered typical. A week in which something unusual is going on, such as a vacation or when relatives are visiting, is probably not a good choice. But then if your purpose is how much the neighborhood

---

8. As you will see, all four types involve decisions about sampling. Because researchers cannot observe 24/7 or over an indefinite period, they must ask, When should I make observations, and should there be a special focus of my observations?

figures into what you do with relatives, friends, or other people when they visit, that might be the time to observe your own comings and goings.

Observation is **event oriented** when researchers pick a special event to give focus to observations. That event may be an evening walk, an annual parade, a neighborhood watch meeting, or a service (e.g., when you visit a house of worship on Sunday, what is that experience like? When you watch people out for an evening walk, what are their interactions like?).

Observation is **situation oriented** when researchers focus on a condition or setting that shapes behavior. How do people out for an evening walk respond in one kind of situation versus another? When evening walkers pass those walking dogs, do they interact differently than when passing someone walking without a dog? Or how do evening walkers interact when they encounter two or more people walking as a group with a dog?

The fourth observation choice is **stream of consciousness.** This involves watching and recording everything without focusing on any specific thing, like people out for a walk. After taking notes absent focus, the researcher reviews those notes looking for patterns or interesting points to highlight.

How do researchers make sense of their observations? One way is to do a **content analysis.** This technique allows researchers to analyze and summarize content of some kind—the content of observations made, news stories, conversation, television commercials, videos, menus, tweets. The kinds of content that can analyzed are endless. Content analysis involves counting the number of times an action, statement, behavior, or something else of interest occurs. The analysis may focus on the number of times people in conversation offer criticism versus praise or the number of times women appear in a series of YouTube videos relative to men. Researchers are looking for content that occurs more or less frequently. For example, as a measure of the perceived safety of a neighborhood, you could count the number of signs posted on or around homes in that neighborhood that contain content that conveys warnings, mistrust, or insecurity ("Beware of Dog"; "Security Cameras in Use"; "No Trespassing") compared to signs with conveying openness and security (welcome mats or invitations to take a book from a free library box). When presenting the results of a content analysis, be sure to mention number of occurrences relative to some total (e.g., the number of security signs relative to all households examined, or the number of signs posting warnings relative to all signs).

Exercise 6.3: Try out two data-gathering strategies

Now that we have briefly reviewed data-gathering strategies, it is time to try a couple. Specifically, you will

- ✓ do a content analysis of news articles featuring something about or in the surrounding neighborhood to assess that neighborhood's reputation; and
- ✓ do a stream-of-consciousness short observation.

Content Analysis

In this exercise, you will do a content analysis of news articles to gauge the reputation of the neighborhood you are studying. Recall that content analysis involves summarizing some form of content by counting the times various themes, behaviors, or references occur in it. The first step of this exercise is to identify a source of news articles such as Google News or some other news aggregator. Use this source to search for articles about things going on in your census tract. Your census tract might *not* have an official name, but it is certainly part of some town or city (e.g., census tract 106 is located in San Francisco, California, and is part of the Castro District). Use Google News to locate articles about the town or city and select those that feature the parts of the Castro District that are in tract 106. You must decide in advance how many days of news and news articles to sample; you can't read every story. You might choose to sample news articles that appear over the course of a typical week or every fifth article generated. You could also choose to set up a news alert and do a content analysis of articles that come in over that alert for a specific period (a week, a month).

Once you have decided how to sample articles, the question becomes what to look for when you read these articles. The key to content analysis is to identify themes and classify articles accordingly. You may determine themes as you make your way through the sample of news articles. For example, articles about the Castro District that relate to census tract 106 over a two-week period (the sample) includes the following themes:[9]

- Reactions to gay marriage rulings—6
- Gay pride celebrations (past, present, upcoming)—14
- Castro shifting to slightly less gay—1
- Demand for retail—5
- Abusive landlord—1
- Renovations of public space—2
- Traffic congestion—2
- Kim Kardashian visits
- High home prices—3
- Gay art defaced—1
- Fire in residential area—1

Model Interpretation

This content analysis suggests that this census tract's reputation revolves around gay events and issues, since 23 of the 37 news articles reviewed fit those themes. References to renovation, traffic congestion, demand for retail, and high-priced housing suggest a shortage of affordable housing, which reflects high demand for space in San Francisco.

Stream-of-Consciousness Self-Observation

Use a stream-of-consciousness self-observation to think about how you imagine residents see you in your role relative to the place that matters to you.

Model Write-Up: Imagine How Neighbors Perceive You and the Place that Matters

As the resident home owner of the place that matters to me, I reflect on how my neighbors see me as resident and home owner. I have wondered quite

---

9. Another suggestion for determining the reputation of the place that matters is to use archival sources to learn the history of the place. Its history can have some bearing on its current reputation.

often how my neighbors perceive me. I think they see me as young, well-to-do, and a single female. I also think they see me as an outsider moving into a nice home in a lower-income area that is changing. I know that I bought my house at a reasonable price, and not everyone in the neighborhood can afford this house or even qualify for a loan. I do not feel as if I am hurting anyone by being here. I think my neighbors benefit because I am a good resident. I get that I am living in a house that at one time someone did not have the financial means to keep up. I don't have kids, but I pay taxes. I particularly wonder what the kids think about me and my house as they walk to school in the morning. Do they see me as someone who thinks she is "better" than their parents since my house is so nice and well kept? When I see these kids walking to school, I wonder what I can do to help the elementary school.

MODULE 6.4: VARIABLES, OPERATIONAL DEFINITIONS, AND LEVELS OF MEASUREMENT

WHAT YOU WILL DO

- Read background information.
- Complete two exercises about variables and operational definitions.
- Follow instructions for creating, measuring, and assessing variables.

Background on Variables and Operational Definitions

As the word suggests, a **variable** is something that varies about the chosen unit of analysis which may be individuals, groups, households, territories, artifacts, documents, or social interactions. Individuals can vary on an incalculable number of characteristics, including their sex, employment status, and level of optimism. The variable *sex* is typically treated as a two-category (or binary) variable: male and female. Employment status is often treated as a three-category variable: (1) employed, (2) unemployed, and (3) looking for work and not part of the labor market. Level of optimism might be treated as a five-category variable (e.g., on a scale of 1 to 5, with 1 being "not optimistic at all" and 5 being "extremely optimistic," and with 2, 3, and 4 being something in between). Trash collected along riverbanks is a variable as it can vary by weight (*the weight of litter per square mile will vary*). News headlines can vary by theme (crime, tabloid, local, etc.).

An **operational definition** is a precise definition of a variable, including instructions for how it is to be observed or measured. Consider an operational definition for annual income. While on the surface this variable seems straightforward, there are actually many ways that annual income can be defined and measured. One definition is money earned from paid employment only. Another definition is money a person secures from any source. We could think of that income as before taxes or after taxes or income claimed on the last tax return after deductions.

The U.S. Census Bureau defines **income** as money secured in the past year *before deductions* from the following sources considered regular: wages, salary, tips, bonuses; self-employment income; interest; dividends; net rental income; royalties; social security; supplemental security income; public assistance received by check or electronic transfer; retirement, survivor, or disability pensions; and any other sources (U.S. Bureau of the Census 2016). How exactly does the census bureau measure annual income?[10] It does so by asking respondents to look at a list of income sources and indicate the amount received from each source over the course of the past year. From that information, the census bureau calculates total income.

Operational definitions are assessed on reliability and validity. A **reliable** measure produces consistent results. When we ask someone their annual income before deductions from a list of sources, are the answers reliable or consistent? Will people give the same answer today that they did last week? To make answers reliable, we want to know what they earn after, not before, deductions.

A valid measure is one that captures what researchers claim it is measuring. In the case of income, does asking people to list the amount of income secured from each of 15 sources capture the true amount of income secured over the course of a year? Some might argue that is does not, because the question does not ask respondents to reveal income from savings withdrawals, capital gains or losses from sale of a home or stocks; and inheritance, loans, and payments-in-kind as income. When problems of reliability and validity are identified, the first step is to try to correct the

---

10. You can find the operational definition and measure using the search terms "ACS Census Code Lists, Definitions, and Accuracy"

measure or operational definition. If corrections cannot be made, the shortcomings should be disclosed when data are presented.

Exercise 6.4: Assess validity and reliability

For this exercise choose a variable from the American Community Survey and determine how it is operationalized or measured. Then that measure's reliability and validity. Google "ACS Code Lists, Definitions, and Accuracy" for a list. Notice that the variable's name is stated in a very precise way. Keep the ACS wording. Do not, for example, change the name of the variable *dollar value of an occupied unit* to *home value*. An example of how to assess reliability and validity of a variable follows.

Model Write-Up about a Measure's Reliability and Validity

The census bureau collects data on the variable, *dollar value of an owner-occupied unit*. It divides dollar values into eight categories, ranging from "less than $50,000" to" $1,000,000 or more." The eight categories are

Less than $50,000

$50,000 to $99,999

$100,000 to $149,999

$150,000 to $199,999

$200,000 to $299,999

$300,000 to $499,999

$500,000 to $999,999

$1,000,000 or more

The census bureau defines the *value of owner-occupied housing unit* as the dollar value the owner believes the unit would sell for in the housing market. The value is measured or operationalized by asking the survey question shown in figure 6.2.

Now that we know the variable, the categories, and how it is defined and measured, we can assess the validity and reliability of the operational definition. To assess validity, we ask, Is asking owners (or a responsible party living in the owner-occupied household) how much they think their unit would sell for on the market a valid way to measure the actual value? Does that question really help us to know market value? We might argue NO, because most respondents are very likely to under- or overvalue a unit's

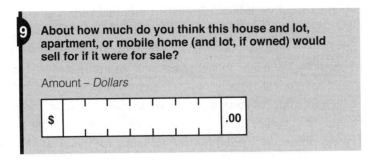

Figure 6.2. American Neighborhood Survey Question on Home Value
SOURCE: American Community Survey.

selling price. On the other hand, we might argue YES, because owners are likely to have a broad sense of property values in the context of the neighborhood in which they live and therefore give a reasonably accurate estimate of value. Furthermore, people may under- or overvalue their homes by tens of thousands of dollars, but it is less likely that they would under- or overvalue their homes by $100,000, for example. In other words, residents are likely realistic in their estimate even if it is undervalued or overvalued.

In assessing reliability, ask, is it reasonable to assume that when asking respondents about home value at two different points in time, they would give the same value? In other words, if we ask an owner to estimate what they think their unit would sell for today and ask the same question again one week later, would that answer change? If we assume housing values have not risen or fallen and that owners know the approximate value of their home, then we can also assume this is a reliable way to get at home value.

You can be sure that the census bureau has tested questions for reliability and validity because that government agency has the financial resources and staff to test their survey instruments before administering them[11].

Levels of Measurement

When we establish operational definitions, we also must specify a level of measurement. There are three levels of measurement: categorical, ordinal, and cardinal.

---

11. For a description of ways that the census bureau tests and evaluates survey instruments, visit www.census.gov/about/policies/quality/standards/appendixa2.html.

Categorical-level variables, also called nominal variables, consist of categories. Each category is assigned a name and number for coding purposes. But there is no natural ordering or rank to categories, so any numbers assigned to them are meaningless. For example, sex is typically treated as a categorical variable (1 = female; 2 = male), and there is no ranking such that one category is presented as more important or greater in value than the other.[12] Likewise, race is a categorical variable with six official categories in the United States. Religious and political affiliation are other examples of categorical variables. As we learned in chapter 4, thinking about humanity in categorical terms can be problematic. There will always be people whose experience falls outside the official categories. For example, there is growing recognition that people can be male, female, or transgender (Facebook presents people with 56 different gender categories, including gender questioning, gender fluid, and pangender).

Ordinal-level variables are those with an implied ranking (e.g., 1 = low-crime neighborhood; 2 = high-crime neighborhood). An ordinal variable can be rank ordered and assigned a value, but that value has no meaning in a relative sense. That is, we cannot say a high-crime neighborhood has two times more crime than a low-crime neighborhood. Level of optimism is another example of an ordinal variable. If we ask respondents to check their level of optimism on a scale of 1 to 4, with 1 = not optimistic at all, 2 = not optimistic, 3 = optimistic, and 4 = very optimistic, we cannot say a score of 4 is twice as optimistic as a score of 2 or a score of 4 is four times more optimistic than a score of 1. Likewise, we could rank the top 10, top 50, or top 100 cities on some quality, like livability. But the rankings alone do not tell us how much more livable city #50 is than city #1. There is no way from looking at just the rankings to know how much better life is in city #1 than city #50.

Other variables that we would consider ordinal are be social class categories, IQ scores, SAT scores, and GPA. In all cases values can be rank ordered from highest to lowest (or lowest to highest). While we can say know some scores are higher or lower than other scores, we cannot say what the magnitude of difference means. That is, a person may score zero on an IQ test, but we cannot conceive of a person as having no IQ. We also

---

12. We can think of a category as more advantaged than another depending on setting.

know that a score of 110 is 55 points higher than a score of 55. However, we cannot say that someone with a 110 IQ has twice the intelligence of someone with a 55 IQ. Nor can we say that the 30-point difference between a score of 60 and 90 has the same meaning as the 30-point difference between 120 and 150. Therefore, IQ is a measure that does not describe an amount of intelligence (anonymous reviewer 2017).[13]

Cardinal-level variables, like categorical and ordinal variables, can be rank ordered. Unlike categorical and ordinal data, however, cardinal-level measures allow us to gauge how much bigger or smaller a value is relative to another, and we can attribute meaning to difference. We can say someone who is 90 years old has lived twice as many years as someone who is 45. We can also say that the difference in amount of time lived is the same between someone who is 35 and someone who is 25 as between an 85-year-old and a 95-year-old.

As we will see, establishing the level of measurement is important, as it places restrictions on what calculations researchers can make. If your variables are categorical-level (such as sex or race), then we cannot calculate an average, mean, or median (e.g., average race is meaningless). But we can express the percentage of residents who classify themselves as each racialized category.

Exercise 6.5: Explore a variable of interest

For this exercise, choose one variable from the American Community Survey that interests you. After you identify that variable, specify whether it qualifies as categorical, ordinal, and cardinal.

Model Interpretation

I chose the variable *percentage of households headed by females with children under 18*. It tells me that of the 883 households in census tract 511.01 in Dayton (Campbell County), Kentucky, 17.1% (n = 151) are headed by females with children under 18 (no husband / partner present).

---

13. IQ scores are typically presented as to where they fall relative to other scores. The score will be associated with a **percentile,** a measure used to indicate the percentage of scores (or observations) below a score of interest. For example, a score that falls in the 90th percentile means that 90% of scores fall "below" it.

Since that variable is expressed as a percentage, it is easy to gauge how much bigger or smaller a percentage value is relative to another percentage value and to specify the magnitude of difference when comparing two percentages. Therefore, percentage of households headed by females with children under 18[14] is a cardinal variable.

MODULE 6.5: VARIABLES AND HYPOTHESES

Now that you have some idea about what is involved in data and understand what variables are, we are ready to discuss relationships between variables and hypotheses. Researchers are always interested in why things vary. Why do people, groups, households, territories, artifacts, or interactions vary on some characteristic, experience, or quality? For example, why do some households have internet access and not others? What role, if any, does being male, female, or transgender play in the income they earn and otherwise secure over the course of a year? Why when walking around the census tract do you notice the absence of some people who appear to be a particular race, age, or gender? Why do some census tracts have a greater percentage of households with children headed by women than others?

WHAT YOU WILL DO

✓ Complete one exercise about variables.

✓ Read about independent and dependent variables and about hypotheses.

✓ Identify two variables and specify a hypothesis.

Variables

Research revolves around variables. As one example: a researcher studying farming communities believes that rural communities (as opposed to

---

14. You cannot compare the number of men and women 85 years or older across census tracts because some census tracts have more residents than others. When making comparisons, it is best to standardize your data—to present data as a percentage of, or a rate per 1,000, or an average or median. One census tract may have more women than other census tracts, but that does not mean that relative to the total population of census tracts there are more women.

urban or suburban communities) expose their residents to a lifestyle that reinforces environmental consciousness. The variables of interest are *type of community* (rural, suburban, urban) and *lifestyle reinforcing environmental consciousness*. The researcher has reason to believe that urban and suburban lifestyles do not support, even undermine, environmental consciousness. Here environmental consciousness is measured by overconsumption (defined as buying things that are never worn, used, or eaten).

Because this researcher is interested in how variables are related to or influence one another, she puts forth a **hypothesis,** a statement that predicts the nature of the relationship between two variables. This prediction can be grounded in theory, personal experience, or existing scholarship. The prediction can be that there

1. is no relationship between variables. That is, there is no relationship between the type of community and residents' level of environmental consciousness.
2. is a relationship between the two variables such that residents choose to live in a community with an environmentally conscious lifestyle that matches their consciousness. Here residents' level of environmental consciousness is the independent variable and the type of community is the dependent variable.
3. is a relationship between the two variables such that the type of community cultivates environmental consciousness such that people who live in rural communities are socialized to have a higher level of environmental consciousness relative to those who live in urban and suburban communities. In this case, residents' level of environmental consciousness is the independent variable and the type of community is the dependent.

Imagine that the findings support a relationship between the type of community in which residents live and their level of environmental consciousness. Before researchers can claim a relationship exists, they must consider whether some third variable could make it appear that there is an association between the type of community and an environmentally conscious lifestyle. That third variable is known as a **control** variable. A control variable is one that is related to the independent and dependent variable in ways that make it appear as if there is a relationship between the two when there is not. The relationship could be the result of a third variable, *opportunities to consume*.

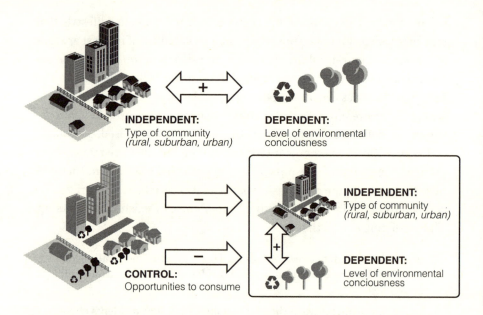

Figure 6.3. Visualization of Hypothesized Relationship between Type of Neighborhood and Level of Environmental Consciousness

Source: Joan Ferrante and Tabitha Kelly

Typically, rural communities, because of their remote locations, have fewer outlets to consume goods and services, which makes rural residents appear environmentally conscious. But if rural residents had the opportunities to consume, they would consume just as much as their urban and rural counterparts. Environments that support or constrain overconsumption are ultimately the source of environmental consciousness.

In figure 6.3, the + sign tells us that the category "rural," which is arbitrarily placed at the top of the rural-suburb-urban ranking, is hypothesized to increase level of environmental consciousness. To put it another way, rural communities are associated with a higher level of environmental consciousness. When we add the control variable to the analysis, we see that opportunities to consume as measured by number of retail stores per 1,000 people is smaller in rural communities than the other two (the minus sign references this). Opportunities to consume also affect level of environmental consciousness (as measured by actual consumption). We are hypothesizing that the control variable is the factor behind the positive relationships between our independent and dependent variables.

Exercise 6.6: Specify a hypothesis and a control variable

For this exercise, choose a variable to study that speaks to something you find interesting about your census tract. Select a variable that is expressed as a percentage, a median value, or an average (mean). Examples of variables you might choose are percentage of residents 18 and over who are veterans, percentage of single-parent households, median household incomes, or average time in minutes to drive to work. Think about how the chosen variable may be related to a second variable. Perhaps you believe that census tracts with a high percentage of veterans are also those with lower median household incomes. Your rationale is that people from communities with lower median incomes disproportionately enlist, and on returning to civilian life, they return to lower-income communities. Figure 6.4 visualizes the relationships between these two variables. Note that the double arrow suggests no clear direction of influence; the minus sign indicates that as one variable rises, the other falls (the *greater* the percentage of residents age 18 and over who are veterans, the *lower* the median household income).

In choosing the control variable, think about how the hypothesized relationship between the two variables may be affected by a third variable. For example, census tracts with high percentages of veterans are those where enlisting in the military is treated as an alternative to going to college. Therefore, we would expect that the more veteran heavy the neighborhood, the lower the percentage of residents with college degrees. And if the percentages of residents with college degrees is low, then so is the median household income. If this is indeed the case, the percentage of residents over age 24 with a college degree is a good choice for a control variable because it predicts both percentages of veterans and median household incomes.

Use the following format to present your analysis.

Unit of analysis: census tracts

Variable 1: % of residents age 18 and over who are veterans

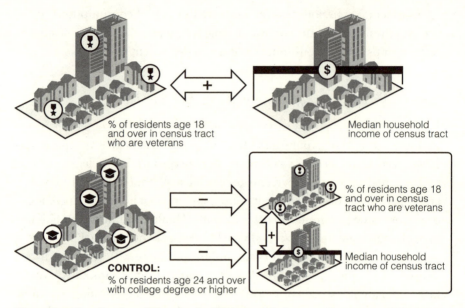

Figure 6.4. Visualization of Hypothesized Relationship between Percentage of Veterans and Median Household Income and Control Variable Percentage with College Degree or Higher

SOURCE: Joan Ferrante and Tabitha Kelly

Variable 2: median household income

Hypothesis (direction not clear): Census tracts with a high percentage of veterans are also census tracts with lower median household incomes.

Rationale: People from communities with lower median incomes disproportionately enlist, and on returning to civilian life, they return to lower-income communities.

Control Variable: % of residents age 24 and over with college degree or higher

Rationale: Neighborhoods with high percentages of veterans are places where residents view the military as an alternative to college. We would expect that the higher the percentage of veterans in a census tract, the lower the percentage of residents with college degrees. Therefore, the percentage of residents with college degrees is hypothesized to predict both the percentage of veterans and lower household income.

WORKING DRAFT OF RESEARCH BRIEF, SECTION 5

Preschool Enrollment, Key Demographic Characteristics, and Reputations

When writing this section keep the following points in mind:

- The content analysis of news provides useful information on your census tract's reputation. That reputation—founded or unfounded—including the reputation of certain streets within the neighborhood, affects both the neighborhood and its residents' lives (Wutich et al. 2015). Reputation can be negative, positive, or unremarkable. As such, the content analysis provides clues about neighborhood strengths and weaknesses and areas where support is needed.
- The research on a third places speaks to neighborhood strengths.
- Preschool enrollment serves as an indicator of investments made in the youngest residents. Research shows that in comparison to children who don't go to preschool, children who do go are less likely to fail a grade or to be placed in special education, more likely when they reach adulthood to secure higher-paying jobs, less likely to be abused and neglected, and less likely to engage in delinquent acts as teens.
- The variable you selected for special focus is important to you for some reason. Offer a rationale for giving it special attention in this report.
- Always keep in mind that the research brief is in the draft stage and is open to refinement and revision.

Model Write-Up, Section 5

Self-Asssessed Reputation: As a home owner, I reflected on how my neighbors perceive my presence. I think they see me as young, well-to-do, and single. I also think they see me as an outsider moving into a nice home in a lower-income area that is changing. I know that I bought my house at a reasonable price, and I know that not everyone in the neighborhood would be able to afford this house or even qualify for a loan. I don't feel as if I am hurting anyone by being here. My neighbors benefit because I am a good resident. I get that I am living in a house that at one time someone else couldn't afford to keep up. I don't have kids, but I pay taxes. I particularly wonder what the kids think about me and my house as they walk to school in the morning. Do they see me as someone who thinks she is "better" than their parents since my house is so nice and well kept? When I see these kids walking to school, I wonder what I can do to help the elementary school.

Neighborhood Reputation: A content analysis of news found on Google News in the month of August featuring Northside and my census tract, in particular, offers insights about the neighborhood's reputation and challenges. Of the 50 articles reviewed, 12 (24%) focused on crime or shootings, 8 (16%) focused on new apartment complexes, and 25 (50%) focused on local businesses in transition, in decline, or new to the scene. Distilleries, breweries, bars, gelato shops, and burger joints are moving in to serve young professionals and college students. The content analysis supports Northside's reputation as a diverse, mixed-income neighborhood in transition that is part of the growing national trend toward center or urban city living. It is a low-income, working-class neighborhood in transition, as evidenced by the focus on filling luxury apartments and townhouse developments built to draw young knowledge-economy professionals attracted to walkable communities, short commutes to work, and convenient social venues.

Preschool Enrollment Rates: Census tract 78 has a higher percentage of 3- and 4-year-olds enrolled in preschool than neighboring census tract 74. About 38% (49 of 130) of 3- and 4-year-olds in census tract 78 are enrolled in preschool, compared to 52% (60 of 115) in census tract 74. That is a 14.2% difference. For my census tract to equal census tract 74's enrollment rate of 52%, it would have to enroll 23 more students.[15]

Knowing this difference in preschool enrollment rates prompts me to consider what it is about census tract 74—its residents or households—that explains its relative success compared to census tract 78. Perhaps residents in census tract 74 have higher or lower household incomes than those in census tract 74. What accounts for the 14.2% difference?

Key Demographic Characteristics: Percentage of Households with Children under 18 Headed by Women. In census tract 78, there are 167 households with children under 18. Of those 286 households, 115 (69%) are married couple households. Fifty-two (31.0%) are female-headed (no spouse or partner present). There are no male-headed households. My rationale for choosing the percentage of households with children under 18 headed by females as a key demographic characteristic is that it opens my eyes to those who carry on day-to-day without the support of a partner. Of course, these females find support from friends and family. Still, it is important to know something about the third of households raising children under 18.

---

15. To get this number, multiply the number of 3- and 4-year-olds in census tract 78 by .873 or (130 * .55 = 71.5). Take that total and subtract the number currently enrolled (71.5 − 49 = 23).

REFERENCES

Arteaga, Irma, et al. 2014. "One Year of Preschool or Two: Is It Important for Adult Outcomes?" *Economics of Education Review* 40: 221–37.

U.S. Bureau of the Census. 2016. "Code Lists, Definitions, and Accuracy." American Community Survey.

Wutich, Amber, et al. 2014. "Stigmatized Neighborhoods, Social Bonding, and Health." *Medical Anthropology Quarterly* 28 (4): 556–77.

7 Types of Investigative Research

While there are many different types of research, all are grounded in the **scientific method,** an approach to data collection and analysis that is driven by two assumptions:

1. knowledge about the world is acquired through observation; and
2. the truth of knowledge is confirmed by verification.

From a scientific method point of view, **observations** include anything researchers can know through their senses—what they see, hear, taste, touch, and smell.[1] In presenting their work, researchers report how they made observations and also what they observed. They do this so that experts and other stakeholders can review the findings and the process (for quality control purposes) and to even repeat the study. If the reported observations cannot be duplicated or if when repeating the study it yields

---

1. As an example, when touring a neighborhood, researchers see people interacting or they see the structures; they hear what people say, music playing, and sounds of traffic (or not); they can taste food and drink and sometimes even odors in the air; they can touch handrails and public art (even feel the worn surfaces resulting from others' hands); and they smell different odors as they move across spaces: gasoline, food grilling, a sewer leaking.

observations that differ substantially from those reported, the study and findings are suspect.

Findings endure when they can withstand **verification** (reexamination and duplication). Verification is at the heart of good research. When researchers know that others are checking and monitoring their work, they have an added incentive to do careful and conscientious research. They also have an incentive to be objective. Researchers are **objective** when they hold in check personal biases that may interfere with what they observe and how they write about those observations. While it is not easy to be objective, being open to criticism helps in the struggle to hold biases in check.

Regardless of the type of research employed, there are steps to prepare and guide researchers in choosing what to observe, how to make observations, and how to interpret the observations. These steps are to

- ✓ decide on a research question that is answerable;
- ✓ review literature that will help to frame and answer that question;
- ✓ identify core concepts;
- ✓ collect data or make observations;
- ✓ analyze and interpret data and observations; and
- ✓ draw conclusions.

All researchers adhere to the scientific method, but the type of research they do depends on the goals of the research and the core questions driving the research. In choosing a type of research, always consider which type is best suited to help you answer the core questions. In the broadest sense, the types of research can basic or applied.

BASIC VERSUS APPLIED RESEARCH

In sociology, **basic research,** sometimes called pure research, is done with the aim of gaining knowledge about how human activity, interactions, and relationships are structured, sustained, and change. Basic research does not place the emphasis on how that knowledge can be applied or used. It is done with the aim of contributing knowledge about how things are, work, and change. As such, basic research presents and tests concepts and theories (the building block of a discipline such as sociology). Some titles of published research that qualifies as basic research are

- "Social and Economic Determinants of Adult Health: Conceptualizing Pathways between Neighborhood Environments and Risk of Cardiovascular Disease" (Lehning et al. 2017)
- "The Health Effects of the Foreclosure Crisis and Unaffordable Housing" (Downing 2016)
- "Neighborhood Effects on Heat Deaths: Social and Environmental Predictors of Vulnerability in Maricopa County, Arizona" (Harlan et al. 2013)

Notice that each of the titles suggests that understanding is the goal: how does neighborhood environment shape risk of cardiovascular disease? how do foreclosures impact health? and what social and environmental predictors increase vulnerability to heat death? Note that most basic research typically concludes with some brief thoughts about how what is learned might be applied. Regardless, understanding, not application, is the driving force. Ultimately basic research lays the groundwork for applied research.

In contrast, **applied research** involves drawing on basic research with the aim of using it to address an important problem. Specifically, the aim of applied sociological research is to test whether an intervention relieves a social distress, an inequality, or other suffering. The following titles illustrate the focus of applied research.

- "How Can Psychological Theory Help Cities Increase Walking and Bicycling?" (Dill, Mohr, and Ma 2014)
- "Neighborhood Factors and Six-Month Weight Change among Overweight Individuals in a Weight Loss Intervention" (Mendez et al. 2016)
- "Evaluating a Community Intervention to Reduce the Risk of Child Abuse: Methodological Strategies in Conducting Neighborhood Surveys" (Earls et al. 1994)
- "Bringing Produce to the People: Implementing a Social Marketing Food Access Intervention in a Rural Food Desert" (Ramirez et al. 2017)

Notice that each title points to a problem or issue and a suggested intervention. That is, something about psychological theory can help city leaders increase walking and bicycling; the neighborhood environment can be structured such that it supports interventions aimed at weight loss; a community can intervene to reduce child abuse; and produce can be introduced into a rural food desert. Basic and applied research can be qualitative or quantitative or both. When both are involved the researcher is engaged in mixed methods.

QUALITATIVE VERSUS QUANTITATIVE RESEARCH

Qualitative research places emphasis on deep understanding of human activities and experiences, most notably, meaning-making. In its purest form, qualitative research yields rich, nuanced, and contextualized analyses of the human condition. It is a method of research that is especially known for giving voice to marginalized, stereotyped, misunderstood, and misrepresented populations. Qualitative researchers do not reduce people to categories or standardize their experiences; they aim to achieve sympathetic knowledge. Consider as one example the study "Lived Neighborhood: Understanding How People with Dementia Engage with Their Local Environment." For this study, Richard Ward and colleagues (2017) did qualitative research to learn how people living with dementia relate to their neighborhoods. The researchers focused on lived experiences to inventory "the capabilities, capacities, and competencies of people living with dementia" and to highlight the important role of social engagement and neighborhood support. The research showed that "the neighborhood plays an active role in the lives of people with dementia, setting limits and constraints but also offering significant opportunities, encompassing forms of help and support as yet rarely discussed in the field of dementia studies" (Ward et al. 2017, 1).

In contrast to qualitative research, **quantitative** researchers count, classify, and assign numerical value to social identities, roles, experiences, behavior, contexts, and processes. For example, human subjects are counted and classified by race, gender, age, and other categories. Experiences are counted as occurring or not (e.g., attended college or not;

living with diagnosed dementia or not). If some object, say, automobile ownership, is the target of study, ownership may be divided into the type of cars owned or the percentage of households with at least one car. Behaviors such as commuting are quantified in terms of minutes to drive from home to work. Opinions can be scaled by intensity, with 1 representing "disagree strongly" and 5 representing "agree strongly." As you will learn later in the chapter, the resulting numbers can be subjected to manipulation and statistical analysis.

One example of a quantitative study is "The Importance of the Neighborhood in the 2014 Ebola Outbreak in the United States: Distress, Worry, and Functioning" (Jose, Holman, and Silver 2017). The researchers were interested in how neighborhood concentrations of West African foreigners, non–West African foreigners, and non-Hispanic blacks[2] affected residents' responses to the Ebola outbreak. About 1,300 residents living in Boston and New York City neighborhoods were studied. Among other things, the researchers asked questions about psychological distress, functional impairment, and Ebola-related worry. They found that the higher the concentration of West African foreigners, non–West African foreigners, and non-Hispanic blacks, the higher the reported sleep problems, anxiety, and Ebola-related worry. The study points to the importance of making research and policies to assist not only "at-risk individuals but also at-risk neighborhoods during and after an infectious disease crisis" (Jose, Holman, and Silver 2017, 1181).[3]

SPECIFIC TYPES OF RESEARCH

The sections that follow offer a brief overview of specific types of qualitative, quantitative, and mixed-method research that can be used to do applied or basic research. Some types are more oriented to qualitative

---

2. Concentrations are typically presented as rates. In this study, the number of West African foreigners, non–West African foreigners, or non-Hispanic blacks per 1,000 residents.

3. It would be a mistake to conclude that quantitative and qualitative research are incompatible. Most researchers employ some mix of these methods. Even those who identify themselves as one type of researcher acknowledge the need to incorporate elements of the other method into their observations, analysis, and interpretation.

research than quantitative. Other types mix the two. The specific types are descriptive, interpretive, historical, longitudinal, comparative, correlational, multivariate, experimental, and mixed methods. While this may seem like a long list, just knowing the many types of research can open your eyes to investigative possibilities. As you will see, there is overlap between types. Researchers also incorporate more than one type when doing research studies. No one type should be considered superior or inferior, as each has its strengths and shortcomings. The choice of research type depends on purpose and the kind of data or observations needed.

Descriptive Research

Like the term suggests, **descriptive research** describes the ways things are or the way they once were. For the most part, the observation and data gathering we have done to this point have been descriptive. Descriptive research is often criticized as the least sophisticated type of research. However, it is a necessary component of other types of research that are considered more complex. That is, we must know and be able to describe what we are studying before making inferences, establishing associations, or attributing cause. For example, one cannot examine the relationship between educational attainment and income without first being able to describe a target population's educational attainment and income and how both are distributed across the population targeted for study. One example of a descriptive study is "Free Range Kids? Using GPS-Derived Activity Spaces to Examine Children's Neighborhood Activity and Mobility" (Loebach and Gilliland 2016). The authors used GPS to identify the locations of children ages 9 to 13 in seven Canadian and London neighborhoods when they were not in school and over the course of a typical week. They found that almost 95% of children's time was spent within 0.3 mile, or 500 meters, of their homes. Researchers found that the children monitored spent very little time outdoors (Loebach and Gilliland 2016).

Descriptive research has shortcomings; for one thing, it is impossible to take in or give a complete account of everything that is going on. Recall in exercise 2.2 when you took an imaginary tour of the census tract with Durkheim, Weber, Marx, Du Bois, and Addams; each influenced you to focus on a slice of reality. For example, Durkheim directed our attention to social ties, while Marx directed our attention to issues centered on conflict and exploitation of labor. The point is that researchers "can never, and will likely never want to, describe everything that is 'there'" (Sandelowski 2000, 336). Rather they observe and describe slices of reality.

Interpretive Research

Interpretive research puts meaning-making front and center. Meaning-making is the complex process by which people glean, understand, interpret, or otherwise make sense of who they are and what is going on in some social context. This type of research seeks to uncover meaning-making processes with an eye to revealing how those meanings came to be and are embedded in behavior, interactions, and human activity. Those who call themselves interpretive researchers make a concerted effort to suppress any preconceived views they may hold about a population targeted for study, and they make a commitment to reveal "reality" in all its complexity. Interpretive researchers' accounts are based on what they are able to glean from observing interactions, engaging in conversation, conducting interviews, and otherwise interacting with the target population.

If the target population happens to be veterans returning to their neighborhoods or moving into a neighborhood, interpretive researchers work to suppress any preconceived notions they may hold about veterans and then work to know and understand veterans—what it means *to them* to return to civilian life. Sympathetic knowledge must inform any interpretation. Of course, the meaning-making varies according to the contexts in which veterans find themselves, whether a VFW center, a welcome home parade, home life, or a new workplace.

The study "Fading, Twisting, and Weaving: An Interpretive Ethnography of the Black Barbershop as Cultural Space," conducted by Brian Keith Alexander (2003), emphasizes meaning-making and seeks to capture "the physical labor of work, care, and cultural communion that occur within the space of the barbershop/salon" (123). Alexander presents the neighborhood barbershop as a site where black-identifying and black-classified people interact "through touch, the manipulation of hair (length, shape, texture, and form), the sounds of talk, information sharing, and the deep penetration of cultural memory" (123).

Historical Research

Historical research studies something considered in the past. It examines the past with the purpose of gaining insights into something that exists in the present or will exist in the future. Historical researchers typically rely on primary sources as a window into what occurred in some past that must be reconstructed. Primary sources are documents and other archived materials that were created during the time period under study, such as photographs, correspondence, diaries, sales receipts, census records, eyewitness accounts, birth certificates, transcripts of court cases, legal writings, and audio recordings. For example, learning what parts of its history a neighborhood celebrates with landmarks and monuments also offers clues about the histories it suppresses or does not want to preserve. In other words, what is celebrated and suppressed often sheds light on the origins of some long-standing and unresolved tensions that exist in the neighborhood.

Safe Space: Gay Neighborhood History and the Politics of Violence, by Christina Hanhardt (2013), focuses on the history of GLBTQ activism, which centered on establishing and protecting safe spaces, most notably, bars and clubs that serve as refuges in the wake of withdrawn family support, as sources of health services (free HIV-testing, condom distribution), as places of entertainment, and as a haven from discrimination, prejudice, and disapproving stares. Given the importance of safe spaces, any attacks on a neighborhood's bars and clubs symbolized an attack on the wider GLBTQ community. As such, the bars, clubs, and other safe spaces became cultural anchors for GLBTQ activism extending far beyond the neighborhood setting. In reconstructing the history of GLBTQ activism, Hanhardt finds that the attacks on safe places and protective responses were always part of something much larger such as the War on Poverty, segregation, and gentrification.

Comparative Research

Comparative research uses comparison as an investigative tool. Most research has a comparative component. This is because a researcher cannot speak to the situation of a person, a group, neighborhood, state, or school system in isolation. The process of comparing and contrasting yields insights into a neighborhood, for example, that it is among the poorest or wealthiest. Cross-cultural research is especially eye-opening because comparing different cultures (especially a researcher's home culture and another culture) not only sharpens what researchers see and hear but also awakens the other senses (Anderson 2016).

Making comparisons encourages a person to notice similarities and differences. Noticing differences drives curiosity and questions. What accounts for differences? Why are there differences? What accounts for similarities? Consider the importance of comparison in determining the availability of healthy food in a neighborhood. If a researcher only inventories stores in one neighborhood to determine the proportion of healthy foods relative to processed foods, there is no way of knowing if the available inventory for that neighborhood is above average, below average, or normal without comparing it against neighborhood inventories.

Kevin Kane and colleagues (2016) at the University of Massachusetts Medical School surveyed convenience and grocery stores in the neighborhoods in Worcester, Ohio, to compare and assess healthy and unhealthy food availability as well as residents' access to fresh produce, unprocessed foods, and other healthy food options, In doing their inventories, Kane found that when compared to grocery stories, regardless of neighborhood socioeconomic status, convenience stores had fewer healthy food options. He also found that the lower the median household income and lower the rate of car ownership within a neighborhood, the higher the number of convenience stores per 100 residents. But people who lived in neighborhoods with higher median household income and car ownership had a higher number of grocery stores per 100 residents.

Longitudinal Research

We can think of any research study as a snapshot in time. Once data are collected, the results are in the past. When researchers put together two or more snapshots of data over some time frame, they are doing a **longitudinal study**. This type of research offers insights about the extent to which something has remained the same or changed and how quickly. Longitudinal researchers follow a target population (individuals, households, groups, or territories) over days, weeks, years, decades, lifetimes, or even centuries. For example, researchers interested in the gentrification process may look at changes in the percentage of residents who classify themselves as black, the median household income, or the percentage of residents age five and under at various points over a decade or more to document shifts (or stability) in neighborhood demographics.

Courtney Shultz and colleagues (2017) did a longitudinal study to see if park use and park-based physical activity in a low-income neighborhood in Columbia, Missouri, had changed after a five-lane highway was constructed in 2012. The highway created a barrier between housing units and the local park. In 2013 a signalized pedestrian crosswalk was installed to improve access. The researchers observed activity prior to and after the crosswalk installation and again in June 2014. Park use increased from 2012 to 2013 and remained constant after that. But physical activity within the park decreased. It is not clear why this was the case, but Schultz plans future research on this question.

Correlational Research

Correlational research seeks to establish whether there is a relationship between two variables such that a change in one variable is associated with a change in another. The strength or weakness of that relationship is measured by calculating a correlation coefficient. If the correlation coefficient is strong and statistically significant we can say that the data support a relationship. That is, there is predictive value such that if we know the value of one variable we can predict the value of the second. A statistically significant coefficient correlation tells us that that result is not a matter of chance. In one study by Lee, Vaughn, and Lim (2014), the researchers secured data on violent crime rates for neighborhoods and police use of force, including level. They found that the higher the rate of violent crime, the more police force was used.

Multivariate Analysis

Life is complex. Many factors converge to shape behavior, achievements, experiences, attitudes, and so on. Thus, for example, if we are interested in understanding why some 3- and 4-year-olds are in preschool (the outcome to be explained) we might want to identify factors that shape parents' decision to enroll their children. Those factors might be household income, parents' beliefs about the value of preschool education, cost of preschool, parents' employment status, and so on. These factors converge to affect any decision to enroll children in preschool, and then, of course, there are factors that explain those factors. For example, any number of factors shape parents' beliefs about the value of education, including their experiences in school. Likewise, the variable *cost of preschool* depends on whether a school district offers public preschool free of charge. Multivariate analysis allows researchers to assess many variables' direct and indirect effects on outcomes.

As you can tell by the title, the study "Social Capital and Adolescent Substance Use: The Role of Family, School, and Neighborhood Contexts" qualifies as multivariate analysis. This study examines the ways family, school, and neighborhood contexts encourage and discourage substance use (cigarettes, alcohol, and illicit drugs) among a sample of adolescents who live in California neighborhoods. The study found that family variables are the most influential in preventing substance use. The most important variable is parental monitoring of adolescent's friendships and social life (Wen 2017).

Experimental Research

Experimental research is used with the goal of isolating an independent variable as the cause of some dependent variable. That dependent variable may be a behavior, an attitude, or something else. In classic experimental research, an independent variable and a dependent variable are chosen for study such that the researcher can manipulate (or change) the independent variable (holding all else constant) to evaluate its impact on the dependent variable. The classic experimental design randomly assigns subjects to one of two groups known as control and experimental. Those assigned to the experimental group are exposed to the independent variable and those assigned to the control group are not. In theory, those who are part of the control group are exposed to the same environment and conditions as those assigned to the experimental group. The only difference, then, between experimental and control groups is the exposure to (or withholding of) the independent variable.

Another variation on the experimental design involves a context in which people who live or work or socialize with each other are presented with an "intervention" (a new member, a new starting time, a training, a tragedy) and researchers study how group dynamics or other behaviors change. Experimental research is not widely used in sociologically oriented research because it is difficult to manipulate variables and the context in which people live their lives such that researchers can make everything the same for experimental and control groups except the introduction of a independent variable. Sometimes, however, the right conditions emerge and sociologists can study what is called natural experimental design. To put it another way, experimental and control-like conditions present themselves and the researcher notices and takes advantage of the opportunity to study the intervention.

In a study of the effects of a grocery store opening in a Philadelphia food desert[4] neighborhood on residents' awareness of food access, the researchers found that awareness of the new food source did not alter residents' dietary habits or obesity rates (Cummins, Flint, and Matthews 2014). The researchers determined that this intervention (a new store) moderately increased residents' perceptions of food accessibility but was not associated with changes in reported fruit and vegetable intake or body mass index. These findings suggest that improving access is one step but steps must also be taken to change food purchase and consumption habits.

Mixed-Methods Research

Mixed-methods research employs both qualitative and quantitative methods such that the findings and analysis include the in-depth, contextualized, and rich insights of qualitative research and the breadth and

---

4. According to the U.S. Department of Agriculture (2009), food deserts are defined as "parts of the country vapid of fresh fruit, vegetables, and other healthful whole foods, usually found in impoverished areas. This is largely due to a lack of grocery stores, farmers' markets, and healthy food providers. . . . [F]ood deserts are often short on whole food providers, especially fresh fruits and vegetables. Instead, they are heavy on local quickie marts that provide a wealth of processed, sugar, and fat laden foods that are known contributors to our nation's obesity epidemic." To qualify as a low-access community, at least 500 people or 33% of the census tract's population must reside more than one mile from a supermarket or large grocery store (for rural census tracts, the distance is more than 10 miles).

statistical insights of quantitative research. The balance between qualitative and quantitative methods can take many forms. In one use, researchers can gather both qualitative and quantitative data by designing a survey that includes fixed-choice questions in order to standardize and quantify responses. Then as a follow-up researchers can interview people to give a voice and face to experiences and meaning making. This enriches and adds detail to quantitative findings.

For their research on neighborhood cohesion and mental health well-being among older adults, Elliott and colleagues (2014) confirmed a link between attachment to neighborhood and mental health well-being: the greater residents' feeling of belonging to the neighborhood, the greater their well-being. But the researchers wanted to know how residents experienced belonging (or not), so they conducted qualitative biographical interviews with 116 men and 114 women to learn about this meaning-making surrounding this attachment to neighborhood.

TRY OUT SOME TYPES OF RESEARCH

To this point we have reviewed the various types of research. Now you have an opportunity to try out a selected few.

WHAT YOU WILL DO:

✓ Complete 7 exercises.
✓ Follow instructions to coach you through decision making
✓ Draw on model examples to write up results.

Exercise 7.1: Choose a dependent variable

Choose a data point (estimate) or variable from a past exercise that applies to your census tract. Or you can just go with the variable *percentage of all households headed by females with children under 18* for your census tract. Regardless of your decision, the variable you choose must be a percentage, an average, or a median. Treat that variable as something you would like to explore further and explain. In other words, treat the variable you choose as a dependent variable. For illustrative purposes, consider the percentage of all households headed by females with children under 18 for census tract 9301, Beauford (Beauford County), North Carolina. Table B11005 (Households by Presence of People under 18 Years by Household Type) contains the number and percentage. Write up the estimate as follows.

Of the 2,141 households in census tract 9301 in Beauford (BeaufordCounty), North Carolina, 11.1% (n = 237) are headed by females with children under 18 (no husband/partner present).

What do we make of this estimate of 11.1%. By itself, we cannot know if this is an especially high or low occurrence, nor can we know if it is typical. We need to compare that percentage to other census tracts. A first step in evaluating this estimate is to see how this census tract compares to other tracts in Beauford County, North Carolina, of which there are 11. To get the estimates for all tracts do as follows. When selecting type of geography simply choose your tract and then the relevant state, county, and "all census tracts within a county." Note that some very rural counties can consist of only one tract and some urban counties can have hundreds. If the county has very few census tracts, add census tracts of adjacent counties until you get at least 10. If the county has more than 10 tracts, you might randomly choose 10.

Once you have secured estimates from at least 10 other tracts, create a frequency distribution modeled after table 7.1 below. A **frequency distribution** is a table that displays the number and percentage of times something occurs or exists for each case. For this research each of the census tracts counts as a case. Table 7.1 shows the percentage of households with children under 18 headed by females for each of the 11 census tracts that make up Beauford County, North Carolina. To create this table, you need to look at is Table B11005 to find the total number of households with children under 18 AND the total number of all households with children under 18 headed by females. Once percentages are calculated, rank order the census tracts from lowest to highest percentage.

Table 7.1 Number and Percentage of Households with Children under 18, Headed by Females (No Husband / Partner Present) for 11 Census Tracts in Beauford County, North Carolina

Census tract Number	Number of Households with Children under 18	Number of Households with Children under 18 Headed by Females	% of Households with Children under 18 Headed by Females
9309	260	12	2.4
9307	184	70	8.3
9305.1	367	60	14.4
9308	839	40	15.4
9301	662	237	27.5
9310	497	177	27.5
9303	489	223	35.6
9302	861	192	39.2
9306	353	80	43.5
9305.2	415	159	45.0
9304	626	307	49.0

SOURCE: American Community Survey, latest data (2015) accessed Nov. 15, 2017.

Model Interpretation

Notice that the percentage of all households with children under 18 headed by females varies from a low of 2.4% to a high of 49.0%. Of the 11 census tracts that make up Beauford County, census tract 9301 is tied with census tract 9310 for the 5th lowest percentage of households headed by females with children under 18. Five census tracts have a higher percentage.

Exercise 7.2: Secure descriptive statistics for the dependent variable

Descriptive statistics are calculated with the aim of summarizing data gathered about a variable—in this case, the variable of interest is the percentage of all households with children under 18 headed by females. Taken together, descriptive statistics help us to assess the level of variability across the 11 census tracts. **Descriptive statistics,** considered the most basic form of statistical analysis; are the foundation for any advanced statistical analysis. Descriptive statistics include the mean (average), median, standard deviation, variance, minimum, and maximum. You can easily calculate these basic statistics using an online calculator such as "the descriptive statistics calculator" (use these words as search terms). Type the relevant values into the statistics calculator, or simply copy and paste the column of values from the table you created. As an example, if we wish to secure descriptive statistics for the variable *percentage of all households with children under 18 headed by females* for the 11 counties, simply copy and paste or type in the percentage for each census tract of Beauford County. When you click "calculate," a list of descriptive statistics like those shown below appears.

Minimum:	2.4
Maximum:	49.0
Range:	46.6
Count:	11.0
Mean:	28.0
Median:	27.5
Standard deviation:	15.9
Variance:	254.1

Before writing up the results as shown in the model interpretation, keep the following in mind.

The *count* (n) is the total number of distinct values in the data set. For this data set there are 11 distinct values, one for each of the 11 tracts that make up Beauford County. The *minimum* is the smallest value in the data set (2.4%), and the *maximum* is the largest value in the data set (49.0%). The *range* is the difference between the minimum and the maximum (49.0% – 2.4% = 46.6%). The *mean* is the average or sum of each value divided by the count (28%). The *median* is the point at which half the values in the data set are smaller and half are larger (27.5%).

Standard deviation is a measure of dispersion or spread of the values in relation to the mean. The standard deviation for the percentage of all households with children under 18 headed by females is 15.94%. We can think of this number as the average distance of the 11 values from the mean. To interpret the meaning of standard deviation, first consider the size of the mean. If the mean is in the millions, a standard deviation of

1000 suggests that the values are all very close to the mean; there is not much dispersion. On the other hand, if the mean is 28.0% and the standard deviation is 15.9%, there is considerable variability relative to the mean. The standard deviation is the square root of the variance

Variance is a measure that also captures how close or far the values are to the mean. In mathematical terms, the variance is the average of the differences of each value from the mean squared. As an example, 2.4% of households with children under 18 in census tract 9209 are female headed. That value is 25.6 percentage points lower than the mean (28.0%). To calculate that difference, subtract 2.4 from 27.98 to get 25.58. Next square that difference (-25.6 * -25.6 = 654.36). Add up all the squared differences and divide by the count (in this case the count is 11), and you have the variance. The variance for the 11 census tracts that make up Beauford County is 254. In the context of statistical analysis, the variance is what needs to be explained.

Model Interpretation

There are 11 census tracts in Beauford County. Among the 11 census tracts, the minimum or smallest percentage of all households headed by females with children under 18 is 2.4%. The largest percentage is 49.0%. The range is 46.6%. The mean or average percentage of households with children under 18 headed by females is 27.98%. The median is 27.5%. So 50% of the census tracts fall above 27.5% and 50% fall below 27.5%. The standard deviation is 15.9. Given that the mean percentage is 28.0, we should note that there is considerable variability.[5]

Explaining Variability

Researchers are interested in questions of why some outcome, experience, or situation varies (e.g., why does the percentage of households with

---

5. The dispersion is considered a normal distribution of values when 68% of the values are within +/- 1 standard deviation of the mean; 95% of the values are within +/- 2 standard deviations of the mean, and 99.7% are within +/- 3 standard deviations from the mean. But keep in mind that data may not be distributed normally. One way to tell if your distribution of values is normal is to compare the mean, mode, and median. If the three are the same or similar in value and 50% of the values are smaller than the mean and 50% are greater than the mean, then the distribution is normal. Why is this important? Some statistical tests assume a normal distribution. For now, that is all we will say about this.

children under 18 headed by females vary?). If the variable targeted for study does not vary or have much variation there is nothing to study or to explain. Why? Imagine you are doing research about why test scores vary—specifically, why do some students score higher than others? There is nothing about the students that can help you explain variation when everyone earns a 90% or if everyone scores between 90% and 95%. But if scores range between 40% and 100% you have something to explain. The same goes for percentage of all households with children under 18 headed by females. If every census tract had the same percentage there would be nothing to explain. The variability in the percentages in table 7.1 tells us that this is something to be explained.

Exercise 7.3: Choose an independent variable

In this exercise, you will go beyond simply looking at the percentages and rankings from highest to lowest. You will look for a second variable (an independent variable) that you think might help you predict or explain our dependent variable. Review one of more of the following documents with an eye to choosing an independent variable to explain the variation in the percentage of all households with children under 18 headed by females (or some other dependent variable of your choice):

1. Selected Social Characteristics in the United States
2. Selected Economic Characteristics in the United States
3. Selected Housing Characteristics in the United States
4. ACS Demographic and Housing Estimates

Scan each of these four documents to find a suitable variable that you believe may help you predict why the percentages of households with children under 18 headed by females vary from 2.4 to 49.0%. What is it about a census tract that draws or repels households with children under 18 headed by females? There are many variables that could help explain this variation. For illustrative purposes, we will choose as the independent variable, *median dollar value of occupied homes,* an estimate that can be found in Selected Housing Characteristics in the United States (see appendix C). Once the independent variable is chosen, state the hypothesis:

H: **The higher the median dollar value of occupied homes, the lower the percentage of households with children under 18 headed by a female (no husband / partner present).**[6]

To summarize, we are seeking to *understand* why our dependent variable *% of households with children under 18 headed by females* varies across the 11 census tracts of Beauford County. We have hypothesized that the independent variable, *median dollar value of occupied homes*, will help us predict that percentage. That is, we expect that when the median value of a home is high, the percentage of households with children under 18 headed by a female is low.

When presenting a hypothesis, always offer a rationale. One rationale might be that households with children under 18 headed by females (no husband or partner present) are typically one-income households, and women in general tend to earn lower wages than men. It makes sense that females with children under 18 would be drawn to census tracts where housing is most affordable. Now we will create a table that includes the median value of housing and the percentage of households with children under 18 that are female headed (see table 7.2).[7]

Model Interpretation

The data in table 7.2 do not appear to support my proposed hypothesis (that the highest median dollar value of occupied homes will be associated with lowest percentage of households with children under 18 headed by females). In fact, the lowest median dollar value of occupied homes is associated with the highest percentage of households with children under 18 headed by females. The second and third highest median dollar values of occupied homes are associated with two of the lowest percentages. Those findings are not in line with my hypothesis.

---

6. We could also hypothesize that the higher the median rent per month, the lower the percentage of female-headed households with children under 18 (no husband or partner). The point is that there are other variables to explain the independent variable.

7. For ease of statistical analysis, the independent variable (percentage of households with children under 18 headed by females, no husband or partner present, in this example) needs to be in a column to the right of the dependent variable column (% median value of housing).

Table 7.2 Median Value of Housing and Percentage of Households with Children under 18 That Are Female Headed for 11 Census Tracts of Beauford County, North Carolina.

Census Tract	Median Home Value	% of Households with Children under 18 Headed by Females
9309	$161,900	2.4
9307	$134,300	8.3
9305.1	$169,700	14.4
9308	$84,100	15.4
9301	$84,200	27.5
9310	$77,000	27.5
9303	$101,200	35.6
9302	$119,400	39.2
9306	$118,600	43.5
9305.2	$112,600	45.0
9304	$182,900	49.0

SOURCE: American Community Survey, latest data (2015) accessed Nov. 15, 2017.

Exercise 7.4: Create a scatterplot and calculate a correlation

Copy and paste your table 7.2 into an Excel file to create a scatterplot like that shown in figure 7.1.[8] A scatterplot offers a way to visualize the relationship between an independent and a dependent variable. (See appendix G for instructions.)

Note that each circle (sometimes a diamond shape) on the scatterplot represents one of the 11 census tracts. The diamond marks the value of the independent variable (median dollar value of occupied homes) and dependent varaible (% of all households with children under 18 that are female headed). To find the values for each diamond, look directly down from the diamond to the horizontal axis to establish the median dollar value of occupied homes for a census tract; if you look directly across to the left you can

---

8. When creating a scatterplot, your independent variable must be placed on the vertical axis and your dependent variable must be placed on the horizontal axis. Your variables need to be in the correct column order for this to happen. Make sure when creating your table that you put your independent variable in the second column and your dependent variable in the third column.

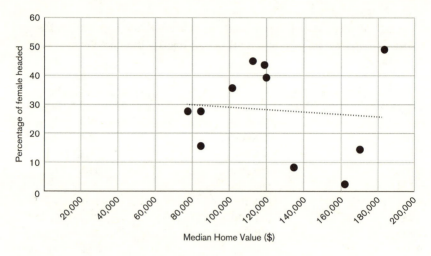

Figure 7.1. Scatterplot of Percentage of Households with Children Headed by Females and Median Value of Housing
SOURCE: Tabitha Kelly

determine the % of all households with children under 18 headed by females. We can see from the scatterplot that there is no pattern to the data. The trendline tells us that the association between the two variables is flat. A flat line tells us there is no discernible pattern such that as one variable increases, the other decreases, or as one increases, the other increases.

We can obtain a measure that quantifies the strength of that association by calculating the correlation coefficient, or r. Google "Pearson Correlation Coefficient Calculator" and follow the directions, which involve copying and pasting (or typing) the two columns of data in table 7.2 into the designated spaces. The Pearson Correlation Coefficient Calculator will give the r for the independent and dependent variables. The calculator will also give you an explanation like that which follows.

The r is -0.104. Although technically a negative correlation, the relationship between the variables is only weak (the nearer the correlation value is to zero, the weaker the relationship).

As you can see, the Pearson Correlation Coefficient Calculator calculates the r and makes the interpretation. With a little bit of background information, you can interpret the r value on yourself. To do that look at the r value—the sign and the correlation coefficient (e.g., -0.104). That sign can be a plus or a minus. A negative, or minus, sign in front of the correlation tells us that as one variable increases in size, the other variables decreases. A positive, or plus, sign in front of the correlation tells us that as one variable increases or decreases, the other does as well.

The size of the r value can be as large as 1 or as small as 0. A correlation coefficient of 1 or -1 indicates that the association between the independent and dependent variables is a perfect one; a correlation coefficient of 0 indicates there is no association. As a rule of thumb, a correlation coefficient that is .40 or higher suggests at least a moderate relationship. The closer to 1, the stronger the relationship.

Model Interpretation of Scatterplot and r Value

The positioning of the diamonds (representing each of the 11 census tracts) and the flat trendline suggest that knowing median dollar value of occupied homes does not help us predict the percentage of households with children under 18 headed by women. The negative sign in front of the r value (-0.104) tells us that as the median housing value rises, the percentage of female-headed households declines. But an r value of .104 tells us that the association or relationship between the two variables is weak.

Exercise 7.5: Compare your census tract to other geographies

You may want to include in the research brief a comparative analysis of your census tract relative to the city, county, state, or nation to highlight some characteristic that distinguishes your census tract or neighborhood. That is, your neighborhood may stand out as significantly different from surrounding tracts in the county, city, state, or nation (see chapter 3). This exercise shows you how to make such comparisons. The comparion will be the wages of full-time employed women relative to their male counterparts.

- Request Table B24042 (most recent 5-year estimates) for Sex by Industry and Median Earnings in the Past 12 Months (in 2015 Inflation-Adjusted Dollars) for the Full-Time, Year-Round Civilian Employed Population 16 Years and Over.
- Follow the directions for calculating the wages of women who work full-time, year-round relative to their male counterparts.

Table 7.3   Aggregate Earnings for Women and Men Age 16 to 64 in Tract 9552 in Mora (Mora County), New Mexico, Who Work Full-Time, Year-Round

Geography	Median Income Females	Median Income Males	Women's Earnings for Every Dollar Earned by Men
Census Tract: 9552	$26,742	$25,446	$1.05
County: Mora	$26,742	$25,446	$1.05
State: New Mexico	$34,692	$42,550	$0.85
Nation: USA	$39,315	$49,828	$0.79

SOURCE: American Community Survey, latest data (2015) accessed Nov. 15, 2017.

Ideally, when making wage comparisons it is best to compare the wages of men and women in the same occupations, working the same number of hours per week, at the same workplace, with the same experience or credentials and performance reviews. In this situation, if the wages of men are higher than those of women, we can place the blame squarely on discriminatory practices in the workplace. But getting the data to make this kind of comparison is difficult if not impossible. The ACS wage data give us a broad look at the money men and women working full-time earn, that is, money they can, in theory, call their own. The census bureau defines **full-time** as all people 16 years old and over who usually worked 35 hours or more per week for 50 to 52 weeks in the past 12 months. We can treat wages as a broad measure of worth in the workplace and as an indicator of the economic clout or power a man or woman working full-time brings to any partnership. We know that money is power, and the data tell us something about power differences between full-time working men and women as a group (however complex the reasons for those differences). See table 7.3.

Model Interpretation

For men and women age 16 and over who work year-round, full-time and live in census tract 9552 in Mora (Mora County), New Mexico, the median income for women is $26,742 versus $25,446 for men—a difference of $1,296 in favor of women. This means for every $1.00 a man earns, a female earns $1.05. Mora County has only one census tract (9552), so the median wage data for the county is the same as the census tract. Relative to their male counterparts, women in census tract 9552 and Mora County earn more money than men. But median wages for both men and women are lower than median wages at the state and national levels.

Exercise 7.6: Do historical research on celebrated local history

History is not static; accounts of what went on in the past are celebrated, lamented, resurrected, revised, rewritten, and reinvented. Anyone who investigates the past will surely uncover "hidden or suppressed histories that have the potential to revise our understandings of the past and thus help us see our own moment in new ways" (McFadden 2014, 139). Every neighborhood celebrates selected parts of the past and suppresses or silences other parts. The past is celebrated in historical markers, street names, and spaces named after the living and the dead or named or known for once was. The past is celebrated through archived materials displayed in museums, stored in libraries, and posted on neighborhood Web pages. What a neighborhood preserves and makes accessible is a window onto what it residents celebrate. This process of remembering and celebrating is also a process of forgetting and concealing. There is no such thing as a neighborhood history on which everyone will agree. Rather there are many neighborhood histories (Lau 2014). Gathering the facts of history requires being alert to what and whose history is showcased. Reflect on the history of your neighborhood by asking the following questions:

- What history does a neighborhood most visibly celebrate through landmarks and named spaces?
- In reviewing names and events celebrated, are there clues to other histories that have been suppressed or silenced?

The territory that houses your census tract was "founded" by a person (or persons) who is typically celebrated on the associated city's websites or remembered with a landmark. In this assignment your task is to find the name of someone credited with founding the town or city of which your census tract is part. On identifying the founder, look for clues that offer insights into the larger historical context at the time of the founding. Do follow-up research on that historical context to learn about whose lives were advantaged and disadvantaged by the founding. As an example, we consider census tract 9602, which is part of Hailey (Blaine County), Idaho.

Model Write-Up

The history of Hailey, Idaho, posted by the Hailey Historic Preservation Commission, proclaims the town's founder is John Hailey, a pioneer who was part of the Boise Basin Gold Rush in 1862. He established an extensive stagecoach and freight line and at one time controlled 2,000 miles of service. Betting the Wood River Valley was going to be a center of mining and commercial activity, Hailey filed a homestead on the future town site in 1879. The next year, he increased his holding with a desert land claim of 440 acres. Calling themselves the Hailey Town Company, Hailey, A. H. Boomer, U.S. Marshal E. S. Chase, and W. T. Riley had the town site surveyed on April 20, 1881, and officially platted at the county seat in Rocky Bar on May 10, 1881. The speculation paid off. By July 6, $30,000 worth of lots had been sold.

This excerpt refers to several larger historical events (Boise Basin Gold Rush and homesteading) that give context to the founding of Hailey, Idaho. Since John Hailey's filing of a homestead is directly related to the founding of the city of Hailey, I did further research on homesteading. Homesteading likely holds clues about those who benefited from Hailey's homesteading and those who were disadvantaged.[9]

The Homestead Act, passed in 1862, was designed with the goal of settling the West by offering 160 acres of "free" land to "any adult citizen, or intended citizen, who had never borne arms against the U.S. government," providing that they live on the land for 5 years and improve it by building a house and cultivating the land (Ourdocuments.gov 2015). Homesteading provided immigrants, freed slaves, the urban poor, and women with an opportunity to begin anew. However, few people in these groups had the skills or, more important, the necessary resources (machinery and materials to build a home and make land productive) to comply with these requirements. While the Homestead Act did provide a new beginning for some, most of the land fell into the hands of those who had the resources to buy it, to develop it, or to hire squatters to hold it.[10] In fact, records show that in

---

9. There is a website that focuses on history from the point of view of ordinary people and those left out of the story. It is founded in honor of Howard Zinn, author of *The People's History of the United States*. https://zinnproject.org/teaching-materials/explore-by-theme/.

10. Subsequent legislation allowed speculators to hire men (squatters) to apply for and stake a claim on the land but then turn the deed over to the speculators. Most of the land

Idaho 60% of homestead properties were never developed into farms (Gates 1964). Of course, we know the lands homesteaded were previously occupied by Native Americans, but an online search shows virtually no record of their plight beyond references such as, "To make way for the homesteaders, the federal government forced Native American tribes off their ancestral lands and onto reservations" (History.com 2018).

References
Gates, Paul W., 1964. "The Homestead Law in Iowa." *Agricultural History* 38 (2): 67–68.
History.com. "1862 Lincoln Signs Homestead Act." This Day in History. www.history.com/this-day-in-history/lincoln-signs-homestead-act.

Exercise 7.7: Do longitudinal research

For this exercise you will do research to document change in your neighborhood over time. In other words, you will present a snapshot of demographic characteristics at three points in time, 2000, 2010, and 2016. This type of research offers insights into the degree to which something has remained the same or has changed and how dramatically. Estimates for 2000 and 2010 can be obtained by going to American Factfinder and choosing Decennial Census (instead of American Community Survey) and then choosing geography and tables in the same manner as you have done for the American Community Survey.

Model Write-Up of Longitudinal Research

Because my neighborhood is aging. I decided to focus on the following characteristics over three points in time, 2000, 2010 and 2015. The characteristics are

- Median age—7.5 (in 2000); 40.6 (in 2010); and 45.1 (in 2015).
- % households with children under 18–32% (in 2000); 29.8% (in 2010), and 22.7% (in 2015).
- Vacancy rates—16% (in 2000); 25.2% (in 2010); and 22.7% (in 2015).

---

purchased under the act went to speculators, cattlemen, miners, lumbermen, and railroads. Of the 500 million acres marked for dispersion by the General Land Office, only 80 million acres went to homesteaders (www.ourdocuments.gov).

Interpretation: The median age has increased by 7.6 years since 2000. The percentage of households with children under 18 has decreased by almost 10% in the past 15 years. Vacancy rates rose by almost 10% between 2000 and 2010 and then declined slightly. But vacancy rates are still quite high.

WORKING DRAFT OF RESEARCH BRIEF, SECTION 6
Key Demographics and Local History

Now we are ready to do Section 6 of your research brief draft. You will draw on what you learned about your census tract doing the seven exercises, which involved descriptive, comparative, correlational, historical, and longitudinal research. Keep the following points in mind as you write the draft of Research Brief, Section 6.

- You gave special attention to one data point that stood out over the course of your research as worthy of further exploration. To determine if that data point suggests something very unusual or normal about your neighborhood, you compared its value to the corresponding value in at least 10 nearby census tracts. This allowed you to establish how your neighborhood compares on the chosen data point to neighboring census tracts.

- Mention what you learned about women's earnings relative to men's and to the longitudinal research that shows how the neighborhood has changed or stayed the same since 2000.

- Your analysis of a chosen landmark allows you the chance to present ways the past has informed the present way of life in the neighborhood.

- As always, avoid making claims the data cannot support. Consider the data on the median income of women working full-time relative to men. Whatever your findings, you must do more research to explain the wage inequality (or equality) that exists in your census tract. For example, research tells us that women tend to "choose" lower-paying jobs with flexible schedules so that they can meet the demands of childcare and other household responsibilities. The point is that we can only speculate about what the data tell us, and further research is necessary (at another time).

- Always keep in mind that the research brief is still in the draft stage and is always open to refinement and revision.

Table 7.4 Demographics for Census Tract 78, Northside (Hamilton County) Ohio, 2000, 2010, 2015

Demographic	2000	2010	2015
% of Population, Less than High School (age 25+)	23.7	17.5	17.2
Vacancy rates census tract 78	13.6	31.8	23.2

SOURCE: American Community Survey, latest data (2015) accessed Nov. 15, 2017.

Model Write-Up, Section 6

Households with Children under 18 Headed by Females: For census tract 78 there are 201 households with children under 18, and 100, or 50%, of these households are female headed (no spouse or partner present). When compared to 20 surrounding census tracts, tract 78 ranks as the sixth lowest percentage. The 20 surrounding tracts range from a low of 11% to a high of 100% of households with children headed by women. So, while in census tract 78, 50% of all households in with children are headed by females (no partner present), that percentage did not stand out as particularly high when compared to percentages in the surrounding census tracts. When compared to percentages for the city of Cincinnati (32%), Hamilton County (29%), the state of Ohio (30.4%), and the United States (27.8%), 57% stood out as very high. There is a correlation of -.41 between the percentage of all households with children under 18 headed by women and median home prices, suggesting that the greater the percentage of households with children headed by women, the lower the home prices in a census tract. While census tract 78 is undergoing gentrification, the median home price is low relative to those in the county, city, and country.

Labor Force Participation Rates and Earning for Males and Females: 56.1% of men 16 and over work full-time, compared to 51% of women. For those men who work full-time, the average salary is $44,645.66, compared to $34,783.00 for women who work full-time—a difference of $9,862.66 in favor of men. This means, on average, that for every $1.00 a man in this neighborhood earns, a woman in this neighborhood earns $0.77.

Changing Demographics: A sign that census tract 78 is in transition is vacancy rates, which are 10% higher than in 2000 but lower than 2010, when the rate was 31.8%. We can see also that the percentage of the population with less than a high school education is declining. These trends are in keeping with a neighborhood undergoing gentrification.

Landmark—American Can Lofts: The history of the American Can Company, which is now the American Can Lofts, is a window into census tract 78 and Northside. The American Can Company opened in 1921. At its peak it employed 2,500 workers. When it closed in 1965 the factory employed 500. The American Can Company's demise occurred the same year the pop-top and ring-tab openings on cans were introduced and when aluminum and other lighter materials, rather than tin and steel, came into use. These innovations were revolutionary, and the can-making machines that American Can Company manufactured were now outdated. The closing of this plant was the first in what would be a long list. Eventually 105 of the American Can Company's factories across the country were shut down or sold, and a new network of 62 plants took their place. Many of the new plants were located in low-wage, less unionized areas inside and outside the United States.

The American Can Company building stayed largely vacant, with some spaces occupied by artists in the 1990s. In September 2011, the building reopened as the American Can Lofts, a 110-unit apartment complex that included Ruth's Parkside Café, a bocce ball court, conference rooms, a music rehearsal room, artist space, and an exercise room Rents range from $610 for one bedroom to $1,480 for the three-bedroom loft (American Can Loft 2017). The cost of renovation was $22 million, assisted by an $8.7 million HUD-backed loan.

The story of the American Can Loft and its transformation from factory to New York–style apartments over the course of 45 years mirrors the restructuring of the U.S. economy from manufacturing based to service and knowledge based. The loss of manufacturing plants and jobs in urban spaces and the simultaneous exodus of working- and middle-class white-classified families to suburbs resulted in the closing of hundreds of local businesses, including drugstores and other service-oriented establishments. These changes profoundly affected the demographics of the populations left behind. In recent years, American Can Lofts is part of what is attracting a new demographic that mirrors a national trend of urban living. That trend is driven by young professionals and retiring baby boomers.

REFERENCES

Alexander, Bryant Keith. 2003. "Fading, Twisting, and Weaving: An Interpretive Ethnography of the Black Barbershop as Cultural Space." *Qualitative Inquiry* 9 (1): 105–28.

Anderson, Benedict. 2016. *A Life beyond Boundaries: A Memoir*. New York: Verso Books.

Cummins, S., E. Flint, and S. A. Matthews. 2014. "New Neighborhood Grocery Store Increased Awareness of Food Access But Did Not Alter Dietary Habits or Obesity." *Health Affairs* 33 (2): 283–91.

Dill, J., C. Mohr, and L. Ma. 2014. "How Can Psychological Theory Help Cities Increase Walking and Bicycling?" *Journal of the American Planning Association* 80 (1): 36–51.

Downing, Janelle. 2016. "The Health Effects of the Foreclosure Crisis and Unaffordable Housing: A Systematic Review and Explanation of Evidence." *Social Science & Medicine* 162 (August): 88–96

Earls, F., J. McGuire, and S. Shay. 1994. "Evaluating a Community Intervention to Reduce the Risk of Child Abuse: Methodological Strategies in Conducting Neighborhood Surveys." *Child Abuse & Neglect* 18 (5): 473–85.

Elliott, J., C. R. Gale, S. Parsons, D. Kuh, and the HALCyon Study. 2014. "Neighborhood Cohesion and Mental Well-Being among Older Adults: A Mixed Methods Approach." *Social Science & Medicine* 107: 44–51.

Hanhardt, C. B. 2013. *Safe Space: Gay Neighborhood History and the Politics of Violence*. Durham, NC: Duke University Press.

Harlan, S. L., J. H. Declet-Barreto, W. L. Stefanov, and D. B. Petitti. 2013. "Neighborhood Effects on Heat Deaths: Social and Environmental Predictors of Vulnerability in Maricopa County, Arizona." *Environmental Health Perspectives* 121 (2): 197.

Ingulstad, Mats, Andrew Perchard, and Espen Storli, eds. 2014. *Tin and Global Capitalism: A History of the Devil's Metal, 1850–2000*. New York: Routledge.

Jose, R., E. A. Holman, and R. C. Silver. 2017. "The Importance of the Neighborhood in the 2014 Ebola Outbreak in the United States: Distress, Worry, and Functioning." *Health Psychology* 36(12): 1181–85.

Kane, K., M. Hoffman, J. Cheng, B. C. Olendzki, and W. Li. 2016. "Neighborhood Differences in the Availability of Healthy Foods in the City of Worcester." *Center for Clinical and Translational Science*. May.

Koenig, Caitlin. 2015. "American Can Reunion Scheduled for September 27." *Soapbox Cincinnati*. www.soapboxmedia.com/devnews/092215-american-can-building-reunion-sept-27.aspx. Retrieved October 1, 2017.

Lau, Amy. "Making Space for Silenced Histories: National History, Personal Archives, and the WWII Japanese American Internment." *Progressive Librarian* 42 (2014): 82.

Lee, H., M. S. Vaughn, and H. Lim. 2014. "The Impact of Neighborhood Crime Levels on Police Use of Force." *Journal of Criminal Justice* 42 (6): 491–99.

Lehning, A. J., C. Mair, S. Waldstein, E. Onukwugha, M. K. Evans, and A. Zonderman. 2017. "Social and Economic Determinants of Adult Health:

Conceptualizing Pathways between Neighborhood Environments and Risk of Cardiovascular Disease." *Innovation in Aging* 1: 92–92.

Loebach, J. E. and J. A. Gilliland. 2016. "Free Range Kids? Using GPS-Derived Activity Spaces to Examine Children's Neighborhood Activity and Mobility." *Environment and Behavior* 48 (3): 421–53.

Low, S. M., and I. Altman. 1992. *Place Attachment: A Conceptual Inquiry.* New York: Plenum.

McFadden, Margaret. 2014. "'People Shouldn't Be Forgotten': Cold Case's Pursuit of History's Ghosts" *Journal of Popular Film and Television* 42 (3): 139–49.

Mecklenborg, Jake. 2011. "$22M American Can Factory Redevelopment to Welcome First Residents This September." *UrbanCincy.* www.urbancincy.com/2011/07/22m-american-can-factory-redevelopment-to-welcome-first-residents-this-september/. Retrieved October 1, 2017.

Mendez, D. D., T. L. Gary-Webb, R. Goode, Y. Zheng, C. C. Imes, A. Fabio, and L. K. Burke. 2016. "Neighborhood Factors and Six-Month Weight Change among Overweight Individuals in a Weight Loss Intervention." *Preventive Medicine Reports* 4: 569–73.

Primerica Corporation History. 2017. "Funding Universe." www.fundinguniverse.com/company-histories/primerica-corporation-history/. Retrieved October 1, 2017.

Ramirez, A. S., L. K. D. Rios, Z. Valdez, E. Estrada, and A. Ruiz. 2017. "Bringing Produce to the People: Implementing a Social Marketing Food Access Intervention in Rural Food Deserts." *Journal of Nutrition Education and Behavior* 49 (2): 166–74.

Sandelowski, Margarete. "Focus on Research Methods-Whatever Happened to Qualitative Description?" *Research in Nursing and Health* 23.4 (2000): 334–340.

Schultz, C. L., S. A. W. Stanis, S. P. Sayers, L. A. Thombs, and I. M. Thomas. 2017. "A Longitudinal Examination of Improved Access on Park use and Physical Activity in a Low-Income and Majority African American Neighborhood Park." *Preventive Medicine* 95: S95–S100.

U.S. Department of Agriculture. 2009. *Access to Affordable and Nutritious Food-Measuring and Understanding Food Deserts and Their Consequences: Report to Congress* Administrative Publication No. AP-036. 160 pp.

Ward, R., A. Clark, S. Campbell, B. Graham, A. Kullberg, K. Manji, K. Rummery, and J. Keady. 2017. "The Lived Neighborhood: Understanding How People with Dementia Engage with Their Local Environment." *International Psychogeriatrics* (May): 1–14.

Wen, M. 2017. "Social Capital and Adolescent Substance Use: The Role of Family, School, and Neighborhood Contexts." *Journal of Research on Adolescence* 27 (2): 362–78.

8 Writing the Research Brief

> Great achievers understand the importance of relentless preparation.... [T]hey are smart enough to know that the quality of their preparation will decide the quality of their performance.
>
> Wale Oladipo, *The Worry Instinct*

This chapter is a guide to writing the research brief.[1] A research brief is a carefully crafted 8- to 10-page, 1.5-spaced report that showcases the most important and relevant findings obtained after doing investigative research. This research brief answers the core questions:

1. In what ways do you currently support, or fail to support, the neighborhood that surrounds the place that matters?
2. Should support be increased? If so, in what ways?

Your answers must be bolstered by data and observations that reinforce your assessment of the census tract's strengths and needs. The brief includes an action plan outlining a strategy for increasing or maintaining your support. That support must be tied to a specific need or to an existing strength. Your job is to review the six draft sections you have written, select the most important and relevant findings, and drop what has the least impact.

If you gave your best effort when doing the chapter exercises and writing up section drafts, you have laid the necessary groundwork to put

---

1. "Research brief" is also a term used to refer to a research project proposal.

together the final version of the research brief. That groundwork is the key ingredient of success. Even though you cannot include all data and observations in am 8- to 10-page brief, the materials you have to draw from give you the confidence to present your neighborhood's needs and strengths, to objectively assess your relationship to the neighborhood, and to lay out concrete steps you can take to increase or sustain your level of support.

The brief should be a piece of polished writing. The final version of the brief is not something to put together the night before it is due. The first attempt to consolidate the six draft sections will likely not result in the final version. It might take two, three, or even four revisions.

SEEK CONSTRUCTIVE CRITICISM

Good writers have people in their lives who read their writing and comment constructively. There is an art to asking and accepting (even welcoming) constructive criticism. Asking someone to review your work sends the message: *I value your criticism, and I trust you to help me make my work better.* Actively look for someone whose judgment and knowledge you respect. Ideally, the person who critiques your work

- ✓ respects you as a person and a thinker;
- ✓ is capable of making thoughtful editorial suggestions;
- ✓ understands that writing is a process that evolves and becomes more effective with feedback; and
- ✓ wants to help you become a powerful and effective writer.

Constructive criticism places the emphasis on assisting writers through the challenges of writing, not on tearing the writers' work down. If you are especially sensitive or easily offended, try to change. If healthy criticism makes you feel defeated, recognize that such feelings get in the way of progress. If you are prone to responding to constructive criticism in an aggressive or defensive manner, you will surely discourage well-meaning critics. Work hard to act gracious. Make a point of listening to and taking in criticism. In time you will learn that thoughtful suggestions are a sign that someone is investing in your success. If your chosen critic is mean-spirited or has self-aggrandizing ways, look to someone else for feedback.

Writing is a skill and a process. As you work to consolidate the six draft sections of the research brief, do so with the goal of making sure every word, line, sentence, and paragraph matter. Make a concerted effort to eliminate repetition and unnecessary words. Work to write in the active rather than the passive voice. Do not editorialize or offer unsubstantiated opinion. Avoid putting things in the research brief that might be nice to know but do not address the core questions or do not help establish a plan of action.

THE FORMAT OF THE RESEARCH BRIEF

The research brief will be about 8 to 10 pages long[2] and include a title page and an introduction followed by 6 sections. Those sections are

Section 1: Background on Self and Place That Matters
Section 2: Key Observations
Section 3: Residents and Households
Section 4: Neighborhood Resources
Section 5: Key Demographics
Section 6: Action Plan

Your brief should convey that you care about the neighborhood that surrounds your place that matters and that you understand its strengths and needs. It should include an assessment of your current level of support, as well as your action plan for sustaining or expanding that support.

In the pages that follow there are two sample research briefs. The first brief is about a neighborhood undergoing gentrification; the second is written from the point of view of a person whose neighborhood is in a

---

2. As long as your decision is not motivated by speed or laziness, of course, you can make the brief longer or shorter depending on goals, purpose, and audience.

rural area. As you review the two samples, read them for insights into how to consolidate and revise your draft sections. Also keep the following points in mind:

- The research brief must answer the two core questions.
- You cannot include everything you have written in an 8- to 10-page brief, so be prepared to make informed choices about what to include and what to leave out.
- Do not worry about length on the first round of consolidation. Include everything you believe important to describing the neighborhood, establishing its strengths and needs, and addressing the two core questions. Then reduce its length to 8 to 10 pages.
- Include a small number of figures and tables, strategically selected to emphasize the most critical information.
- When appropriate, show how your census tract compares on some characteristics to adjacent census tracts, the county, the state, and the nation. Such comparisons support claims of neighborhood uniqueness or typicality.
- If there are residents deserving special attention (households with children under 18 headed by females; veterans; preschoolers), consider doing additional research to give greater depth to your analysis. That extra research can include looking at ACS data, property records, or news stories.
- Avoid using census estimates to learn specifics about a very small category of residents (e.g., .1% Asian identifying; the age or racial classification of 145 people living in poverty of a particular classification; the under 18 population that is about 250 in size). Estimates are based on samples, and it is hard to draw a sample that selects enough people from groups that have a small numerical presence within a census tract. The estimates on the smallest groups are the least reliable. You can learn about such groups by interviewing or observing.
- Remember that your goal is to write a coherent, convincing, and meaningful research brief that culminates in a plan of action. See appendix F for a rubric that acts as a checklist of everything that should to be covered.

* * *

MODEL EXAMPLE #1

RESEARCH BRIEF FOR CENSUS TRACT 78, NORTHSIDE
(HAMILTON COUNTY), OHIO

Section 1: Background on Self and Place That Matters

This research was conducted with the goal of addressing two core questions:

(1) In what ways do I, in my role as a home owner and resident of 99 Home Street, Northside, Ohio, which is part of Hamilton County, currently support or fail to support the surrounding neighborhood?

(2) Should my support be increased? If so, in what ways?

As a resident, I have an obligation to care about the neighborhood that supports my home and lifestyle. I recognize that a thriving and healthy neighborhood has a direct impact on my quality of life. Thus, I do not want to take the surrounding neighborhood for granted. I want to be a force for neighborhood improvement.

THE PLACE THAT MATTERS: My home is located in the heart of Northside, census tract 78. It is part of Cincinnati, Ohio, and Hamilton County. I am 32 years old, a college graduate with a major in business management. I work for a large retailer as a sales representative, earning $38,800 a year. Two years ago, before buying this house, I rented an apartment in Northside for 7 years. I believed buying a home in Northside was a good personal investment and a vote of confidence in the neighborhood. My home is within walking distance of many restaurants, bars, and Jacob Hoffner Park.

The county tax records show that my 94-year-old house was in foreclosure on at least two occasions in the past 15 years. In 2015, the Hamilton County Land Reutilization Office took possession of the house and turned it over to Sustainable Transformation (ST), a not-for-profit organization.[3] ST rehabilitated the house, and then I bought it for $150,000. My home is one of many in Northside that ST has renovated. The nonprofit's mission is to fix up and sell homes that have been labeled eyesores

---

3. Some names are fictitious to protect the identity of writers.

CHAPTER EIGHT

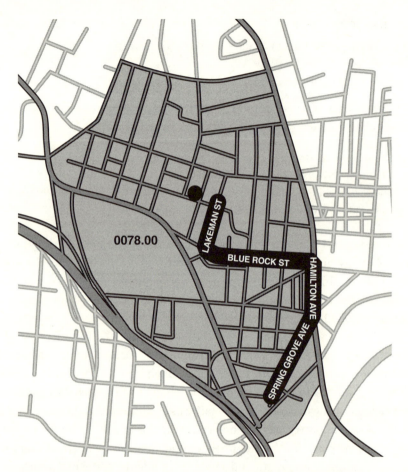

Figure 8.1. Map of Most-Traveled Streets, Census Tract 78 in Northside (Hamilton County), Ohio
SOURCE: American Community Survey Census Tract Maps

and beyond repair at an affordable price. I am someone who earns less than $40,000 a year (gross), so I and others like me benefit from this mission.

Figure 8.1 shows the streets that make up the census tract and its boundaries. The streets on which I routinely drive to work, walk, and ride my bike are Lakeman, Blue Rock, Hamilton Avenue, and Spring Grove.

These streets take me to my favorite eating place, Melt Eclectic Deli, and my favorite place to relax, Jacob Hoffner Park.

Section 2: Key Observations

When driving around my census tract, I notice a divide between the have- and have-nots. One observation is that there is the nonprofit Cincinnati Urban Promise, with a mission of helping children in underresourced communities succeed and avoid negative peer pressure. The apartments and homes around Cincinnati Urban Promise are occupied by residents who appear to be lower income and predominantly Hispanic and black classified. Some houses have boarded-up windows, and most need major repair. This section is in stark contrast to streets in Northside, where housing is occupied by a professional class who appear to be in their late 20s to early 40s; most appear to be white, but there are hints of diversity.

Census tract 78 is a neighborhood in transition. Specifically, it is part of the larger national trend valuing urban or high-density living over suburban or rural living. This trend is associated with gentrification, where socially and economically disadvantaged populations are pushed out by the more economically advantaged. This trend includes a generational bifurcation, as urban environments are attractive to both older and younger adults. The most noticeable symbol of this transition is the many apartment complexes that have been built where abandoned lumberyards, factories, and railroad depots once sat. The apartments capitalize on a swelling millennial-age population attracted to urban living and its conveniences. Studio apartments range from $683 to $970 a month. The most expensive units are two-bedrooms ranging from $1,230 to $1,545 a month.

Section 3: Residents and Households

Census tract 78 is home to 2,411 residents who live in 1,166 occupied households, for an average of 2.1 persons per household.

- 41.8% of households (n = 488) are single resident; that is, the resident lives alone; 7.9% of all households (n = 93) consist of a married couple with children under age 18; 9.0% of households (n = 217) consist of unmarried partners.

CHAPTER EIGHT

- 65.5% of residents self-classify as white, 24.8% self-classify as black, and 3.4% self-classify as more than one race.
- The average income of the bottom 20% of households is $11,219. In contrast, the average income of the top 20% of households is estimated to be $265,132. The average income for the top 20% is 23.6 times that of the bottom 20%.
- The bottom 20% of households in census tract 78 secure 2.63% of all income. Compare this to the households in the top 20%, which secure 63.13% of income.
- The median income of black-classified households is $24,942, compared to $54,942 for white-classified households, a difference of almost $25,000. Almost half the black-classified residents live in households with an income below poverty, compared to 11.2% of white-classified households.
- There are 254 school-age children, or about 10.5% of residenst. Of these 254, 27% are black classified and 70% are white classified. Primary- and middle-school-age residents are noticeable around schools but are less noticeable around the business districts, which draw almost all white-appearing residents and other patrons who can afford luxury coffees, healthy foods, and beverages.

Section 4: Neighborhood Resources

Neighborhood resources can be tangible and intangible. Housing is a tangible resource, as are income, insurance, and cars. Census tract 78 is home to 1,519 total housing units; 353, or 23.2%, are vacant. That is a high percentage when compared to the state of Ohio (10.8%), Hamilton County (12.1%), and the nation (12.3%). The vacant housing units in Northside are not for rent or sale or seasonal. Almost 75% of the 353 vacant units have for all practical purposes been abandoned, compared to about 50% of the vacant households in the state and county and 31% in the nation.

Northside residents bring in a combined income of $99.3 million per year from all sources. That translates to $41,174 per resident or $65,353.80 per household. Sixty-eight percent of this aggregate income is from wages and salary. The next largest source of income is pensions and/or social security combined ($13.9 million), which accounts for 28% of the neighborhood's income.

In the neighborhood, 157, or 13.4%, of households have no vehicle and 10.6% have no health insurance; 398, or 34.1%, of occupied households are considered cost burdened; that is, residents expend 30% or more of household income to meet expenses.

A key intangible human resource is education. Almost 30% (29.6%) of the 561 residents who are age 24 and older have a bachelor's degree or higher, with the three highest fields of study being Visual and Performing Arts (84, or 14.9%), Engineering (63, or 11.2%), and Liberal Arts (50, or 8.9%) and History (50, or 8.9%). The least represented fields are Physical and Related Sciences (16, or 2.9%) and Multidisciplinary Studies (9, or 1.6%).

Another intangible resource is neighborhood reputation. A content analysis of Google News articles published in August 2017 featuring my census tract offers insights on the neighborhood's reputation and its challenges. Of the 50 articles reviewed, 12 (24%) focused on crime or shootings, 8 (16%) focused on new housing or special event developments, and 25 (50%) focused on local businesses in transition, in decline, or new to the scene.

Section 5: Key Demographics

This section presents information about my census tract that peaked my interest as I worked to learn about its needs. I give special attention to (1) households with children under 18 headed by females, (2) male-female wage differences and labor force participation, and (3) the history of American Can Corporation, which mirrors the history of Northside.

HOUSEHOLDS WITH CHILDREN UNDER 18 HEADED BY FEMALES: In census tract 78 there are 201 households with children under 18; and 100, or 50%, are female headed (no spouse or partner present). When compared to 20 surrounding census tracts, tract 78 ranks as the 6th lowest percentage. The 20 surrounding tracts range from a low of 11% of households to a high of 100% of households with children headed by women. So while 50% of all households with children are headed by females (no husband or partner present), that percentage did not stand out as particularly high when compared to percentages in the surrounding census tracts. When compared to percentages for the city of Cincinnati

Table 8.1 Changing Demographics for Census Tract 78, Northside, Ohio

Tract 78	2000	2010	2015
% of population, less than high school (age 25+)	23.7	17.5	17.2
Vacancy rates	13.6%	31.8%	23.2%

SOURCE: American Community Survey, latest data (2015) accessed Nov. 15, 2017.

(32%), Hamilton County (29%), the state of Ohio (30.4%), and the United States (27.8%), 50% stood out as very high.

There is a correlation of -.41 between the percentage of all households with children under 18 headed by women and median home price. The correlation shows that the greater the percentage of households with children headed by women, the lower a census tract's home prices. While census tract 78 is undergoing gentrification, the median home price ($111,900) is low relative to home prices in the county ($142,000), the state ($129,900), and the nation ($178,600).

LABOR FORCE PARTICIPATION RATES AND EARNINGS FOR MALES AND FEMALES: Just over 56% of men 16 and over work full-time, compared to 51% of women in that age group. For those men who work full-time, the average salary is $44,645.66 versus $34,783.00 for women who work full-time—a difference of $9,862.66 in favor of men. This means, on average, that for every $1.00 a man in this neighborhood earns, a woman in this neighborhood earns $0.77. That 23-cent pay gap is wider than it is for the county (20-cent gap) and nation (20-cent gap) but narrower than the state (.25-cent gap.

CHANGING DEMOGRAPHICS: Two signs that census tract 78 is in transition are vacancy rates, which are 10% higher than in 2000 but lower than 2010, when the rate was 31.8%. We can see also that percentage of population with less than a high school education is declining. These shifts are in keeping with a neighborhood undergoing gentrification.

The history of the American Can Company, now the American Can Lofts, is a window into the history behind the gentrification and changing demographics taking place in census tract 78 and Northside. The company opened in 1921. At its peak it employed 2,500 workers. When it closed in 1965 the factory employed 500. The American Can Company's demise occurred the same year the pop-top or ring-tab opening was introduced and when cans were made of aluminum and other lighter materials rather than tin and steel. These innovations were revolutionary, and the can-making machines that the American Can Company manufactured became outdated. The closing of this plant was the first in what would be a long list. Eventually 105 of the American Can Company's factories across the country were shut down or sold, and a new network of 62 plants took their place. Many of the new plants are located in low-wage, less unionized areas inside and outside the United States.

The American Can Company building stayed largely vacant, with some spaces occupied by artists in the 1990s. In September 2011, the building reopened as the American Can Lofts, a 110-unit apartment complex that included Ruth's Parkside Café, a bocce ball court, conference rooms, a music rehearsal room, artist space, and an exercise room. Rents range from $610 for one bedroom to $1,550 for the three-bedroom loft (American Can Loft 2017). The cost of renovation was $22 million, assisted by an $8.7-million HUD-backed loan.

The story of the American Can Loft and its transformation from factory to New York–style apartments over the course of 45 years mirrors the restructuring of the U.S. economy from manufacturing based to service and knowledge based. The loss of manufacturing plants and jobs in urban areas and the simultaneous exodus of working- and middle-class white-classified families to the suburbs resulted in the closing of hundreds of local businesses, including drugstores and other service-oriented establishments. These changes profoundly affected the demographics of the populations left behind. American Can Lofts is attracting a new demographic that mirrors a national trend of urban living. That trend is driven by young professionals and retiring baby boomers.

Section 6: Action Plan

The action plan begins with a self-assessment of my reputation as a resident and home owner.

SELF-ASSESSED REPUTATION: I have often wondered how my neighbors perceive me. I think they see me as young, well-to-do, and single. I also think they see me as an outsider moving into a nice home in a lower-income area that is changing. I know that I bought my house at a reasonable price and that not everyone in the neighborhood would be able to afford this house or even qualify for a loan. I don't feel as if I am hurting anyone by being here. I think my neighbors benefit because I am a good resident. I get that I am living in a house that at one time someone else couldn't keep up. I don't have kids, but I pay taxes. I particularly wonder what the kids think about me and my house as they walk to school in the morning. Do they see me as someone who thinks she is "better" than their parents since my house is so nice and well kept? When I see these kids walking to school I wonder what I can do to support the elementary school.

SPECIFIC PLAN OF ACTION: The strengths of census tract 78 include Jacob Hoffner Park and the business district. Census tract 78's most pressing needs revolve around vacant housing (23.2%) and income inequality, especially between the black- and white-classified households. The median income of black-classified households is $24,942, compared to $54,942 for white-classified households, a difference of almost $25,000. Almost half the black-classified residents live in a household with an income below poverty, compared to 11.2% of white-classified households. The census estimates are too unreliable to allow me to learn more about the 10% of school-age residents. My observations tell me that this is a neglected group, overshadowed by gentrification and the economic development supporting it.

After reviewing a Yelp Inventory of businesses in census tract 78, it is clear to me that I currently support only a handful of local businesses: Sidewinder Coffee (4181 Hamilton Ave.), Melt Eclectic Deli (4165 Hamilton Ave.), Northside Tavern (4163 Hamilton Ave.), and Shake-It Records (4156 Hamilton Ave.). I plan to continue patronizing these local businesses and increase the number I support. I have already identified an independent pharmacy and a shoe repair shop.

Using the resource GuideStar, I identified five nonprofits to support. I am interested in volunteering at (1) Sustainable Transformation (ST), which focuses on increasing home ownership; (2) CAIN (Churches Active in Northside), which attempts to build a more vibrant community by providing various resources such as food and crisis assistance; (3) Wordplay Cincinnati, located in the business district of Northside, which offers free tutoring and creative writing programs for K–12 students, who connect with caring volunteers working in partnership with parents and teachers to realize success in and beyond the classroom; (4) Mobo Bicycle Co-op, a nonprofit in neighboring census tract 74 that also serves census tract 78 dedicated to making cycling accessible to people of all ages by offering access to tools and parts to repair and maintain their bicycles; and (5) Happen Inc. and Happen Toy Lab Program, which offer free art programs and give children a chance to be toy inventors. Children can invent their own toys, drawing on the massive supply of recycled toy parts, and seek advice from toy professors.

Since I was able to purchase an affordable home through ST, I will make it my highest priority to give back to this agency. One way is through AmazonSmile. When I order from Amazon, I will designate ST as the recipient of 0.5% of the purchase price on eligible AmazonSmile purchases. I learned that ST has an annual fund-raiser that I will support.

References

American Can Lofts. 2017. "Northside." www.americancanlofts.com/availability. Retrieved October 1, 2017.

Barton, Michael. 2014. "An Exploration of the Importance of the Strategy Used to Identify Gentrification." *Urban Studies Journal* 53 (1): 92–111.

Daga, Sanat. 2015. "Who Cares about the Neighborhood? Gentrification and Educational Outcomes in Oakland Unified School District Elementary Schools." www.econ.berkeley.edu/sites/default/files/Sanat%20Daga.pdf. Retrieved October 1, 2017.

Moos, Markus. 2015. "From Gentrification to Youthification? The Increasing Importance of Young Age in Delineating High-Density Living." *Urban Studies Journal* 53 (14): 2903–20.

U.S. Census Bureau. 2017. "American FactFinder: American Community Survey. 2011–2015 American Community Survey 5-Year Estimates." https://factfinder.census.gov/faces/nav/jsf/pages/searchresults.xhtml?refresh=t. Retrieved October 1, 2017.

* * *

MODEL EXAMPLE #2

RESEARCH BRIEF FOR CENSUS TRACT 704 IN DENISON
(CRAWFORD COUNTY), IOWA

Section 1: Background on Self and Place That Matters

This research was conducted with the goal of addressing two core questions:

(1) In what ways do I, in my role as a new resident to Denison, Iowa, currently support or fail to support the surrounding neighborhood?

(2) Should my support be increased? If so, in what ways?

As a resident to be, I want to get to know my new neighborhood and learn about its residents. Census tract 704 is the city of Denison, Iowa. To put it another way, one census tract makes up Denison, and that tract is 704. I will be living with my great-aunt who needs assistance now that she is older. She lives in a two-story house at 100 Assist Avenue,[4] Denison (Crawford County), Iowa. My new neighborhood will have a large effect on my lifestyle. As a new resident, I want to contribute to the quality of life there.

THE PLACE THAT MATTERS: The place that matters to me is my great-aunt's house, which is located near Denison High School in the city of Denison, Iowa, in Crawford County. I am 22 years old and plan to take a few classes at the community college, which is also located in census tract 704.

Figure 8.2 shows my census tract and the streets that I will travel to get from my great-aunt's home to Western Iowa Tech Community College. I start out on North 16th Street, take a left onto North 20th to BelAire Drive. Then 24th Street takes me to US 30. I turn left on North 36th and then on North 35th. I know when I live here I will be a regular visitor to Yellow Smoke Park, a 359-acre recreation area where people go to picnic, hike, bike, camp, swim, and engage in all kinds of water activities (boating and canoeing, sailing, and fishing). Whenever I visited my great-aunt's house in the past, we always went to this park.

---

4. The address is a stand-in to protect the identity of an informant. The research brief is based on real events.

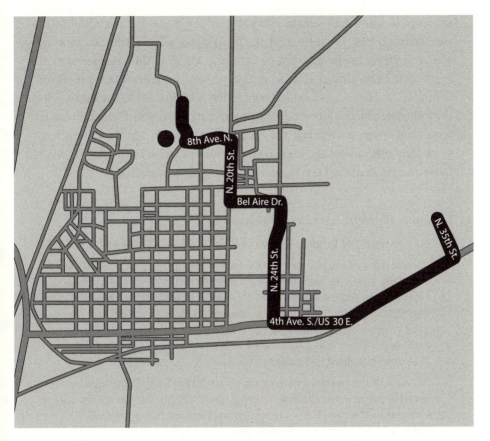

Figure 8.2. Map of Most-Traveled Steets, Census Tract 704 in Denison (Crawford County), Iowa
SOURCE: American Community Survey Census Tract Maps.

Section 2: Key Observations

According to ACS Demographic and Housing Estimates, there are 2,844 housing units in census tract 704. Almost 95% of all housing is occupied. There are four meat processing/packing plants within the boundaries of census tract 704: Smithfield (800 Industrial Dr.), Quality Food Processors (710 US 59), Tyson Fresh Meats (2490 Lincoln Way), and Tyson Foods (2490 Lincoln Way).

There are a large number of residents who appear Hispanic, and when I walk around the streets I hear many people speaking Spanish. This Hispanic presence is verified by census estimates: of the 8,304 people who live in census tract 704, an estimated 3,978 (47.9%) self-classify as being of Hispanic ethnicity. Twenty-two percent (n = 1,946) of the total population are foreign born, almost all of whom (97%) were born in a Latin American country. The Hispanic-classified population is connected to the meatpacking industry, which is known to draw most of its employees from this census tract (and from surrounding tracts). A simple Google search of "Denison, Iowa Hispanic" shows the area has come to depend on Hispanic-classified labor and residents to keep the once-thriving town operating.

Section 3: Residents and Households

- Census tract 704 is home to 8,304 residents who live in 2,844 households.
- Almost 50% of the people who live in the census tract self-classify as of Hispanic ethnicity. Seventy-one percent of the 3,978 who identify as Hispanic are from Mexico or are the children and grandchildren of Mexican immigrants. Other than those who identify as Mexican, the next largest presence identifies as Guatemalan (n = 498) and Salvadoran (n = 469). These two nationalities account for about 24.3% of the Hispanic-classified residents.
- About half the population of census tract 704 classify themselves as non-Hispanic white (48.8%) (n = 4,259). The top national ancestries claimed by the non-Hispanic whites are German (2,519, or 55.6 %), Irish (450, or 10.0%), and Norwegian (320, or 7.5%)
- The median age of residents classified as non-Hispanic white is 49.4 and for the Hispanic-classified residents, 21.9—a difference of 27.5 years. Seventy percent of primary school students are classified as Hispanic; and 63.5% of middle school students and 47.2% of high school students are also classified as Hispanic.

There seems to be two distinct populations living in census tract 704, the Hispanic classified who identify racially as white and the non-Hispanic white classified. It is fascinating that 84.8% of Hispanic-classified (who can be of any race) residents also classify themselves as white. When the percentage who self-classify as Hispanic white are combined with the percentage who consider themselves non-Hispanic white, the total proportion of white-classified residents is 87%. About 14% of Hispanic-classified residents self-classify racially as "some other race" or "two or more races."

Section 4: Neighborhood Resources

Housing is an important tangible resource. Of the 1,779 non-Hispanic white-classified households, 75% (n = 1,349) are occupant owned. Of the 854 Hispanic-classified households, 55% (n = 471) are occupant owned. To put this another way, 25% of the households classified as non-Hispanic white are renter occupied, compared to 45% percent of the Hispanic classified who rent.

Household income is another tangible resource, as money is what opens the door to purchasing goods, services, and leisure. The median household income for the non-Hispanic white-classified residents is $44,013; for the Hispanic-classified households, it is $43,017. While the two incomes seem similar, the margin of error of +/- $6,304 for non-Hispanic white residents suggests their income is less volatile; the margin of error for the Hispanic household is +/- $21,898. Other evidence of income inequality is that 19% of non-Hispanic white classified households have incomes higher than $100,000, compared to 8% of Hispanic-classified households.

Of course, occupation is an important source of income. The census bureau divides jobs into 18 broad categories, one of which is production, transportation, and material moving. Fifty percent of the Hispanic workforce is employed in that job category (which encompasses meatpacking, processing, and transportation), compared to 12% of the non-Hispanic white-classified workforce who are employed in this line of work. No non-Hispanic white-classified women work in production, transportation, and material moving, in contrast to the 43% of Hispanic-classified women in the workforce who do.

A key intangible human resource is education. Twenty percent of non-Hispanic white classified residents age 25 and older have a college degree. The census bureau estimates show no Hispanic-classified residents of that age with a college degree (the margin of error is +13). The proportion with some college (no degree) is 17% for non-Hispanic white classified residents and 4.6% for Hispanic classified. (Note: there are 3,063 non-Hispanic white-classified residents age 25 and over versus 1,874 Hispanic classified).

An intangible resource is neighborhood reputation. A content analysis of Google News articles posted the first week of October 2017 shows that there is no one theme that dominated. Of the 25 articles reviewed

8 (32%) focused on crashes/crime/shootings/drug use;

4 (16%) focused on changes in leadership, most notably at the community college or as a result of the death of a prominent figure;

3 (12%) focused on residents with connections to people who were caught up in large events such as Hurricane Maria that hit Puerto Rico or the Las Vegas high-rise shooting;

5 focused on special community events like school sports; and

4 focused on business news (a business opening or closing).

There was one article on the Hispanic-classified population as the future of Denison and other small towns.

Section 5: Demographics

In this section I give special attention to (1) percentage of residents self-classifying as Hispanic, (2) percentage of one-person households, and (3) the history of Denison Job Corps Center. The center is a landmark with a history that is intertwined with the city of Denison.

PERCENTAGE SELF-CLASSIFYING AS HISPANIC: Among residents, 47.5% classify themselves as Hispanic. When compared to the 13 surrounding census tracts, tract 704 ranks number one in the percentage of Hispanic-classified residents. The 13 surrounding tracts range from a low of 0% to a high of 14% of Hispanic-classified residents. The figure 47.5% stands out as very high when compared to the percentages for Sioux City (28%),[5] Crawford County (26.9%), the state of Iowa (5.4%), and the United States (17.0%). There is a correlation of +.30 between the percentage of Hispanic-classified residents and the median age of those who are classified as non-Hispanic white. This suggests that the higher the median age of non-Hispanic whites, the higher the percentage of Hispanic classified.

LIVING ALONE: There are 854 Hispanic-classified households. Forty of the 854 are households where people live alone. That translates to 4% of Hispanic-classified households. There are 1,779 non-Hispanic white classified households. Of these, 605 are households where people live alone.

---

5. This is the city closest to Denison. Denison is small city that *is* census tract 704.

That translates to 34% of households. That is a remarkable difference of 30%. There are likely many explanations, one being median age of the two populations. Given that the white classified median age is close to 50, we might speculate that children have left the nest, couples divorce, and spouses die. Still this difference says something very important about the two populations. For the most part, Hispanic households are not empty nests or empty of family, roommates, or unmarried partners.

CHANGING DEMOGRAPHICS: The most significant demographic change has to do with the percentage of residents who self-classify as Hispanic. It was 17.4% in 2000 and jumped to 47.5% by 2015 (an increase of 30.1%). It is also interesting to see that the median age of the non-Hispanic white classified residents rose by almost 10 years between 2000 and 2015. At the same time, the median age of Hispanic-classified residents dropped by 1.2 years.

% Hispanic Classified 17.4% (2000) to 37.0% (2010) to 47.5% (2015)

Median Age, Non-Hispanic White Classified 40.9 (2000) to 49.5 (2010) to 49.4 (2015)

Median Age, Hispanic Classified 23.1 (2000) to 21.6 (2010) to 21.9 (2015)

The Denison Job Corps Center is a landmark in census tract 704. The center has a history that speaks to the demographic changes. Job Corps is a low-cost education and career technical training program funded and administered by the U.S. Department of Labor. Its mission is to offer people ages 16 to 24 career, technical, and academic training.[6] The Job Corps Center sits on the campus of what was once Midwestern College, which opened as a for-profit institution in 1965. The college's mission was to reach out to the college-age population that had tried college and dropped out. This school was there to give them a second chance. The funders projected that the enrollment would reach 3,000 and would pump $2 million annually into the local economy. The first year, 588 students enrolled, and 1,000+ the second year. The school even had a football team for a few

---

6. The Job Corps program is authorized by Title I-C of the Workforce Innovation and Opportunity Act of 2014 (supersedes WIA 1998).

years. By the fall of 1970 enrollment was 450. The college officially closed, $3 million in debt.

The college's fate was tied to the town of Denison, which was in transition and not able to support a college-age population. It was a farming town that came under economic strain during the depression and after. It turned to meatpacking plants as a way to build its economy in the 1950s. When the plants first opened they were unionized and wages were good. A strike at the Farmland meatpacking plant ended by favoring the owners when workers took a pay cut and the union imploded. Now Denison had two major exports: beef and pork products and young people leaving in search of better futures (Maharidge 2005). To me, the history reads like the wages were lowered as a result of an unsuccessful strike, young people left, and over time immigrant workers picked up the slack. In 1980 the Denison Job Corps Center moved into the abandoned Midwestern College campus. Today the center offers self-paced classes to help students secure a GED, tutoring programs in math and reading, and a readiness pipeline to Western Iowa Tech Community College (WITCC). It also offers drivers' education and English-language learning.

Section 6: Action Plan

My research on census tract 704 helps me to see that its strengths lie with the Denison Job Corp Center, the Norelius Community Library, Western Iowa Tech Community College (WITCC), and the influx of a young Hispanic-classified population that is bolstering the economy and population of Denison. Census tract 704's most pressing needs include finding ways to bridge two distinct populations: the Hispanic classified who for the most part identify racially as white and the non-Hispanic white classified. The divide is complicated by age differences: the median age of the non-Hispanic white classified residents is 49.4 and for the Hispanic-classified residents, 21.9—a difference of 27.5 years.

The action plan begins with a self-assessment of how residents in my census tract perceive me as a newcomer and my current level of support.

MY PERCEIVED REPUTATION: As someone who will be coming to stay with and help my great-aunt, I will probably interact at first with her friends and neighbors. I have been to Denison many times to visit her, so I do know a little about the neighborhood. I identify as non-Spanish-speaking Hispanic (Guatemalan, mistaken for Mexican), but my father is non-Hispanic and identifies as an American "mutt" (no nationality). My great-aunt considers herself "German mixed with other unknown ancestries." I am going to go to the local community college, where tuition is about $2,500 a semester. I imagine I will lead two lives—one that involves my great-aunt and her social circles and one with my new friends, who will likely be a mix of Hispani- and white identifying. I know I will be perceived as the good niece. My new friends might see me as "coconut" ("white" on the inside and "brown" on the outside).

BUSINESSES I WILL SUPPORT: There are hundreds of businesses in census tract 704. In looking over the list, I see many kinds of businesses I will support. My number one need is a chiropractor. There are seven to choose from in the census tract. I also want to connect with a physical fitness gym (there are two to choose from). There are two nail salons and seven hair stylists. As far as food, my favorite is Guatemalan or Italian. There does not appear to be a Guatemalan restaurant; there are many Mexican restaurants (chain and independent). I am intrigued by Tacopocalypse, described as a "vibrant counter-serve eatery featuring Asian-inspired tacos, burritos, fries & vegan options." There are really no Italian restaurants in Denison outside of chain pizza places.

SUPPORT AND COHESION RESOURCES: The GuideStar website shows a handful of nonprofits whose missions I am attracted to. One is a Catholic church (St. Lima) that says it is open to diversity. There are about a dozen churches in census tract 704, and there only seems to be one that is Catholic. I visited the website and could see a picture of a recently renovated church. This church holds Spanish-speaking services. I also would like to join the Friends of the Norelius Community Library, which has about 68 members. It raises funds "to be used by the Library for activities not ordinarily covered under the Library's operating budget since ongoing Library operations are paid for by city and county dollars."

There are five schools in Denison: Denison High School, a middle school, and primary schools. There is also Broadway Elementary. About

60% of the high school students are economically disadvantaged, qualifying them for the Free and Reduced-Price Lunch Program. Thirty-four percent of all high school students are considered to have limited English proficiency (U.S. News and World Report 2017; Start Class 2018). The low percentage tells me that proficiency in English is not just a problem of the Hispanic-classified. The statistics are similar for the primary and middle schools.

SPECIFIC PLAN OF ACTION: My research on census tract 704 helps me to see that its strengths are the Denison Job Corp Center, the Norelius Community Library, Western Iowa Tech Community College (WITCC), and the influx of a young Hispanic-classified population that is bolstering the economy and population of Denison. Census tract 704's most pressing need is finding ways to bridge two distinct populations: the Hispanic classified who for the most part identify racially as white and the non-Hispanic white classified. The divide is complicated by age differences: the median age of the non-Hispanic white-classified residents is 49.4 and for the Hispanic-classified residents, 21.9—a difference of 27.5 years. The median age of the two populations puts them at different stages of the life cycle, which also contributes to the divide.

After learning about census tract 704—its history, needs, and population—I am very interested in supporting the Hispanic-classified population and organizations, programs, and school events that make a concerted effort to bring the non-Hispanic and Hispanic populations together.

My number one priority will be to volunteer at the schools as a tutor or mentor to any child in need. I will join St. Rose of Lima Catholic Church because it seems open to Hispanic classified people. I also would like to join the Friends of the Norelius Community Library and support its fundraising efforts to expand services beyond those the budget allows. Finally, Yellow Smoke Park has always been my favorite place to go when I visited my great-aunt in the past. Perhaps this park has events that bring the communities together.

I will look to local businesses to meet my consumer, health, and social needs. Those needs include a chiropractor, a physical fitness gym, nail salons, and a stylist. I plan to eat Asian-inspired tacos, burritos, fries, and vegan options at Tacopocalypse. After researching businesses and learning about my new hometown, I understand the importance of *shopping local*. I have always heard that phrase, but I did not really understand its meaning until I thought about what this kind of support means to Denison.

References

Denison Job Corps Center. 2017. "Find Your Purpose." https://denison.jobcorps.gov/about-us.

Grimes, William. 2005. "In This Small Town in Iowa the Future Speaks Spanish." *New York Times,* September 19.

Maharidge, D. 2005. *Denison, Iowa: Searching for the Soul of America through the Secrets of a Midwest Town.* New York: Free Press.

Norelius Community Library. 2018. "Join the Denison Library Friends."

Start Class. 2018. "Denison High School in Denison, Iowa." Graphic IQ.

U.S. News and World Report. 2017. Best High School and High School Rankings. www.usnews.com/info/blogs/press-room/articles/2017-04-25/us-news-announces-the-2017-best-high-schools.

REFERENCES

Oladipo, Wale. Forthcoming. *The Worry Instinct: Turn Obsessive Worry, Anxiety and Stress to Calm, Happiness and Confidence.*

Appendixes

APPENDIX A: HINTS FOR MAKING SIGNATURE
CONCEPT-INSPIRED OBSERVATIONS

This list of hints is designed to alert you to possibilities. When writing up each concept-inspired observation, you need only address one question.

Hints for Seeing Signs of Solidarity (Émile Durkheim)

Note activities held inside the neighborhood that bring residents together.

- ✓ Advertisements for concerts, plays, talks, or other events
- ✓ Parades
- ✓ Sports fields in use, parks, play areas

Note organizations that cultivate ties among residents.

- ✓ Place of worship
- ✓ A home owners' association
- ✓ A chamber of commerce

Note things that change the way people meet, who they interact with, or go about their lives.

- ✓ A business closing; a new business opening
- ✓ A building that is boarded up or demolished
- ✓ A building under construction
- ✓ An obituary in the newspaper or a wedding announcement

Note people, organizations, or businesses that connect residents to networks beyond the neighborhood, including those that are international.

- ✓ Major multinational companies (clothes, fast-food chains, grocery store chains, banks, technology)
- ✓ Airports, train stations, freeways

Hints for Seeing Economically Driven Tensions and Conflicts (Karl Marx)

Note the major employers.

- ✓ What kind of labor do they require?
- ✓ Speculate on the wages earned by those who work there.

Note evidence of tension and conflict related to income or the sources of income.

- ✓ Are there signs of worker dissatisfaction (high turnover, protests)?
- ✓ Are there flyers for an election, a vote, or a town hall meeting topic?

Note evidence of tension and conflict between residents.

- ✓ Are there signs that some residents of the neighborhood are better off economically than others?

Hints for Seeing Social Forces That Shape Thought and Behavior (Max Weber)

Note any settings that cultivate or honor tradition.

- ✓ Are there any statues, streets, building, or parks named after a person or an event?
- ✓ Are there any places of worship?
- ✓ Are there any specialized restaurants or grocery stores with food you associate with a specific culture?

Note any settings in the neighborhood that evoke some emotion.

- ✓ Are there any parks, gardens, murals, or special buildings?

Note any settings in the neighborhood that cultivate or honor a code of conduct.

- ✓ Are there any signs along the street or in the store windows reminding people how to behave or what not to do?
- ✓ Are there crests, seals, or standards on buildings?
- ✓ Are there businesses that cater to a way of life, purpose, or set of ideals?

Are there any settings in the neighborhood that cultivate (or reject) achieving a valued goal at any cost?

Hints for Seeing the Color Line (W. E. B. Du Bois)

- ✓ Is just about everyone in the neighborhood perceived to be a member of one racial group?
- ✓ Do people perceived to be members of one racial group predominate among the employees of some businesses or among those who frequent public spaces?
- ✓ Are there streets where only residents who appear to be a particular race live?

Hints for Seeing Need for Sympathetic Knowledge (Jane Addams)

- ✓ Is there evidence of marginalized groups in the neighborhood (people for whom life is likely made difficult because of the status they occupy—the frail elderly, the disabled, the poor)?
- ✓ Do you notice a category of residents who appear marginalized, misunderstood, and susceptible to stereotypes?

✓ Are there social problems in the neighborhood that are the result of larger social and economic forces (foreclosures, a food pantry, a social service agency, a property in disrepair)?

APPENDIX B: ACCESSING FOUR ACS DOCUMENTS

To access four overview American Community Survey census documents for the census tract or for other geographic space, follow the instructions below.

1. Google "ACS Data Tables on American FactFinder"
2. Under Data Profiles, choose the latest 5-year DP
3. You will see the following documents listed (do not check boxes next to each yet)

    Selected Social Characteristics in the United States

    Selected Economic Characteristics in the United States

    Selected Housing Characteristics in the United States

    ACS Demographic and Housing Estimates

4. Before checking the box next to each, specify the geography of interest. Do this by choosing Geography (to lower left), and then from the dropdown menu choose "Census Tract-140." Then select the appropriate state, county, and census tract number for your home census tract. Click "Add to Selections." Close the box.
5. Now check the four boxes and choose "View."
6. Move from one document to the next by clicking on the arrow at the top of the page.

APPENDIX C: USING GOOGLE SCHOLAR

Google Scholar is a search engine that give you access to scholarly (expert-written) books, articles, and other sources. Your job is to enter a search term(s) that relates to an observation you have made about your neighborhood or some data point. As an example, imagine that you notice a locally owned auto care center located in your census tract that has an outstanding reputation. Imagine also that you are seeking to connect this observation to notions of order and stability (Durkheim). You want to find a scholarly article that supports such a connection. A good search term is "local business," followed by the word *sociology* outside the quotes. Scan the titles and choose those that seem to support notions of order and stability. Some examples follow.

- ✓ Rupasingha, Anil. 2017. "Local Business Ownership and Local Economic Performance: Evidence from US Counties." *Regional Studies* 51 (5): 659–73.
- ✓ Shuman, Michael H. 2007. *The Small-Mart Revolution: How Local Businesses Are Beating the Global Competition.* Oakland, CA: Berrett-Koehler.
- ✓ Steenbeek, W., B. Völker, H. Flap, and F. V. Oort. 2012. "Local Businesses as Attractors or Preventers of Neighborhood Disorder." *Journal of Research in Crime and Delinquency* 49 (2): 213–48.
- ✓ Tolbert, Charles M., Michael D. Irwin, Thomas A. Lyson, and Alfred R. Nucci. 2002. "Civic Community in Small-Town America: How Civic Welfare Is Influenced by Local Capitalism and Civic Engagement." *Rural Sociology* 67 (1): 90–113.

Click on the title of interest. The link may take you to a short description known as an abstract or to a page of the article, or sometimes to the full article. For the purposes of these exercises, simply reading the abstract may be enough to give you the support you need. It is up to you whether you want to access the full article.

APPENDIX D: ACCESSING AN ASC TABLE

To access specific tables, follow these steps.

1. Google American FactFinder Census.
2. Look for link to American Community Survey, then select "Get data."
3. Click arrow button at geographies.
4. Choose "Census Tract-140" from the drop-down menu for "Select a geographic type," then select the state, select the county, and select the

census tract *number*. Click "Add to Selections." Close the box. If you are looking to compare your census tract with another census tract, the county, state or nation, just add the needed geographies to the selection.

5. In the search box type in search terms (e.g., households, race, Italian) or a specific table number (e.g., "B01001 Sex by Age")
6. Check the box for the most recent 5-year data set.
7. Select "View."

APPENDIX E: ACCESSING THE CENSUS TRACT NUMBER OF AN ADDRESS

You can find the census tract number for any address by typing in the search terms "FFIEC Geocoding System." Then type in the address and wait for a map to pop up. Look for the dot (marker) that shows the location of the place that matters. Notice that the marker is inside a set of boundaries and that the tract number is also printed inside those boundaries.

APPENDIX F: CREATING A SCATTERPLOT

1. Copy and paste the data from table 7.2 into an Excel file. Click the top of the column with the independent variable ("median value of housing"); hold the Control button down on the keyboard and click the top of the column with the dependent variable ("% of households with children under 18 headed by females/no husband").
2. Click on the Insert tab of the Excel menu and then choose "scatter" and then "scatter with only markers." A chart will pop up.
3. Click on the + sign by hovering the mouse to the left of the scatterplot, choose "Axis Titles" and then "Primary Horizontal Axis Title" and enter the variable title (e.g., Median Value of Housing). Then choose "Primary Vertical Axis Title" and enter the variable title (e.g., "% of female-headed households with children under 18").
4. Click on + sign again and choose trendline.
5. Right click on the chart; choose "copy" and then "paste" it in the appropriate spot.

APPENDIX G: RUBRIC

	Capstone	Milestone-Upper	Milestone-Lower	Novice
Empirically based evidence: Presents an empirically based overview of community (including its residents and resources), the place that matters and existing support for community, setting the stage for recommendations/ plan of action.	Demonstrates exceptional ability in making empirically based overview of community, the place that matters and existing support for community.	Demonstrates an ability to make empirically based overview of community, the place that matters and existing support for community but with minor inaccuracies.	Demonstrates some ability to make empirically based overview of community, the place that matters and existing support for community but with noticeable problems.	Demonstrates little to no ability to make empirically based overview of community, the place that matters and existing support for community; glaring inaccuracies that suggest little understanding of meaning of empirically-based evidence.
Organization and structure of research brief: Purpose and goals are clearly stated; each section of report contributes key points and insights that support recommendations/ action plan.	Demonstrates outstanding ability to clearly state research brief's purpose and goals and to make key points in each section of the brief that support recommendations/ plan of action.	Demonstrates an ability to state research brief's purpose and goals and to make key points in each section of the brief that support, recommendations/ action plan, with some minor inaccuracies in logic.	Demonstrates an ability to state research brief's purpose and goals and to make key points in each section of the brief that support recommendation/ action plan but with noticeable problems.	Demonstrates little to no ability to state research brief's purpose and goals and to make key points in each section of the brief that support recommend-ation/ action plan; has glaring inaccuracies.
Recommendation/ Plan of Action: Presents recommendations/ action plan grounded in and supported by empirically based evidence.	Exceptionally articulated recommendations/ action plan grounded in and supported by empirically based evidence.	Effectively articulated recommendations/ action plan grounded in and supported by empirically based evidence with minor inaccuracies.	Articulates recommendations/ action plan grounded in and supported by empirically based evidence but with noticeable problems.	Shows little to no ability to articulate recommendations/ action plan grounded in and supported by empirically based evidence; has glaring inaccuracies.

Figure 8.3. Rubric for Research Brief
SOURCE: Joan Ferrante

Index

action-based learning, xi-xii
action-based research experience, 2, 3, 11
action stage of proficiency building, 10, 11
Addams, Jane: great thinker, 32; observations inspired by ghost of, 57; review data with ghost of, 40, 43, 48, 49; sympathetic knowledge, 39; take a tour with ghost of, 32, 39, 40, 49, 153; see also, *Second Twenty Years at Hull-House, The*, 58
age: categories, 68; composition, 68
age-sex composition, 60, 68, 69-73, 85
Alexander, Bryant Keith., 154, 176
Altman, I., 178
American Community Survey, 20, 60, 78, 206-208
Anderson, Benedict., 156, 177
ancestry as defined by U.S. Bureau of Census, 63
Anselin, Luc, 51
applied research, 149, 150, 151
applying sociological concepts, 31-58
Arteaga, Irma, et al., 120, 147
artifacts (or traces), 116, 118, 119, 122, 134, 140

Barnet, Richard, 108, 114
Barton, Michael, 111, 191
basic research, 8, 115, 149, 150
Beard, Virginia R. 54

beliefs, 101-103
Benabou, Roland, 82, 86
Berger, Peter, 31, 45, 58, 83, 86
Burger, William C., 54
Bertot, John Carlo, 52
Bohmann, C.R., 81, 87
Bjork, Sofia, 69, 87
Blumenfeld, P.C., et al., xii, xiii
Bracken. Cheryl, C., 105, 114
Brighton Center, Inc., 107
broken window theory, 12
Brotherton, R., 12,
Bryant, Clifton D. 19, 30
Burawoy, M., xiii

Callan, Victor J., 83, 87
Campbell, S., 151, 178
cardinal-level variable, 137, 139, 140
case study, 126
categorical-level variable, 137, 138, 139
census tract: defined, 20; map of a, 21; as a neighborhood, 20
chance and race, 64-65
Chang, Leslie T., 35, 58
Cheng, B, C., 156, 177
Choice and race, 65-66
Clark, A., 151, 178
color line, 37-38, 43, 57, 66, 110, 205

211

community, definitions of, 18–19
comparative research, 8, 153, 155, 174
conflict perspective, 49, 50, 51–52
confidence interval, 47–49
constructive criticism, 180–181
content analysis, 127, 129, 131–133, 145–146, 187, 195
context and race, 65
control variable, 141–144, 148, 158, 159
convenience sampling, 125, 127
core research questions: answering, XX; answered in research brief; 179, 181, 182, 183, 192; coaching answers to, xx; driving research, 5, 149; exercises and, 32, 56; neighborhood resources and 88, 112; and organizing concepts, 14; as part of purpose statement, 27; and residents, 59; and sociological perspectives, 49; and types of research, 149
core concepts, 7, 31–58
correlation coefficient, 167–169
correlational research, 8, 157, 174
Cummins, S., 159, 177

data-gathering strategies, 127–134
descriptive research, 8, 116, 153, 174
descriptive statistics: count, 163; defined 162; maximum, 163; mean, 162–163; median, 162–163; minimum, 163; standard deviation, 163–164; variance, 163–165
Dill, J., 150, 177
disability, 54, 59, 60–63, 73, 78
documents, 118, 122, 123, 125, 134, 155
doing research: challenges to, ix-x; basic vs. applied, 149–151; meeting the challenges, 9–11; qualitative vs. quantitative, 151–152
Downing, Janelle, 150, 177
DuBois, W.E.B: on color line, 37–38, 57, 205; a great thinker, 32; review data with ghost of, 40, 43, 48; take a tour with ghost of, 32, 38, 49, 153; see also *Souls of Black Folk*, The, 37, 58
Durkheim, Èmile: on economic and social crisis, 35; great thinker, 32; observations inspired by ghost of, 57; on order and stability, 207; review census data with ghost of, 40, 41, 42, 57, 49; on social ties, 35, 36, 37; on solidarity 32, 34, 35,42, 203; take a tour with ghost of, 32, 35–36, 49, 153; see also, *Suicide*, 58

Earls, F., 150, 177
educational attainment, 95–97, 153

Economy and Society, 58
Elliott, J., 160, 177
Emerson, Michael O., 66, 87
Epstein, I., x, xiii
estimates, 20, 40, 41, 45–50
ethnic categories (official), 63–64
event oriented observation, 130, 131
experimental research, 8, 153, 158, 159

feminist perspective, 45, 50, 54–55
first place, 15
Fitzsimmons, Terrance W., 83, 87
fixed-choice responses, 128, 129, 160
FFIEC Geocoding System, 20; 24, 208
Flap, Volker H., 207
Flint, S., 159, 177
Flunk, Winfried, 1, 12
food deserts, 151, 159nn
French, C.C., 12
frequency distribution, 161
full-time work, 170, 174
functionalist perspective, 45, 50, 54–55

Gale, C.R., 160, 177
Gates, Paul W., 173
Gary-Webb, T. L., 150, 178
gender, 54, 55, 68, 69
generalizability, 123
gentrification: define, 58, 111; accompanying attacks on safe places, 155; and change, 110, 111, 157, 175, 181, 188; and neglected populations, 190; home prices and, 175; as a trend, 185; and youthification, 58
Gieryn, Thomas F., 1, 13, 15–16, 30
Gilliland, J.A., 153, 178
globalization, 108, 110
glocalization, 108, 110
Goode, R., 150, 178
Great Good Place, The, 15
groups, 117, 119, 122, 125, 134, 140, 157
growth stage of proficiency building, 10, 11
GuideStar USA, 105, 106, 107
Guzman, Gloria G., 78, 87

HALCyon Study, 160, 177
Hanhardt, C.B., 155, 177
Harlan, S.L., 150, 177
Heflinger, C.A., 81, 87
historical research, 8, 155, 171, 174
history: celebrated, 171; hidden, 171; local, 176, 176
Holam, E.A., 152, 177
Hoffman, J., 156, 177

INDEX   213

Holman, E.A., 152, 177
household: income, 77–82; types, 75–77
householders, 45
human capital, 95–99
hypothesis, 115, 140–141, 143–144, 166

impairment, 39, 60–61
income: defined, 78, 135; household, 77–82; income inequality, 77–78; sources of, 90–92
individuals, as unit of analysis, 116–117, 119, 122, 134, 156
Ingulstad, Mats, 177
inertia stage of proficiency building, 9, 11
insiderness, 15–17
instrumental social ties, 34
intangible resources, 7, 89, 187, 195
interpretive research, 8, 153, 154
investigative research, 8, 148–178
Irwin, Michael D., 207

Jaeger, Paul T., 52
Jeffres, Leo W., 105, 114
Jian, Guowei, 105, 114
Johnston, Lynda, 55
Jose, R., 152, 177

Kane, K., 156, 177
Kelling, George L., 12, 13
Koenig, Caitlin, 177
key questions, xii
Kuh, D., 150, 177

landmarks, 20, 22, 100–104, 171, 176, 196, 197
Lau, Amy, 171, 177
launching the project, 6–7; 15–30
Lee, H., 157, 177
Le Goix, R., 82, 87
Lehning, A.J., 150, 177
Lennon, M.C., 82, 87
Lim, H., 157, 177
Loebach, J.E., 153, 178
longitudinal research, 153, 156, 173, 174
Lopez, Ian F. Haney, 64, 87
Low, S.M., 178
Lyson, Thomas, A., 207

Ma, L., 150, 177
Macfarlane, Alan; 18; 30
MacQueen, Kathleen, et al., 19, 30
Maharidge, 198, 201
Mair, S., 150, 177
margin of error, 31, 40, 42, 45–47

Marx, Karl: on economically-driven tensions, 33, 44, 204; and Friedrich Engles, 58; a great thinker, 32; on materialism, 33; on relationships between capitalists and laborers, 33, 44; review data with ghost of, 40, 43, 48, 49; view of society, 33; take a tour with ghost of, 32, 34, 49, 153
Marx, R.W., xii, xiii
Matthews, S.A., 159, 177*mattering* defined, xi–xii
McClure, Charles R., 52
McFadden, Margaret, 171, 178
McGuire, J., 150, 177
Mecklenborg, Jake, 178
Mendez, D.D., 150, 178
mixed methods, 8, 151, 152, 153, 159
Milford, K., ix, xiii
Mohr, C., 150, 177
Moos, Markus, 58, 191
multivariate analysis- research, 8, 153, 157, 158

neighborhood: best definition of, 19; census tract as a, 20; as a concept, 18–20; and daily routines, 23–24, 28–29; establishing boundaries of, 20; landmarks, 100–104; operational definition of, 28; reputation, 99–100; resources, 7–8, 88–114; as a support context, 11–12; personal support for, 25; why care about? 11–12
neighborhood resource, 7, 88–89, 112, 186, 195
nonparticipant observation, 130
nonrandom samples, 125
norms, 101, 102
Nucci, Alfred R., 207

Obama, Barack, 64, 65, 66, 87
observations: defined, 148–149; event oriented, 130–131; nonparticipant, 130; participant, 130; self, 133–134; situation oriented, 131; stream of consciousness, 131, 133–134; time-oriented, 130–131
Onukwugha, E., 150, 177
Oladipo, Wale, 201Oldenburg, Ray, 15, 30, 105, 114; See also, *Great Good Place, The*
Oort, F.V., 207
open-ended questions, 128, 129
operational definition, 134, 135, 136, 137
ordinal-level variable, 138, 139
outsiderness, 15–16

Parsons, S., 160, 177
participant observation, 130

Pearson Correlation Coefficient Calculation, 168–169
Pease, Donald E., 1, 12
Peck, Dennis L. 19, 30
percentile, 139
Pickering, A.D., 12
place that matters: agentic qualities of, 15; as emotional anchors, x, 3; defined, 2, 16–17; the concept of, 14–16; examples of, x, 3–4; neighborhood that surrounds, 2,3; personal statement about, 17–18; power of, 1; self and, 1
population pyramids, 70–72
Posner, Richard A., 36, 58
proficiency building: action stage, 9, 10; four stages of, 9–11; growth stage, 10, 11; inertia stage, 9, 11; realization stage, 10, 11
purposive sampling, 125

qualitative research, 8, 151, 152, 153, 159, 160
quantitative research, 8, 151, 152, 153, 159, 160
questionnaires, 125, 127, 128

race: defined, 64; a four-hundred-year history; 66; an illusion with real consequences, 66; product of chance, choice and context 64–65;
racial categories, 63–68
racialized, 66, 139
Ramirez, A.S., 150, 178
random sample, 123, 124, 126
Rawlings, Marjorie Kinnan, 1, 13
reliability, 135–137
realization stage of proficiency building, 10, 11
Relph, Edward, 15, 16, 30
resources: global and local businesses, 107–109; intangible, xxi, 7, 25, 89, 95, 112, 115, 186, 187, 195; support and cohesion, 104–107; tangible, xxi, 7, 89–94, 112, 115, 186–187, 195
research brief: cover/title page, 26; format of, 181–183; model #1, 183–191; model#2, 192–201; purpose statement 27; section 1 of, 26–29; section 2 of, 56–58; section 3 of, 85–86; section 4 of, 112–114; section 5 of, 145–146; section 6 of, 174–176; writing the, 8–9
Rios, L.K.D., 150, 178
Rowe, John Carlos, 1,12
Rupasingha, Anil, 207

sampling: convenience, 125–127; nonrandom, 125–126; random, 123–125; snowball, 125–126
Sandelowski, Margarete, 154, 177
scatterplot, 167–169, 208
Schultz, Courtney L., 157, 178
scientific method, 148
second place, 15
secondary questions, 5
Second Twenty Years at Hull-House, The, 58
self-administered survey, 128
sex, 69, 128, 134, 138, 139
sex composition, 68–69
Shay, S., 150, 170
Shuman, Michael, 207
Silver, R.C., 152, 177
situation-oriented observation, 130, 131
Slayers, S.P., 150, 178
Small, Mario, 81, 87
Smith, Christian, 66, 87
snowball sampling, 125
social action, 36–37, 204–205
social categories, 60, 83–85
social change, 109–111
social interactions, 52, 116, 118, 134
social location, 82–84
socialization needs by age categories, 74
solidarity, 32, 34–36, 42, 110, 203–204
Sonnenberg, Elissa, 107
Soloway, E. xii, xiii
Souls of Black Folk, The, 37, 58
standard of deviation, 163–164
Stanis, S.A.W, 157, 178
stream of consciousness observation, 131
structured interview, 129
subtle skills, 6
support as a concept: 24–25
supporting questions, 5
symbols: black rose as, 40; buildings as, 104, 111, 113, 155, 185; defined, 53;
symbolic interactionist perspective, 50, 52–54
sympathetic knowledge, 32, 39–40, 44, 57, 84, 151, 154, 205–206

tangible resource, 7, 89, 92–95, 187, 195
target population, 119–122
territories, 117, 119, 122, 125, 134, 140, 157
third places, 15, 104, 105, 126
Thurber, A., 81, 87
time-oriented observation, 130
Tolbert, Charles M., 207
transnational corporations, 108

Unhomely Places, xii
U.S. Bureau of the Census: annual surveys, 19–20; definition of disability, 62; definition of full time work, 170; definition of household, 73–74; definition of income, 78, 134; official job categories, 19;
U.S. Department of Agriculture, 159, 178
U.S. Department of Labor, 197
unit of analysis, 115–120, 143
University of Kansas, Work Group for Community Health and Development, 12
unstructured interviews, 129

Valdez, Z., 150, 178
Vaughn, M.S., 157, 177
validity, 135, 136
values, 101, 102–104, 118
variability, 164–165
variables: cardinal level, 137, 139, 140; categorical level, 137, 138, 139; control, 141–144, 148, 158–159; defined, 134; dependent, 142; hypothesis, 140–143; independent, 142; ordinal level, 138, 139

verification, 148, 149
Vesselinov, E., 82, 87

Waitt, Gordon, 55
Waldstein, S., 150, 177
Ward, R., 151, 178
Weber, Max: a great thinker, 32; on social action, 36; on forces that shape thought and behavior, 36, 204; review data with ghost of, 40, 43, 48; take a tour with ghost of, 32, 36, 37, 49, 153; see also *Economy and Society,* 58
Weinberg, Daniel H., 81, 87
Wen, M., 158, 178
Werlen, Benno, 15, 30
Wheeler, Christopher H., 82, 87
Wilson, James Q., 12, 13
Wilson, William J. 82, 87
Wutich, Amber, et al., 99, 114, 145, 147
working draft defined; 25–26

Zager, Masha, 104